CONTENTS

D1432465

The Official
GameSalad®
Guide to Game Development

Jeannie Novak

DELMAR
CENGAGE Learning·

Australia • Brazil • Japan • Korea • Mexico • Singapore • Spain • United Kingdom • United States

The Official GameSalad Guide to Game Development

Vice President, Careers & Computing:
Dave Garza

Director of Learning Solutions:
Sandy Clark

Senior Acquisitions Editor: **Jim Gish**

Managing Editor: **Larry Main**

Senior Product Manager:
Nicole Calisi

Editorial Assistant: **Sarah L. Timm**

Brand Manager: **Kristin McNary**

Market Development Manager:
Deborah Yarnell

Senior Production Director:
Wendy A. Troeger

Production Manager: **Andrew Crouth**

Senior Content Project Manager:
Kathryn B. Kucharek

Art Director: **Jack Pendleton**

Media Editor: **Debbie Bordeaux**

Cover Image ***Raptor Storm***
Image courtesy of GameSalad ®

For product information and technology assistance, contact us at
Cengage Learning Customer & Sales Support, 1-800-354-9706
For permission to use material from this text or product,
submit all requests online at **www.cengage.com/permissions.**
Further permissions questions can be e-mailed to
permissionrequest@cengage.com

Library of Congress Control Number: 2012944317

ISBN-13: 978-1-1336-0564-5

ISBN-10: 1-1336-0564-8

Delmar
5 Maxwell Drive
Clifton Park, NY 12065-2919
USA

Cengage Learning is a leading provider of customized learning solutions with office locations around the globe, including Singapore, the United Kingdom, Australia, Mexico, Brazil, and Japan. Locate your local office at: **international.cengage.com/region**

Cengage Learning products are represented in Canada by Nelson Education, Ltd.

To learn more about Delmar, visit **www.cengage.com/delmar**

Purchase any of our products at your local college store or at our preferred online store **www.cengagebrain.com**

Notice to the Reader

Printed in Canada
1 2 3 4 5 6 7 16 15 14 13

Chapter 2   Interface: eye of the beholder 24

Chapter 3 Protopying: practice makes perfect.............................. 48

Chapter 5 Mac Game Development: garden of digital delights..................................92

Chapter 6 Mobile Game Development: play as you go 110

Chapter 7   Online Game Development: deploy everywhere 138

Part III: Focus 159

Chapter 8   Social Games: "you've got to have friends" 160

Chapter 9 Serious Games: why so serious? 178

Appendix: Basic Terms & Tutorials 200

Resources 214

Index 226

Introduction

"Game Creation for Everyone"

Game Salad Creator enables developers who have little to no programming experience to create, test, and publish compelling and fun games in a variety of genres with a simple drag-and-drop process. Creator is understandably being adopted in high schools and colleges around the country due to its ease of use, versatility, and extensive support. Projects developed in Creator can be played on both Mac and Windows systems (including online through HTML5)—and all iOS and Android mobile devices.

GameSalad lives up to its slogan ("game creation for everyone")—not only through its flagship product but the many features available to its customers. It was clear that an official textbook could be a key supplement to this supportive infrastructure consisting of several elements: *Arcade* (arcade.gamesalad.com), where developers can show off their projects in a user-friendly environment; *Community* (forums.gamesalad.com), where a thriving developer community of more than 550,000 developers can swap advice and announce new releases; *Cookbook* (cookbook.gamesalad.com), which provides a wealth of tutorials, Q&A, a dictionary of terms, and tips/techniques for making the most of Creator; and *Marketplace* (marketplace.gamesalad.com), where developers buy and sell art, audio, and game templates. GameSalad developers have produced more than 150,000 games—at least 65 of which have reached the top 100 in the Apple App Store. (One title even hit #1!)

This book is the first of its kind: a new type of software guide that goes beyond the confines of its contemporaries. It's truly an *official* guide—the *only* textbook written with close support, review, and feedback from the GameSalad team. Rather than being a traditional software manual, it's an instructional tool, reference guide, and game development primer all rolled into one. The bonus Appendix provides definitions of terms and tutorial walkthroughs for readers who need a basic refresher course in the general workings of Creator.

Providing an overview of topics that are relevant to those who want to broaden their knowledge of game development, each chapter covers material that might be taught in a course associated with a particular topic. For example, each of the three chapters in the first section of the book focuses on a primary subject that could be taught in an entire course: gameplay, interface, prototyping. The four chapters in the next section explore all the different formats associated with Creator: Windows, Mac, mobile (iOS and Android), and online (HTML5). Courses focusing on a particular format might use one of these chapters. The final section of the book contains two chapters that explore social and serious games—two industry trends that deserve close attention. With Creator's links to social networks such as Twitter and the ability to track a player's progress during a serious game, the brave new world of game development is ready to be explored through this versatile and empowering tool.

Whether you're new to Creator or you've been hoping to broaden your knowledge, this book will provide you with the additional tools needed to make the most out of this groundbreaking software.

Jeannie Novak
Santa Monica, CA

About the Book

This book provides an overview of GameSalad Creator—including associated versions, operating systems, hardware/technology platforms, and game development techniques.

This book contains the following unique features:

- Key chapter questions that are clearly stated at the beginning of each chapter
- Coverage that surveys the topics of gameplay style, interface design, prototyping, Windows/Mac desktop, Android/iOS mobile, online (HTML5), social games, and serious games
- A wealth of case studies, quotations and profiles of game developers that feature concise tips and techniques to help readers focus in on issues specific to GameSalad Creator
- Discussions that go beyond a general reference guide into historical context, tutorial content, real-world solutions, and future predictions
- In-depth analysis of GameSalad Creator's core and enhanced functionality with regard to both Windows and Mac versions and desktop, mobile, and online (HTML5) deployment
- An abundance of full-color screenshots, photos, diagrams, and illustrations throughout that expand on the concepts and techniques discussed in the book
- Thought-provoking review exercises at the end of each chapter that help promote critical thinking and problem-solving skills (with annotated responses included in the Instructor Resources)

There are several general themes associated with this book that are emphasized throughout, including:

- Using GameSalad Creator as a gameplay development, interface design, and prototyping tool
- Comparing Windows Creator and Mac Creator--and understanding how each version of the software can be used to create desktop, mobile, and online (HTML5) games
- Creating games for distinct platforms and operating systems--such as Android and iOS (mobile)
- Understanding the significance of online game development using HTML5
- Utilizing specific features of GameSalad Creator that lend themselves to social and serious game development

How Is This Book Organized?

This book consists of three parts—providing foundational game development concepts, a comparison of formats associated with GameSalad Creator, and two areas of focus: social and serious games.

Part I / Foundation—focuses on how gameplay, interface, and prototyping concepts can be addressed with GameSalad Creator. Chapters in this section include:

- **Chapter 1 / Gameplay: the game's the thing**—provides an overview of gameplay styles and genres best suited to GameSalad Creator
- **Chapter 2 / Interface: eye of the beholder**—discusses ways in which GameSalad Creator can be used to enhance a game's interface
- **Chapter 3 / Prototyping: practice makes perfect**—delves into how GameSalad Creator can enable rapid prototyping in games

Part II / Format—focuses on the differences between Windows Creator, Mac Creator, mobile operating systems (iOS and Android), and online (HTML5) deployment. Chapters in this section include:

- **Chapter 4 / Windows Game Development: every screen is a playground**—explores distinct features of Windows game development and breaks down Windows Creator components
- **Chapter 5 / Mac Game Development: garden of digital delights**—explores distinct features of Mac game development and breaks down Mac Creator
- **Chapter 6 / Mobile Game Development: play as you go**—explores distinct features of mobile game development and how GameSalad Creator can be used to create and publish games for both iOS and Android devices
- **Chapter 7 / Online Game Development: deploy everywhere**—explores distinct features of online game development and how GameSalad Creator exports to HTML5

Part III / Focus—focuses on two important game development trends: social and serious game development. Chapters in this section include:

- **Chapter 8 / Social Games: "you've got to have friends"**—covers features of social game development and discusses how GameSalad Creator can add social components to a game
- **Chapter 9 / Serious Games: why so serious?**—covers features of serious game development and discusses types of serious games that are best suited to GameSalad Creator

The book also contains a **Resources** section—which includes lists of game communities, directories, libraries, organizations, news, reviews, research, events, books, and articles.

How to Use This Book

The sections that follow describe text elements found throughout the book and how they are intended to be used.

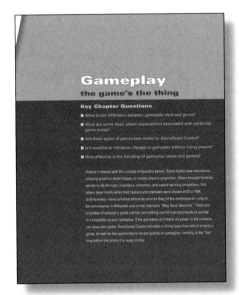

key chapter questions

Key chapter questions are learning objectives in the form of overview questions that start off each chapter. Readers should be able to answer the questions upon understanding the chapter material.

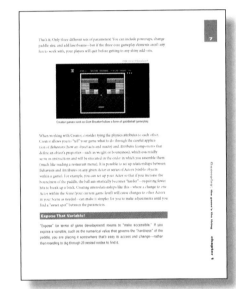

notes

Notes contain thought-provoking ideas intended to help readers think critically about the book's topics.

tips

Tips provide advice, inspiration, and techniques from industry professionals and educators.

case studies

Case studies contain anecdotes from industry professionals (accompanied by game screenshots) on their experiences developing specific game titles.

quotes

Quotes contain short, insightful thoughts from industry professionals and educators.

sidebars

Sidebars offer in-depth information on topics of interest—accompanied by associated images.

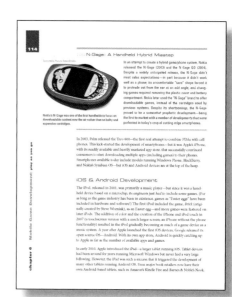

profiles

Profiles provide bios, photos and in-depth commentary from industry professionals and educators.

tutorials

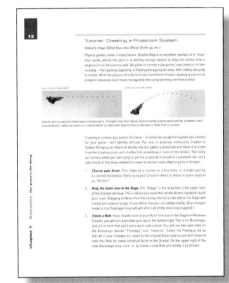

Tutorials provide step-by-step instructions and walkthroughs associated with software applications and associated topics.

chapter review exercises

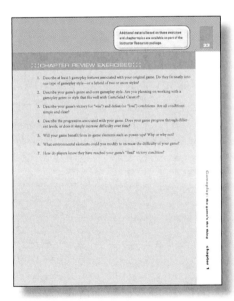

Chapter review exercises at the end of each chapter encourage readers to apply what they've learned. Annotations and answers are included in the Instructor Resources, available separately.

Photo by Luis Levy.

About the Author

Jeannie Novak is the Lead Author & Series Editor of the widely acclaimed *Game Development Essentials* series (with more than 15 published titles), co-author of *Play the Game: The Parent's Guide to Video Games*, and co-author of three pioneering books on the interactive entertainment industry—including *Creating Internet Entertainment*. She is also Co-Founder of Novy Unlimited and CEO of Kaleidospace, LLC (d/b/a Indiespace, founded in 1994)—where she provides services for corporations, educators, and creative professionals in games, music, film, education, and technology. Jeannie oversees one of the first web sites to promote and distribute interactive entertainment and a game education consulting division that focuses on curriculum development, instructional design, and professional development. As Online Program Director for the Game Art & Design and Media Arts & Animation programs at the Art Institute Online, Jeannie produced and designed an educational business simulation game that was built within the *Second Life* environment—leading a virtual team of more than 50 educators, students, and industry professionals. She was a game instructor and curriculum development expert at UCLA Extension, Art Center College of Design, Academy of Entertainment & Technology at Santa Monica College, DeVry University, Westwood College, and ITT Technical Institute—and she has consulted for several educational institutions and developers such as UC Berkeley Center for New Media, Alelo, and GameSalad. Jeannie has also worked on projects funded by the National Science Foundation and Google for Lehigh Carbon Community College and the University of Southern California (USC) Information Sciences Institute.

An active member of the game industry, Jeannie has served as Vice Chair of the International Game Developers Association-Los Angeles (IGDA-LA) and Vice President at Women in Games International (WIGI). She has participated in the Online Gameplay and Connectivity selection committees for the Academy of Interactive Arts & Sciences' DICE awards since 2003 and has developed game workshops, panels, and breakout sessions for events and organizations such as the Penny Arcade Expo (PAX), GDC Next, Macworld Expo, Digital Hollywood, USC's Teaching Learning & Technology Conference, and the Los Angeles Games Conference. Jeannie has been profiled by CNN, *Billboard Magazine*, *Sundance Channel*, *Daily Variety*, and *The Los Angeles Times*.

Jeannie received an M.A. in Communication Management from USC's Annenberg School (where her thesis focused on using massively multiplayer online games as online distance learning applications) and a B.A. in Mass Communication/Business Administration from UCLA (where she graduated summa cum laude/Phi Beta Kappa and completed an honors thesis focusing on gender role relationships in toy commercials). A native of Southern California, Jeannie grew up in San Diego and currently resides in Santa Monica with her husband, Luis Levy. She is also an accomplished composer, recording artist, performer, and music instructor (piano/voice).

Who Should Read This Book?

This book is not limited to the education market. The audience for this book includes students, industry professionals, and the general interest consumer market. The style is informal and accessible, with a concentration on theory and practice—geared toward both students and professionals. Readers that might benefit from this book include:

- College students in game development, interactive design, entertainment studies, communication, and emerging technologies programs
- Art and design students who are taking game development courses
- Students in high school or college-level programs who are taking game development courses
- Professionals in the traditional game industry who are interested in creating games on their own or in small groups
- Producers, designers, artists, and audio professionals in other arts and entertainment media who are interested in migrating to the game industry

About the Instructor Resources

The Instructor Resources package was developed to assist educators in planning and implementing their instructional programs. It includes sample syllabi, study guides, projects, presentations, chapter outlines, chapter review exercise annotations, and other valuable instructional resources. All of these features can be found at: http://login.cengage.com. At the CengageBrain.com home page, search for the ISBN of your title (9781133605645) using the search box at the top of the page. This will take you to the product page where these resources can be found.

Questions & Feedback

We welcome your questions and feedback. If you have suggestions that you think others would benefit from, please let us know and we will try to include them in the next edition. To send questions and/or feedback, please contact the publisher or lead author and series editor at:

DELMAR CENGAGE LEARNING
Executive Woods
5 Maxwell Drive
Clifton Park, NY 12065
Attn: Media Arts & Design Team
(800) 998-7498

Jeannie Novak
Lead Author & Series Editor
Game Development Essentials
P.O. Box 5458
Santa Monica, CA 90409
jeannie@indiespace.com

Acknowledgements

The author would like to thank the following people, educational institutions, and companies for their hard work, dedication, and support for this project:

Cengage Learning

Jim Gish (Senior Acquisitions Editor, Delmar) for making this series happen.

Nicole Calisi (Senior Product Manager, Delmar) for her excellent management support during all phases of this project.

Kathryn Kucharek (Senior Content Project Manager, Delmar) for her assistance during the production phase.

Sarah Timm (Editorial Assistant, Delmar) for her ongoing support throughout the *GDE* series and related projects.

Aishwarya Dakshinamoorthy (Project Manager, PreMediaGlobal) for providing support during pre-press and delivering the manuscript to the printer.

Alexandra Ricciardi (Rights Acquisitions Specialist) for reviewing image clearances.

David Koontz (Publisher, Chilton) for starting it all by introducing Jeannie Novak to Jim Gish.

GameSalad

Steve Felter (Chief Executive Officer) for giving this project the green light.

Frank Coppersmith (Chief Operating Officer) for leading the educational outreach program.

Mark Sones (Business Analyst) for taking the reins early on and providing curriculum-related elements.

Robert Hoff (Education & Customer Relations Manager) for his thorough editorial support and feedback throughout the development and review stages.

Anne Coale (Artist) for providing art assets during the cover's initial design phase.

Jonathan Samn (Senior Game Engineer) and Rhiannon Watkins (QA Analyst & Community Liaison) for providing "fact-checking" support during the review stage.

Billy Garretsen for providing early technical review.

Jonathan Hunt for providing early marketing guidance.

Mark Chuberka for jumpstarting this project with Jeannie Novak.

Development & Production

David Ladyman (IMGS, Inc.) for his superhuman efforts during the compositing & layout phase.

Brian McGovney and Sharan Volin for their research and writing assistance.

Per Olin for his organized and aesthetically pleasing diagrams.

Robert Entrekin for the use of his voluminous photo archive.

Contributors

Ace Connell (Mynameisace Ltd)

Bharat Battu

Caleb Garner (Part12 Studios)

Dan Caldwell (Power Up Education Inc.)

Darren Spencer (Utopian Games /
Deep Blue Apps)

David Conover (Connolly High School)

David Javelosa (Santa Monica College)

George Kotsiofides (Quantum Sheep)

Jenny McGettigan (Beansprites LLC /
Hamster Wheel Studios)

John Papiomitis (Papio Games)

Jon Draper (Stormy Studio)

Jonathan Mulcahy (How I Hate the Night)

Luis Levy (Novy Unlimited, Inc.)

Marcin Makaj (The Moonwalls)

Nicolas Palacios (ePig Games)

Thomas Wagner (Gamesmold)

Copyright Holders

Andrew Kirmse & Chris Kirmse

Apple Inc.

Bharat Battu

Bitstorm.org

Caleb Garner (Part12 Studios)

Chris Ulm (Appy Entertainment, Inc.)

Culver Media, LLC

Dan Caldwell (Power Up Education, Inc.)

Darren Spencer (Utopian Games /
Deep Blue Apps)

Duane Blehm (HomeTown Software)

Eclipse Foundation

Ernest Woo (Woo Games)

Facebook

Fire Maple Games

Foursquare Labs

Games Press

GetGlue

Google

Hellenic Game Developers Association

id Software

Interplay Entertainment

iStockphoto

Jon Draper (Stormy Studio)

Jonathan Mulcahy (How I Hate the Night)

Legacy Interactive

Lori Mezoff (US Army)

Marcin Makaj (The Moonwalls)

Martin Campbell-Kelly

Martine Doucet

Microsoft Corporation

Milton Bradley Company

Nintendo

Nokia

Piga Software

Quantum Sheep

Richard Tate (HopeLab Foundation)

Silicon Beach Software, Inc.

Sony Computer Entertainment America

Thomas Wagner (Gamesmold)

Will Crowther

William Volk (PlayScreen, LLC)

Zynga

SPECIAL THANKS

To Kimberly Unger (Chief Executive Officer, Bushi-go, Inc.) for her invaluable contributions to this book—including research, writing, diagrams, illustrations, screenshots, and tutorials. This project would not have been possible without Kimberly—who went far beyond the call of duty to make it the exceptional work that it is. Thank you, Kimberly!

— Jeannie Novak

Part I: Foundation

CHAPTER

Gameplay
the game's the thing

Key Chapter Questions

- What is the difference between *gameplay style* and *genre*?

- What are some basic player *expectations* associated with particular game styles?

- Are there types of games best suited to *GameSalad Creator*?

- Is it possible to introduce *changes* to gameplay without losing players?

- How effective is the *blending* of gameplay styles and genres?

History is littered with the corpses of beautiful games. Some fueled new innovations, amazing graphics technologies, or unique physics properties. Others brought fantastic worlds to life through cinematics, animation, and award-winning storytellers. Still others blew minds when their teasers and previews were shown at E3 or PAX. Unfortunately, many vanished almost as soon as they hit the marketplace—only to be remembered in Wikipedia and on the Internet's "Way-Back Machine." There are a number of reasons a game can fail, but nothing can kill a product quite so quickly or completely as poor gameplay. If the gameplay isn't there, no power in the universe can save your game. GameSalad Creator provides a strong base from which to build a game, as well as the opportunity to iterate quickly on gameplay—locking in the "fun" long before the product is ready to ship.

Under the Sun . . .

For basic GameSalad Creator tutorials, see Appendix. For more information on gameplay, see *Gameplay Mechanics* (Dunniway/ Novak)—part of Delmar Cengage Learning's *Game Development Essentials* series.

A good game is nothing new. Entertaining and thought-provoking games have been around since the beginning of recorded history, from before humanity even thought up harnessing steam, let alone the microchip: Games such as *Tic-Tac-Toe*, *Fox and Hounds*, tag, polo—and games with balls, sticks, mud, and feathers. The rules for these games have been tested and modified though years of repeated play. A game might stay true to its original form or transform so radically that it might become completely different in everything except for its name.

Source iStockphoto. Photo by Martine Doucet.

Traditional children's games such as hide-and-seek that involve simple rules of play continue to be popular today.

Make the jump to digital, and there's potential for further evolution. Early games focused on replicating real-life games such as *Tic-Tac-Toe* and variations of table tennis (ping pong). Still, many early computer games were more like tech demos. Computing resources were limited to mainframes at universities and research firms that could easily cost over $75 per hour, and games were not the best use for them. The first few games and systems to hit the open market, such as *Computer Space* and the Magnavox Odyssey, didn't do as well as expected—in large part due to gameplay issues, such as a steep learning curve and tricky controls. It wasn't until *Pong* was released as an arcade game in 1972 that games found the elusive gameplay "sweet spot."

Elements of Gameplay

Above all, gameplay must be engaging—something your players will enjoy. The controls should be clean and easy to learn—and they must work well with your target device. Consider the joystick control as an example. Early mobile games attempted to use a "virtual" joystick, with only limited success. Controls that were better adapted to the workings of the touchscreen still needed to be invented and implemented. As a result of this gameplay innovation, fewer games use the virtual joystick model; instead, games created for mobile devices such as smartphones and tablets (discussed in Chapter 6) tend to use touch controls—allowing for swiping (*Fruit Ninja*) or tapping (*Diner Dash*). Equally troublesome for joystick-type controls are desktop computers—which are better suited to mouse and keyboard control schemes, and as such can support a much more complex user interface.

It's important to understand that you cannot use yourself as your target audience. You know yourself too intimately, and you will (consciously or unconsciously) end up tweaking the game to your own personal strengths and weaknesses. It's difficult to monetize on an audience of one. Aim for the middle ground—the spot that gives you access to the broadest user base for your type of game. Good gameplay occurs at the intersection of controls and content. Every type of game has a predefined set of conditions for success (e.g., "Collect 10 pellets = WIN," "Shoot all 10 bad guys = WIN"). The *win* (or *victory*) *condition* is the rule that allows players to win and reap rewards for their hard work. Defining this is often the simplest part of the gameplay. It is that condition's *modifiers* (obstacles deliberately put in the way by the developer) that get interesting.

GameSalad Creator ("Creator") is uniquely suited to allow you to experiment with gameplay during development. With the ability to tweak any number of gameplay elements and have the associated changes propagate through the entire game, designers working with Creator can ensure that their games are fun to play without the need for programming.

Unbeatable Strategy

Remember: It's easy to build a game that no one can beat. It's much more difficult to build a game that *almost* defeats the player at every turn!

Genre & Style

Games are broken down into different *genres* and from there into distinct gameplay *styles*. It is entirely possible to blend different gameplay components across genres to come up with new game types. *Genre* describes the broad category of a game: Is it an action game, or is it a strategy game? *Style* refers to the specifics of the gameplay itself—and perhaps most importantly, it sets player expectations with regard to the game's rules. For example, a player will expect a platform game to focus on elements such as timing, puzzles, running, and jumping over obstacles.

Image courtesy of Kimberly Unger.

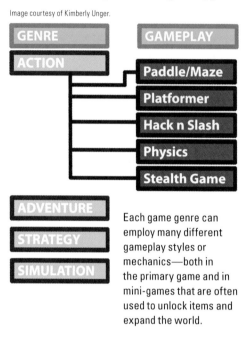

Each game genre can employ many different gameplay styles or mechanics—both in the primary game and in mini-games that are often used to unlock items and expand the world.

Like other game engines and tools, Creator is well suited to particular game genres; conveniently enough, these just so happen to be some of the most expansive and popular gameplay styles on the market—thanks to the resurgence of casual games. Creator's strengths cater to types of games that for the most part can be found consistently in the "Top 10" spots in App Stores for all platforms.

Action

Action games are all about … action—within the game (e.g., animations, procedural motion, explosions, active interface elements) and taken by the player (e.g., button presses, finger twitches, arm wiggles, jumping up and down). Action games incorporate a lot of motion, timing, and "events" happening within its digital confines—and they often contain shorter play times within levels.

Paddleball

The key to *paddleball* games is timing. The speed of the ball must ramp up just right at the correct time to keep things challenging. We've all played a badly coded *Breakout* clone at some point in our lives—where you set the ball and paddle just right so that you can bounce the ball back and forth for all eternity! This gets dull after a while—and you eventually "lose" due to being bored rather than challenged.

The primary gameplay mechanics in a classic paddleball game are:

1. Ball physics
2. Paddle physics
3. Block physics

That's it: Only three different sets of parameters! You can include powerups, change paddle size, and add laserbeams—but if the three core gameplay elements aren't any fun to work with, your players will quit before getting to any shiny add-ons.

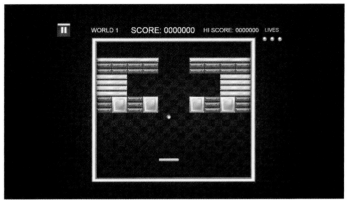

Creator games such as *Gem Breaker* follow a form of paddleball gameplay.

When working with Creator, consider tying the physics attributes to each other. Creator allows you to "tell" your game what to do through the careful application of *Behaviors* (how an object acts and reacts) and *Attributes* (components that define an object's properties—such as weight or bounciness), which essentially serve as instructions and will be executed in the order in which you assemble them (much like reading a restaurant menu). It is possible to set up relationships between Behaviors and Attributes on any given *Actor* or series of Actors (visible objects within a game). For example, you can set up your Actor so that if you increase the bounciness of the paddle, the ball automatically becomes "harder"—requiring fewer hits to break up a brick. Creating interrelationships like this—where a change to one Actor within the *Scene* (your current game level) will cause changes to other Actors in your Scene as needed—can make it simpler for you to make adjustments until you find a "sweet spot" between the parameters.

Expose That Variable!

"Expose" (in terms of game development) means to "make accessible." If you expose a variable, such as the numerical value that governs the "hardness" of the paddle, you are placing it somewhere that's easy to access and change—rather than needing to dig through 20 nested nodes to find it.

Run 'n' Gun

Run 'n' gun games are all about close combat and quick reflexes. They may contain elements used in role-playing games (RPGs)—such as adding new weapons in the form of pickups or power-ups—but at their core, the focus is to mow through all the enemies in a level to reach the big bad boss at the end. Notable examples of this gameplay style include blockbuster titles such as the legendary *Contra*. These games work very well with keyboard and mouse—but they're trickier to manage with only a touchscreen because they traditionally require one set of controls for direction and another for weapon or fighting moves.

Image courtesy of Kimberly Unger.   Source Apple Inc.

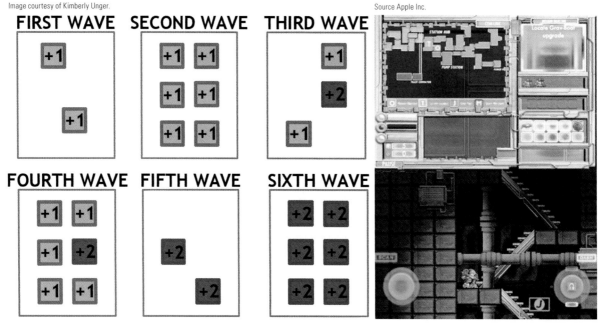

The composition of the waves of enemies is essential toward making "run 'n' gun" games such as *SZCBeyondDead* (right) "fun" to play. Each wave needs to be properly balanced to ensure it is a challenge to the player but not impossible to defeat.

The goal of these games is to defeat waves of enemies in order to reach an end boss. Even modern console shooters such as *Halo* and *Call of Duty* follow this format; however, as the genre has matured, the 'lieutenants" or mini-bosses have often been replaced with mission-based goals such as arming a bomb or saving a hostage. The key to making these games fun is the existence of waves of enemies. Like platform games (covered later in this chapter), run 'n' gun games ramp up the level of difficulty and introduce new classes of enemies as players progress. Players initially fight just a few, easily dispatched enemies—then in greater and greater numbers. The number of enemies diminishes—but new, stronger enemies are introduced. This pattern is repeated until the player reaches the "boss"—who often combines the skillsets and weapons of the smaller enemies. The patterning of these "waves of enemies" is a key component in making these types of games fun and challenging for the player. This is an excellent place to prototype and focus test your game (see Chapter 3) to observe player reactions and explore ways to mix up enemies to keep the game challenging.

Hack 'n' Slash

Similar to run 'n' gun games, *hack 'n' slash* games emphasize close combat and quick reflexes. They can contain RPG-style elements such as improved health, armor, or weapons—but character advancement is not the focus. Instead, goals include room-clearing and collecting with an emphasis on being able to defeat the endgame. Depending on the type, the endgame might be a boss or a puzzle of some kind. Often, being able to defeat the end of the level depends on collecting enough of the correct items to ensure that players live through the final encounter.

Source Apple Inc.

Hack 'n' slash games such as *Hobo with a Shotgun* tend to focus on picking up enough loot drops and finding enough in-game items (e.g., ammo, weapons) to beat the "big boss" at the end of the level.

Viva Piñata!

Enemy characters in hack 'n' slash games are sometimes referred to as "piñatas" because the goal of the player is to smash them to get the loot they are carrying.

Platformer

Platformers are all about timing. How much time is needed to dodge a bullet, rocket, or turtle on fire—or to double-jump across a pit of snakes or get to the top of a stairway before an anvil falls on your head? Famous platformers include the Mario and Sonic The Hedgehog franchises (*Mario World, Super Mario Galaxy, Sonic The Hedgehog, Sonic & Knuckles*) or the wildly popular independently-developed *Braid*.

Image courtesy of Kimberly Unger.

Source Apple Inc.

Tile-based level design allows you to easily build large and complex levels for platformers such as *CheeseMan* (right) out of only a few simple tiles—saving space and time.

An easy way to help keep consistent distances between obstacles and platforms is to build your game on a grid. *Tile-based* level design helps to standardize the size of objects and distances between objects within a level. This will in turn ensure that your level doesn't contain invisible walls or impassible areas because one jump is just two pixels wider than it should be. Creator does not, as of yet, have a built-in "snap-to-grid" function—but if you use the grid in Photoshop or another sketch program as the basis for your mockup, you will find that re-creating the layout in Creator is a much simpler task than trying to create it on the fly.

"You Shall Not Pass . . ."

In games, an *invisible wall* refers to a situation where a player cannot get through a space (such as cross a street) for no apparent reason. This is usually caused either by an inexperienced level designer simply setting up an invisible *collision box* to keep the player out (without providing an appropriate visual "reason" such as a locked gate or a pile of rubble)—or by an in-game object's improperly aligned (or sized) collision box. This can cause the player to get hung up on the object without being able to understand why—which can be extremely frustrating!

Mr. Ninja System

My greatest technical achievement with Creator was to complete a *Mr. Ninja* system in which the main character jumps from one spinning platform to the next and spins around on the platform until the next jump. Creating this system required a fair amount of trigonometry and logic.

Dan Caldwell (Owner & Founder, Power Up Education Inc.)

::::: Case Study: Bartley Does Boston

Image courtesy of Bharat Battu.

My *Bartley Does Boston* prototype is a 2D platformer that incorporates "Mario-style" run-and-jump gameplay—using a keyboard on a typical computer and touch-based controls on iOS devices. Mechanics include collections of coins and special tokens (ducklings), enemies that take a life from the player, moving platforms, and checkpoints to resume progress after a player death.

—*Bharat Battu, M.Ed.*
(educational multimedia developer)

Physics

Physics games can be quite deceptive. They rely on the physics built into the game engine or tool (in this case, Creator) to handle any action and animation on the part of the game objects. This can save a game developer from the necessity of animating walk cycles or flapping wings. Balls can bounce, boxes can tumble, and stones can roll. While physics games *seem* like less work, the gameplay itself (building physics puzzles with a consistently findable solution) can require a little more thought. However, like all styles of gameplay, it's fairly easy to build an insoluble puzzle—but it's much harder to build an *almost* insoluble puzzle. It's possible to create limited character animation (e.g., wobbling arms and legs in *Scribblenauts*) or swap in a physics-animated object for a hand-animated object when appropriate (e.g., ragdoll physics effects seen when a character dies in AAA games such as *Halo* or *Left for Dead*). Developers need to walk a very fine line in order to keep a player coming back again and again.

Source Apple Inc.

Games such as *Zig Zag Zombie HD* give players the power to choose the angle and amount of force applied; the rest is up to physics!

::::: Tutorial: Creating a Projection System

Kimberly Unger (Chief Executive Officer, Bushi-go, Inc.)

Physics games come in many flavors. *Zombie Drop* is an excellent example of a "drop" style game, where the point is to destroy enough objects to drop the zombie onto a target so it can be electrocuted. Slingshot or cannon style games have come to the fore recently—first gaining popularity on Flash game aggregate sites, then making the jump to mobile. With the physics already built into GameSalad Creator, building a cannon or slingshot becomes much more manageable than programming one from scratch.

Image courtesy of GameSalad®.   Image courtesy of GameSalad®.

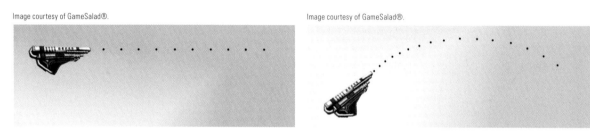

Games can incorporate both types of projections: Straight lines that remain unaffected by gravity work well for elements such as laserbeams, while parabolic arcs work better to represent objects that are thrown or fired from a cannon.

Creating a cannon, goo spitter, fire hose—or whatever projection system you choose for your game—isn't terribly difficult. You are, in essence, instructing Creator to Spawn (bringing an object or enemy into the game) a projectile and move it in a line from the creation point until it either hits something or runs off the screen. The tricky part arises when you are trying to get the projectile to travel in a parabolic arc. Let's take a look at the steps needed to create a cannon-style physics game in Creator:

1. **Choose your Actor.** This might be a cannon or a fire hose, or it might just be a colored rectangle; that's up to you! Creator refers to these in-game objects as "Actors."

2. **Drag the Actor over to the Stage.** The "Stage" is the large box in the upper right of the Creator window. This is where you assemble all the Actors needed to build your level. Dragging an Actor from the Library (the list on the left) to the Stage will create an Instance (copy) of your Actor that you can safely modify. (Any changes made to the Prototype [original] will affect all of the Instances [copies].)

3. **Create a Rule.** If you double-click on your Actor (the one on the Stage) in Windows Creator, you will see a window open up on the bottom right. This is the Backstage, and it's in here that you'll place your instructions. You will see two open tabs on the Backstage labeled "Prototype" and "Instance." Select the Prototype tab so that all of your changes are saved to the original Actor (and so you don't have to redo this Rule for every individual Actor in the Scene). On the upper right of the new Backstage area, click ⊕ to create a new Rule and modify it as follows:

When the mouse is down (the player has clicked the mouse button) and the mouse cursor is also over the Actor, Spawn (create a copy of) an Actor at location X. The drop-down menu in the node will allow you to specify the Actor spawned. Keep this in mind: When you set the location for the object Spawn, Point 0,0 is the center point of your Actor. With the settings from this tutorial,

Image courtesy of GameSalad®.

With Creator, it's possible to choose exactly where on the screen your object Spawns—whether it's related to a particular Actor or all on its own.

Creator will create your new Actor in the exact same position in relation to the original Actor—regardless of the starting Actor's position or rotation. When you run this to test it with the current settings, your Actor (in this case, our little orange projectile) will Spawn at exactly the center point of the weapon Actor.

Image courtesy of GameSalad®.

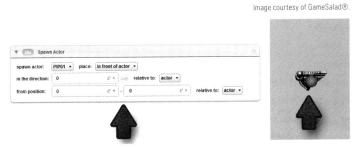

The number values you choose are related to the pixel location on the playfield. If your screen is 320 x 240, a value of 600 will create your Actor offscreen.

Change the "from position" equation. In this example, we have set the "X" attribute to "50" (i.e., 50 units to the *right* of the center of your original Actor) and the "Y" attribute to "20" (i.e., 20 units *above* the center of the original Actor). The projectile Actor will Spawn in this exact relationship from here on out—no matter how you rotate the original Actor or move it about the screen. If you need to Spawn an object in the same spot without tying its location to an Actor, you can change the drop-down setting on the "relative to Actor" menu to reflect an absolute position instead.

Image courtesy of GameSalad®.

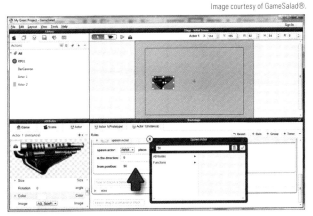

Before you can complete your instructions to Spawn an Actor, you need to be sure that the Actor already exists in your Library. Try to create all Actor objects before adding Behaviors and Attributes.

:::::: Case Study:
d-capitatrix

Image courtesy of Thomas Wagner.
© 2011 Gamesmold.

I wondered if it would be possible to transfer the spirit of *Portal* into 2D space—and to develop this using Creator. It was: After a single day of experimenting, I had a ball rolling in a maze with several portal gates that could be dragged from wall to wall by your fingertips. For the look and the story of the game, I tried to come up with something that would combine a simple ball shaped player object with a little bit more personality. I ended up allowing the player move robot heads back to their decapitated bodies. While the bodies are simply waiting (and eventually start to move slowly when fully charged with batteries), the head keeps talking to the player—commenting on what's happening. It was quite challenging to permanently analyze the progress of the gameplay to determine the correct audio file to play. Much easier than this was the creation of the main physics routine: Depending on what gate the rolling head touched (and at what angle this gate was rotated), I just repositioned it at the opposite gate—flipping and adapting its physical velocities according to the new gate's rotation. The rest was done by Creator's physics engine.

—*Thomas Wagner (Owner, Gamesmold)*

:::::: Case Study:
Escape Artist

Image courtesy of Stormy Studio.

I decided to run a GameSalad design competition called "Think Outside the Box" via the GameSalad forum. I created *Escape Artist* as a "pretend" entry after deciding I couldn't take part because I was running the contest. *Escape Artist* evolved and eventually made it to the app store. Featuring some unique game ideas, this simple shape drawing game was my first to feature some eight-bit graphics. The "Think Outside the Box" contest has now been run four times—with great prizes donated by users; even GameSalad offered up Pro memberships! The most recent contest saw over 30 impressive entries—each of which had been worked on for a full month. The contest is run to push fellow users to share discussions on game design and produce truly original game ideas using the superb Creator software.

—*Jon Draper (Director, Stormy Studio)*

When the mouse is down (the player has clicked the mouse button) and the mouse cursor is also over the Actor, Spawn (create a copy of) an Actor at location X. The drop-down menu in the node will allow you to specify the Actor spawned. Keep this in mind: When you set the location for the object Spawn, Point 0,0 is the center point of your Actor.

Image courtesy of GameSalad®.

With the settings from this tutorial, Creator will create your new Actor in the exact same position in relation to the original Actor—regardless of the starting Actor's position or rotation. When you run this to test it with the current settings, your Actor (in this case, our little orange projectile) will Spawn at exactly the center point of the weapon Actor.

With Creator, it's possible to choose exactly where on the screen your object Spawns—whether it's related to a particular Actor or all on its own.

Image courtesy of GameSalad®.

The number values you choose are related to the pixel location on the playfield. If your screen is 320 x 240, a value of 600 will create your Actor offscreen.

Change the "from position" equation. In this example, we have set the "X" attribute to "50" (i.e., 50 units to the *right* of the center of your original Actor) and the "Y" attribute to "20" (i.e., 20 units *above* the center of the original Actor). The projectile Actor will Spawn in this exact relationship from here on out—no matter how you rotate the original Actor or move it about the screen. If you need to Spawn an object in the same spot without tying its location to an Actor, you can change the drop-down setting on the "relative to Actor" menu to reflect an absolute position instead.

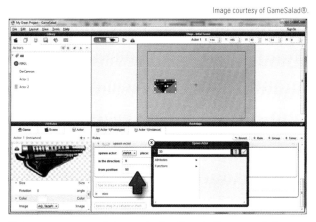
Image courtesy of GameSalad®.

Before you can complete your instructions to Spawn an Actor, you need to be sure that the Actor already exists in your Library. Try to create all Actor objects before adding Behaviors and Attributes.

■ *Tell this newly spawned projectile how to move.* This means adding a new Rule—but rather than attaching that Rule to the weapon, you'll attach it to the projectile itself. Under the "Actor" tab, select the Actor you will be using as your projectile (In this case, for the images being used in this tutorial, the Actor's name is PIP01.) From the Library, select and bring the "Change Velocity" Behavior to the Rule window to create a Rule for this Actor. (We are using "Change Velocity" rather than "Move" to ensure the gravity will affect the speed *and* motion of the projectile.) If you test the game at this point, you'll see that the projectile simply gets spawned and moves from the barrel of the cannon offscreen to the right. Now, you'll need to make some adjustments to the world so that gravity affects this projectile like a cannon ball and drags it earthward the farther out it gets.

Image courtesy of GameSalad®.

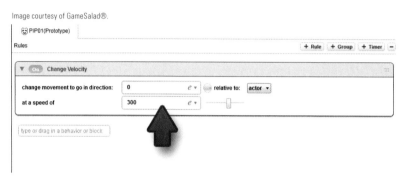

The bottom left of the grid (or Stage) is denoted by "0,0"—and objects move in positive (+) or negative (-) increments from it.

Image courtesy of GameSalad®.

■ *Set Attributes for the Scene at large.* Go to the "Attributes" box on your left and select "Scene." These set the Attributes for the Scene at large, Here, may adjust elements such as gravity and wind that will affect *everything* in your Scene (unless you make an exception, of course). Find "Gravity" and set the "Y" parameter to around 150. This will cause elements in your Scene to be dragged downward along the Y (up/down) axis of your Scene. Any object that *not* flagged as "non-moveable" will be affected by the Gravity you have set for the Scene and will fall off the bottom of the screen the first time you test your game. (Incidentally, if you were to set this value at -150, your objects would float upward.) Keep in mind that a virtual environment has no concept of "up" or "down." Whether you are working in a 2D environment like Creator or a 3D environment like Unreal's UDK, the program is going to determine the direction an object moves in relation to an invisible grid. The bottom left of the grid (or Stage) is denoted by "0,0"—and objects move in positive (+) or negative (-) increments from it.

"Gravity" in Creator can exert a pull in any direction you choose. Set the Y value to a negative number and watch your objects float to the sky; set the Y value to a positive number and watch them drop to the floor. The same goes for the X value: A positive number pulls objects to the right, and a negative number pulls objects to the left.

Image courtesy of GameSalad®.

Set how the object reacts with the Scene Attributes. Go back to the Attributes for the projectile Actor and find the "Physics" Attribute. Don't worry about "Motion"; we have already set those parameters by using "Change Velocity" in the previous step. Under "Physics," we want to set how the object reacts with the Scene Attributes you adjusted. Set the density to around 10. (Density is how much mass your object has; this tells the Creator physics code whether the object is a soap bubble or a bowling ball.)

Next, set your friction to 1 and your bounciness to 1. As you add objects later on, these values will affect how hitting those objects will affect your projectile. Make sure "Moveable" is checked and set your "Drag" to around 100; again, this is information for Creator's built-in physics. "Drag" will tell the game how quickly the projectile will be affected. The lower the drag coefficient, the longer the projectile will go before gravity drags it down. When you go back in to test this, you will find that your projectile (when fired) will move in a long parabolic arc—similar to what is seen in Flash games such as *Crush the Castle* or *Kitten Cannon*.

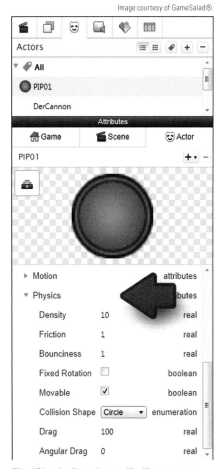

The "Physics" settings will affect every object in your Scene that has been marked as "moveable." Turn this off for any object and it is immediately locked into place.

Variables

Distinctions between variables (e.g., setting Drag at 100 vs. 25) can make the difference between a game that's understandable and easy to learn and one that will have players tearing their hair out. Be sure to playtest these elements thoroughly.

By Any Other Name . . .

It is often better to rename assets that are individualized in order to avoid losing track. *Naming conventions* (naming objects according to a specific set of rules) will help keep things in order—especially when a project involves several people.

Fighting

Fighting games can easily be one of the more frustrating types for a new player—since moves tend to become more complex over time, with straightforward single-key attacks getting superseded by more complicated patterns. Rather than fight waves of enemies in order to get to an "end boss," players fight a series of single, one-on-one matches against various opponents. These games are particularly well-suited to two-player gameplay and were arcade staples during the early 1990s. For a fighting game, the fun comes at the intersection of the complexity of the controls and the reactivity of the game itself. For the novice player, these types of games quickly turn into a long series of frantic button punches (hence the term "button masher"). It's important to allow the player time to get used to the game's basic controls—whether they're keyboard strokes or taps of the fingertip—before introducing more complex structures into the gameplay. A part of the satisfaction, particularly for players who are fans of this type of game, is to be able to execute moves that do more damage (by memorizing more complex controls).

Image courtesy of Appy Entertainment, Inc.

FaceFighter Ultimate provides a unique fighting game experience —where any photo becomes a customized fighting foe.

Gameplay Versatility

Here are just a few examples of gameplay systems created by Creator developers:

Complex physics systems, drawing engines, portal-style teleportation physics, and endless runner engines.

Thomas Wagner (Owner, Gamesmold)

Balance block physics game, point-and-click adventure (with swappable 360-degree rooms), drawing shapes game, submarine control game, and a unique audio game (where you see with your ears).

Jon Draper (Developer, Stormy Studio)

Unlock systems (collect items, unlock levels, characters, music, color), score multipliers, bonus periods (collect 5 objects in 10 seconds), power-ups, achievements (in-game), and an inventory/movement system (adventure game).

George Kotsiofides (The Head Sheep, Quantum Sheep)

Strategy

Strategy games encompass a narrower category than action games and can involve resource management and socioeconomic "simulations" that predict the rise and fall of empires. A tool such as Creator is better suited to pocket-sized strategy games such as *Tower Defense* or *Plants vs Zombies*. These smaller-scale strategy games require a little additional cleverness but can be quite an addictive form of gameplay for the casual player.

Image courtesy of Utopian Games.

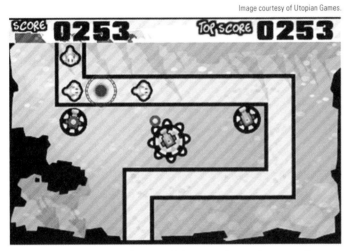

Strategy games such as this tower defense-style template come in all shapes and levels of complexity. One key element in this type of gameplay is player choice and the consequences that stem from it.

A key component of strategy games is the element of player choice. Yes, players make choices in every type of game—but in the strategy genre, forward progression through the story is arguably less important than the player's ability to choose the route taken to get there. This means that multiple solutions and options are important elements of the gameplay.

Trying Out Something New . . .

I test out new gameplay systems and mechanics all the time. Even if I'm not developing a mechanic for a specific game, I find that it's fun and quick to try out new ideas in Creator. I've developed everything from a side-scrolling beat-em-up to complex RPG battle systems.

Ace Connell (Managing Director, Mynameisace Ltd)

Case Study:
d-capitatrix

Image courtesy of Thomas Wagner.
© 2011 Gamesmold.

I wondered if it would be possible to transfer the spirit of *Portal* into 2D space—and to develop this using Creator. It was: After a single day of experimenting, I had a ball rolling in a maze with several portal gates that could be dragged from wall to wall by your fingertips. For the look and the story of the game, I tried to come up with something that would combine a simple ball shaped player object with a little bit more personality. I ended up allowing the player move robot heads back to their decapitated bodies. While the bodies are simply waiting (and eventually start to move slowly when fully charged with batteries), the head keeps talking to the player—commenting on what's happening. It was quite challenging to permanently analyze the progress of the gameplay to determine the correct audio file to play. Much easier than this was the creation of the main physics routine: Depending on what gate the rolling head touched (and at what angle this gate was rotated), I just repositioned it at the opposite gate—flipping and adapting its physical velocities according to the new gate's rotation. The rest was done by Creator's physics engine.

—*Thomas Wagner (Owner, Gamesmold)*

Case Study:
Escape Artist

Image courtesy of Stormy Studio.

I decided to run a GameSalad design competition called "Think Outside the Box" via the GameSalad forum. I created *Escape Artist* as a "pretend" entry after deciding I couldn't take part because I was running the contest. *Escape Artist* evolved and eventually made it to the app store. Featuring some unique game ideas, this simple shape drawing game was my first to feature some eight-bit graphics. The "Think Outside the Box" contest has now been run four times—with great prizes donated by users; even GameSalad offered up Pro memberships! The most recent contest saw over 30 impressive entries—each of which had been worked on for a full month. The contest is run to push fellow users to share discussions on game design and produce truly original game ideas using the superb Creator software.

—*Jon Draper (Director, Stormy Studio)*

The Intersection of "Meh" & "Whee"!

Gameplay occurs at the intersection of controls and content. Every type of game, not just the ones discussed in this chapter, has a pre-defined set of conditions for success—such as "collect all 10 pellets to win" or "shoot all the bad guys and destroy the temple to win." The victory condition is often very simple; the "magic" happens when you modify it, allow things to go wrong in a level, or place obstacles in a player's path. This is where things really get interesting as a designer.

The Big Red Button

A "Big Red Button" game is one that essentially delivers a payout of some kind to the player every time, regardless of that player's skill. Essentially, you give the player a big red button that says, "WIN." When players press the button, they win. This often results in a game that will make players "happy" but is ultimately unfulfilling and short-lived.

For the purposes of illustration, we have created an "imaginary" game called *Pachinko Madness*. It contains (or will contain as we walk you through it) most of the basic precepts you will need to build a game of your own. Elements such as scoring, collision, and basic physics are used in almost every type of game. Learning them here will give you enough grounding to use them in your own game further down the road. The victory condition for the first level of this game is to get 100 points. Points are earned by dropping a ball from the top of the screen and allowing it to bounce downwards until it hits one of the point buckets at the bottom of the screen. Setting this up is simple enough.

Image courtesy of Kimberly Unger.

The victory condition for the first level of *Pachinko Madness* is to earn 100 points by dropping a ball from the top of the screen and allowing it to bounce down between the pegs until it hits a point bucket at the bottom of the screen.

Consider the accompanying image: This doesn't look like much of a challenge, does it? This part of the game might have been built out during prototyping (discussed in Chapter 3) to test the ball physics—ensuring that they drop and bounce like they are supposed to. If you prefer to create a "Big Red Button" game, you might be able to make this work. However, in order for gameplay to be any fun in the classical sense of the word, there must be a chance that the player will lose. With the whole bottom of the screen covered in buckets, there may be no way for players to lose in the short term—but the game would leave them unfulfilled, and they will move onto the next shiny thing that catches their attention. So we have our victory condition: "100 points = WIN." Now, let's make a mess. First things first: Let's cut those buckets down to three. This is the first level, so we're feeling a bit kind. We are going to take that "Big Red Button" and make it more difficult for the player to push.

It turns out that disrupting the buckets will be the simplest way to make this game challenging. The task of players is to figure out where on the top of the screen they need to drop a ball so that it will end up where they want it to be at the bottom. By changing up the buckets at each level or every few levels, you will have the form for the game's most basic challenge. Let's set the rules for our buckets as such:

1. No more than three buckets per level
2. Buckets change size every five levels
3. Buckets change location every level

These rules may be modified later after playtesting—but for now, let's use them as part of the framework. This will yield a proper, if very basic, game. Drop the balls and try to get them in the bucket. It's simple and straightforward. 'How are you feeling, player? Nice and comfy with the ball clicking and bucket-filling mechanic we have going on here?' *Tap the screen and watch the ball drop. Tap the screen and watch the ball drop.* It will not take a player very long to master the basics!

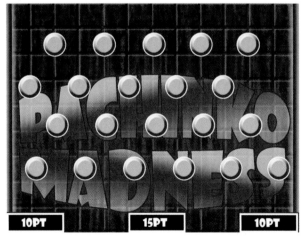

Image courtesy of Kimberly Unger.

By merely adjusting the size and position of the "buckets," you can create a simple game that will still be somewhat fun to play … for a level or two at least.

The game will soon become extremely boring—even with these new rules. Let's consider the gameplay for a moment. This is a physics-based game. The balls drop. The balls ping back and forth between the pegs on their way down to the buckets. So what happens if we alter the physics? Let's choose one of those pegs and make it a "special." We can change the color of the peg—and perhaps even add a little icon to it to inform the player that something is up. (Remember: We want to *challenge* the player—not create an unwinnable game.) Let's make that peg *bouncy* (not "rubber-ball" bouncy; try that and see what happens!): We can just increase the "bounciness" by changing one of the Attributes.

It's important to avoid changing the pegs that are already in the game. Instead, you need to create a new peg Actor with an empty set of rules. Creator does not allow you to simply make a copy of an existing Actor within the Library; you will need to use ✚ to create a new Actor, then use the Backstage to assign new Behaviors and Attributes as needed. You can use the same image for multiple Actors—so do not import a new one, but simply assign it from the Media Library.

					Backstage				

PIP01(Prototype)   PIP01(Instance)

Rules   ↰ Revert   + Rule   + Group   + Timer   −

▼ ⬤ On   Change Velocity

change movement to go in direction: 0   𝑒 ▾   ⬤ relative to: actor ▾

at a speed of   0   𝑒 ▾

Click the lock to modify rules for this specific actor

type or drag in a behavior or block

If you double-click an Actor already in the Scene, you will see two tabs in the Backstage: Prototype and Instance. You want to work with the Prototype (the original version) of your Actor. Any changes made to the Prototype (original) will affect all of the Instances (copies).

You might want to throw in these new pegs after the first few levels, then tweak the gameplay a bit after the player gets comfortable. This approach has an added advantage: You can make a number of different changes to the physics of these pegs and mix them up as the player moves forward by making them more or less bouncy, sticky—or *explosive*! If you test the game by trying it out on a few of your friends, you will most likely find that more than a few players will discover a way to use these new pegs to their advantage.

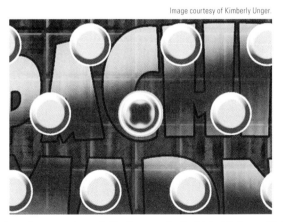

If you make a change to an in-game element, like the pegs in *Pachinko Madness*, it's important to inform the player of this change in some way (such as showing a distinct visual difference). Try to avoid explaining changes to players overtly—unless it's clear that they won't figure this out for themselves.

Depending on how many levels you plan to create, you can take this idea even further—by creating pegs that reverse gravity for a few moments, or pegs that move when struck. The key is to change things in small increments. Introduce a new element, allow players to get used to it, and then change things up again. This way, you reinforce the satisfaction that comes with mastery *and* keep the gameplay fresh.

Avoid Ennui

"Ennui" is a feeling of listless boredom. Although you might not hear the word mentioned often (outside of literature courses), ennui is the perfect description for what a player feels when gameplay gets stale and predictable. Be sure to avoid it!

There is no perfect formula for what makes the gameplay "right" in one game versus another. In fact, there are more than a few instances in which two games with essentially the same gameplay (sometimes even direct clones of one another) have hit the market—and one succeeds wildly while the other fails. The reasons can be as subtle as the hang time of a bird shot out of a catapult, or as clear as erratic controls or inaccurate scoring. One thing that can and will make a difference is getting the game into the hands of live players and seeing how *they* react. This will tell you if the gameplay is *really* as fun as you think it is!

Best Foot Forward

Mashups and *hybrids* (games that mix controls and conditions across two or more genres) are the new "shiny." The emergence of easily accessible and properly supported tools such as GameSalad Creator will break the never-ending cycle of clones and safe "me-you" games. More developers are experimenting with style-bending gameplay—adding strategy elements to paddleball games or a collection element to a fighting game. Players—even the newer breed of "casual" gamers—are being exposed to hybrid styles of gameplay that haven't been widely available, simply because larger studios weren't comfortable taking a risk. However, with players seeking ever newer experiences (coupled with the sheer volume of games available), the pressure to attract the player's attention will drive studios and independent game developers alike to experiment with gameplay in ways never seen before.

Additional material based on these exercises
and chapter topics is available as part of the
Instructor Resources package.

23

:::CHAPTER REVIEW EXERCISES:::

1. Describe at least 5 gameplay features associated with your original game. Do they fit neatly into one type of gameplay style—or a hybrid of two or more styles?

2. Describe your game's genre and core gameplay style. Are you planning on working with a gameplay genre or style that fits well with GameSalad Creator?

3. Describe your game's victory (or "win") and defeat (or "lose") conditions. Are all conditions simple and clear?

4. Describe the progression associated with your game. Does your game progress through different levels, or does it simply increase difficulty over time?

5. Will your game benefit from in-game elements such as power-ups? Why or why not?

6. What environmental elements could you modify to increase the difficulty of your game?

7. How do players know they have reached your game's "final" victory condition?

2

Interface

eye of the beholder

Key Chapter Questions

- What elements comprise a game's *interface*?

- How important are *"look and feel"* vs. *function* in user interface design?

- At what point during development should the user interface be *"locked"*?

- How can *GameSalad Creator* help to enhance a game's interface?

- How do user interfaces differ based on *genre*?

"Connection" is key. The point of contact between the player and the game is possibly one of the most important elements in game design. Interfaces immediately reveal the type of game that's being played—providing players with the information needed to solve a puzzle, stay alive, or navigate dangerous terrain. Some developers have done away with the onscreen interface altogether, while others focus heavily on the interface—leaving the remaining visuals as an afterthought. Interfaces even extend beyond the visual screen—with physical interfaces tied to controllers, keyboards, trackballs, and touchscreens. The interaction of player and interface must be as smooth and effortless as possible; in fact, one cannot talk about interfaces without addressing both halves of the equation: software and hardware.

Points of Contact

For basic GameSalad Creator tutorials, see Appendix. For more information on interface design, see *Game Interface Design,* (Saunders/ Novak)—part of Delmar Cengage Learning's *Game Development Essentials* series.

A game interface is not a single element of a game's design. It is, instead, a string of brightly colored beads—a series of interconnected elements that all affect one another as they execute their assigned tasks. Since the interface exists in both physical and digital environments, players can interact with it in the real world. The two interface categories—hardware (physical) and software (visual)—have evolved alongside each other throughout the history of interface development. As innovations emerged in physical interface development, advances were also made in visual interfaces (and vice versa)—often exceeding expectations.

Hardware

Initially, there was a custom *hardware* design for every game. With the popular arcade games of the late 1970s and early 1980s, it was common to see trackballs, paddle dials, multiple button sets, and joysticks—all depending on the developer's choice of gameplay and the publisher that put it on the market. Every time a gameplay innovation was introduced, a new way to interact with it was presented to players. The experimentation of the early years slowly resolved into several basic control setups. Standardization emerged as the arcade industry reached its peak, and smaller publishers began to experiment with cost-saving measures such as installing new games into old (occasionally refurbished) arcade cabinets. It was common to see inexpensive cabinets with multiple sets of buttons or controls that had been disabled in order to make it simpler for companies to swap in new games.

Source Atari, Inc. Photo by Robert Entrekin.

Source Nintendo. Photo by Robert Entrekin.

The quest for the perfect physical interface led early console manufacturers to try a broad range of designs—from the minimalist Atari joystick (left) to the complex Power Glove controller (right).

Console games followed a similar trend. As in any infant industry, game hardware manufacturers fought to come up with something new that will set their products apart from the competition. A player's first and possibly most important point of contact with any new game was through the use of the *controller*. Size problems (e.g., too large, too small), awkward grip angles, or inconsistent button placement could positively or negatively affect a user's gameplay experience—not to mention the console's sales. Each console manufacturer quickly developed a signature controller style that evolved with each design iteration.

Source Sony Computer Entertainment America. Photo by Robert Entrekin.
Source Sony Computer Entertainment America. Photo by Robert Entrekin.
Source Sony Computer Entertainment America. Photo by Robert Entrekin.

Console manufacturers adopted a distinctive physical interface design that evolved very little over time—retaining a signature "look and feel" and key elements such as button options and placement (PlayStation controllers: DualShock [left], DualShock 2 [middle], and SIXAXIS/DualShock 3 [right]).

Early mobile games took advantage of old-school control schemes. Devices such as the BlackBerry contained built-in trackballs used for menu navigation that were easily adapted to styles of play that had proven successful in the past. It was, in many cases, a simple button-to-button conversion.

When touchscreen handhelds gained popularity at around 2007, virtual versions of these physical interfaces—already proven to be effective with existing styles of gameplay—were developed. For mobile devices such as smartphones and tablets (e.g., iPhone, Galaxy Tab series) that almost exclusively utilize the touchscreen as a physical interface, virtual thumbpads, and joysticks presented early solutions. However, as game developers became more comfortable with touchscreens, games began to take advantage of the unique opportunities offered by touch-focused control systems.

Source Games Press.

However, touchscreen games moved away from the virtual joystick fairly quickly. The evolution of the touchscreen has enabled new modes of play and ways to look at existing gameplay styles. Players accustomed to working with touchscreen devices will often experiment with screen taps first before looking to see if there is a virtual thumbstick available.

Early touchscreen games such as *Street Fighter IV* (iOS) utilized virtual versions of established gameplay controls as an attempt to directly translate the gameplay experience from console and arcade games to touchscreen handhelds.

Software

As the hardware evolved to meet the demands of gameplay, the *software* also followed suit. Early games were extremely restricted in terms of available *screen real estate*—which meant that the interface was often limited to essential components such as player scores, available lives/health, and a *leaderboard* (a public "high-score" list showing player names or initials) allowing players to see the "top dog" in the arcade in any given week. Even with all this early simplicity, the amount of information given to the player grew dramatically over time.

Source Interplay Entertainment. Image courtesy of Kimberly Unger.

Like physical interfaces, visual interfaces evolved to suit the needs of the game—giving players the information needed to complete it. More information meant a more complex interface—as exemplified in early role-playing games (*The Bard's Tale*, shown), in which the UI became a deeper and more integrated part of the gameplay rather than only a feedback mechanism.

Early games displayed more or less the same information: how well a player was doing (usually defined by score), and how much longer a player had to play (usually determined by a timer or number of lives). As games began to compartmentalize even further, types of information became even more game-specific—and designers focused on the visual interface as a key component. For games that required more management on the part of the player—such as role-playing games (RPGs) or real-time strategy games (RTSs)—the interface expanded to include multiple screens that the player could access from the main gameplay screen.

Different software interfaces began their evolution on distinct systems—and it took quite a while for them to cross over from system to system. For example, the desktop computer was the original home of the RTS—in part because early interfaces for the RTS genre contained multiple screens of information that the player needed to access. Early consoles faced a double whammy of poor screen resolution (with access only to 640 x 480 pixels per inch associated with television screens, versus the thousands of pixels available on an average computer monitor) and available memory. This made games with simpler interfaces and gameplay (such as side scrollers) a better fit for consoles. In order to make the jump to console, the whole system of interaction had to be re-designed—something that wouldn't happen with any real success until early 2006.

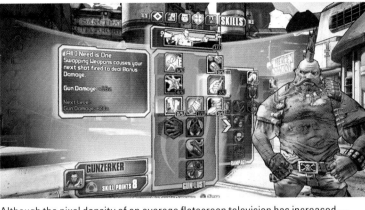

Source Games Press.

Although the pixel density of an average flatscreen television has increased—allowing classic role-playing and real-time strategy style interfaces to make the jump to consoles—the tradition of heavy iconography and images continues, giving console interfaces their own distinctive look (*Borderlands 2*, shown).

"Next-gen" consoles began to appear in 2006 and 2007. These systems were backed by hardware manufacturers that had a vested interest in both sides of the market (computer and console) and aggressively pursued hardware setups that mimicked the mid- to high-end computers available at the time. With dedicated *VRAM* (*Video RAM*), cutting edge processors, and built-in broadband connectivity, these consoles were designed to run the larger and more complex games that had until recently only been found on desktop computers. At the same time, the costs of large, high pixel density televisions began to plummet. No longer crippled by 640 x 480 pixel resolutions, consoles were finally capable of running the complex interfaces found in large-format RPG and RTS games. However, the "lean and symbolic" nature of the console interfaces that came before continued to carry through into the new designs.

Common Ground

The first thing that comes to the average player's mind about the *user interface* (*UI*) is the information that is displayed onscreen during gameplay. While this is one of the key elements of any UI, it is in fact one of the smaller components of the overall UI design. UI refers to the whole interface, from the point at which a player comes into physical contact with the game (usually via a physical controller of some kind, but also through audio or visual cues) until the final credits screen—every button, dial, and other components players can manipulate.

When using a cross-platform tool such as GameSalad Creator, think first about those UI elements that are common to all platforms—those that will not be as affected by different physical interface types.

UI design decisions need to be made early on in the design process—not only because in-game UI elements need to feed into important components such as monetization and social networking, but because the amount and type of information needed to convey to players may end up affecting the gameplay itself. While some developers have experimented with the total absence of a UI (at least during gameplay), most provide the player with the information needed to complete the game. With this in mind, begin by taking a look at the elements that players will need to complete the game.

How does the UI fit in the world? Is it simply an external way of connecting the player to the game, or is it integrated into the game? Does it serve a purpose beyond communicating information to the player? It's okay if it's just an information tool; it just needs to be defined up front to help maintain consistency. In games such as *Dead Space* and *BioShock*, UI components are integrated into their respective worlds through physical objects that are accessed by the player character. For example, in order to access different Plasmids (in-game super skills players can acquire in game) in *BioShock*, the player must confirm that the player character is standing in front of the appropriate machine in game rather than pausing the game to search through the character's inventory whenever the need arises. Unless the player has access to one of these objects, the amount of information and functionality available is limited. Players of casual games such as *Candy Crush Saga* primarily play for high score and social bragging rights, so they may not be as interested in integration; keeping the UI elements separate from the game screen by placing them to the left or bottom of screen will help these players keep track of features that are important to their own game experiences.

Source Games Press.

Integrating the user interface with the game universe can be an effective way to include more elements without sacrificing screen real estate. Even though *Dead Space 2* (shown) was designed for consoles and large-format screens, the integration of the interface with the world was a key design component.

Carefully consider the game's type and genre. There are certain kinds of games that will be extremely well-suited to GameSalad Creator, and each of these types of games will have a different set of expectations associated with them.

Importance of Game Interface Design

The user interface is an often overlooked and underestimated part of game design; especially for the indie developer. Spending time on the interface will not only add extra polish to the game but will increase the user experience—something that should be a focal point at every aspect of game design and execution.

Ace Connell (Managing Director, Mynameisace Ltd)

Progress

Progress can be shown in a number of different ways—such as movement toward a goal on a map, a checklist of tasks to be completed, and even the health bar of your opponent. The key point is to give players an idea of how far they still have to go. Is the boss almost dead? Is the silver key still missing? How much wood *can* a woodchuck chuck? Do you get bonus points if you finish chucking ahead of time? It's important to consider the *goal* of the game and find a way to convey to players just how close they are to attaining that goal. For example, in a beat-em-up game such as *Street Fighter*, the player and opponent's health bars are displayed as easy-to-read objects on the game screen. Since the goal of combat is to defeat the opponent, the health bar does double duty—showing players how successful any given combination of moves was and what remains to be done before the round is over. In an RPG/shooter hybrid such as *Borderlands 2*, players instead have a checklist of items. As players succeed in each piece of the scavenger hunt such as quests, a box is checked off. Players can call this box up at any point in the game and can switch between active quests if they're unable to complete a task. A third example might be a puzzler such as *Bubble Safari* on Facebook where the player is shown a map to indicate progress through the game.

Source Apple Inc.

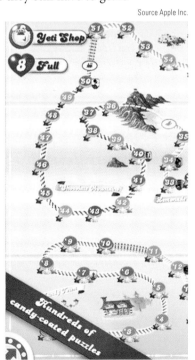

Popular Facebook game *Candy Crush Saga* shows progress toward player goals via a map that ties all levels together.

::::: Tutorial: Scoring Systems

Kimberly Unger (Chief Executive Officer, Bushi-go, Inc.)

Let's revisit our imaginary game *Pachinko Madness* for the purposes of this setup. In *Pachinko Madness*, the player gets points when a ball drops into a bucket at the bottom of the screen. These points are added to the player's overall score—displayed at the top of the screen. There are several different ways to set up this type of scoring in GameSalad Creator. The method shown here compartmentalizes each element so they can be reused later in the game. To begin with, create a new Attribute for your Scene:

Image courtesy of Kimberly Unger.

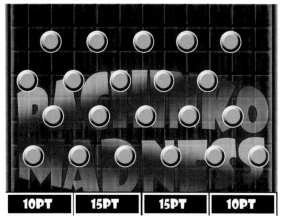

In *Pachinko Madness*, a small ball is dropped from the top of the screen and bounces from peg to peg on its way to the scoring buckets at the bottom of the screen. Points are assigned when the ball hits one of the buckets.

1. In the Attributes area in the bottom left of your screen, select the "Game" tab.

2. Click on the [+] button in the top right corner of the Attributes area to create a new Integer Attribute in the Game. Name this Attribute "GameScore." By placing the new Attribute here, you can access it from anywhere in the game.

Next, create three new Actors—for the scoreboard, ball, and bucket. The interaction of these three Actors will generate and display the score as the game is played. Remember that you want to work with the Prototype Actors—not the Instance.

Actor #1: Game Scoreboard (Pachinko_Scoreboard)

1. Create an Actor and assign an image to it. In our example, a small "scoreboard" will be displayed in the top left of the screen. Name the Actor "Pachinko_Scoreboard".

2. In the "Attributes" of the new Actor, access the Physics Attribute and uncheck the box marked "Moveable." This will keep the Scoreboard from falling under influence of Gravity later on.

3. Drag the Actor to the Stage and place it in the top left corner of the screen.

4. Double-click on the Actor to open up the Backstage at the bottom of the screen and select "Prototype." You will need to click on the lock to unlock the Instance (and break the link between the Prototype and the Instance).

5. Go to the Library and select "Display Text." Drag this Behavior over to the Backstage. This Behavior will display a specific line of text at runtime (when you run the game). You won't be able to see anything until you test the game.

6. Choose the font and size. (Feel free to experiment with this.) Creator will display your text based on the Actor's center point. You can adjust whether it aligns to the left, center, or right—but you cannot fine-tune it on a pixel-by-pixel basis. The scoreboard image used in this example was designed to have the text displayed in the middle of the image in order to minimize any extra work.

7. To the right of the word "display" in your Behavior, you will see an Expression Editor symbol (e). Select this symbol to open the Expression Editor. The Expression Editor will allow you to tie the text displayed here to the "GameScore" Attribute you just created in your Scene.

8. In the Expression Editor, select "Attributes," followed by "Game," and finally "GameScore." Click on the green checkmark in the Expression Editor.

Image courtesy of GameSalad® and Kimberly Unger.

9. When you run the game, you should see a "0" displayed in your score box. If not, return to the editor and select your "Instance" of Pachinko_Scoreboard. On the top, you should see a "revert" button; click it to pull a clean copy of the Actor from the Prototype to the Instance. ("Revert" will make the Instance a clean copy, which is useful as a reset tool if your Behaviors are set up incorrectly.)

The Expression Editor in Creator (Windows, shown) will allow you to tell the game to display the Integer held in the new "GameScene" Attribute you created in the first part of the tutorial.

Actor #2: Game Ball (Pachinko_Ball)

1. Create an Actor and assign an image to it. In the case of our example, we are using a fairly simple circle to represent our Pachinko ball.

2. Drag this Actor to the Stage. Double-click on the Actor to open the Backstage and choose the Prototype for making changes. Remember, the Prototype is the original—so every change made to it will propagate down through all Instances.

3. Under the Attributes for the Actor (window on bottom left), open Physics and set the ball's collision shape to "circle."

4. Go to the Library (top left window) and find the "Collide" Behavior; drag it into the open Backstage for this Actor. (Collide simply tells Creator which objects this Actor can bump into.) In the case of this example we will use the drop-down menu to choose the "Pachinko_Bucket" Actor. If you have not added a "Collide" Property, the Actors will not recognize one another. (You won't be able to choose the Actor in the dropdown menu until you create it.)

Image courtesy of GameSalad® and Kimberly Unger.

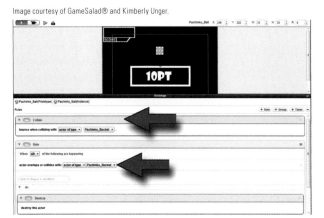

For any collidable object, include the "Collide" Behavior.

5. Click the button on the top right of the Backstage to add a "Rule." Set your Rule to "when *any* of the following are happening" and set the "Actor of type" to "Pachinko_Bucket." (At this point, you will need to skip ahead to the next section of this tutorial and create the Pachinko Bucket Actor; you will not be able to see the Pachinko_Bucket_ Actor until you have created one.)

6. Go to the Library (top left window) and find the "Destroy" property. Drag this property into the open Backstage for this Actor. This will destroy the ball when it comes in contact with the "Pachinko Bucket" Actor; otherwise, it will pass through the bucket and drop off the bottom of the screen.

Actor #3: Collection Bucket (Pachinko_Bucket)

1. Create an Actor and assign an image to it. In our example, we use a fairly simple rectangle with the point value of the bucket printed on it. Under the Actor Attributes (bottom left of window), go to Physics and uncheck the box marked "Moveable." (If you are skipping ahead to here from Actor #2, this is as far as you need to go for now.)

2. Find your Actor in the Library window on the left and double-click on it to open it up in the Backstage window.

3. In the upper right corner of your Backstage area, click the button to add a Rule to your Actor. Set your new Rule to "when all of the following are happening."

4. In your new Rule, set the Actors of type to "Pachinko_Ball" and set your condition to "Collision."

5. Return to the Library and find the "Change Attribute" Behavior. Drag this to the "do" dropdown in your Rule. This tells the game what to *do* when the conditions are met.

6. Next to "Set" in your new Change Attribute Behavior, click [A] to access the Attribute Browser; select Attributes, followed by Game, and finally your custom Attribute "GameScore." This will give you access to the GameScore integer as long as the game is running.

7. Next to "to:" in your new Change Attribute node, you will find another Expression Editor. Click _e_ to open it. We are going to create a simple little equation here. First go to Attributes, followed by Game, and then GameScore; this will retrieve the Integer from the GameScore Attribute (whatever it may be).

Image courtesy of GameSalad® and Kimberly Unger.

8. Next to the _game.GameScore_ Attribute that should now show up in the top box, type in "+10." This will take the current integer from the GameScore Attribute and add 10 to it, then change the GameScore Attribute to reflect the new total. The first time a Pachinko_ Ball collides with a Pachinko_Bucket, it will then return 0 + 10 = 10. The second time, it will return 10 +10 = 20, and so on.

Since you are calling the _game.GameScene_ Attribute, the math for the scoring will update every time. On the first collision, you get 0+10, on the second you get 10+10, the third will give you 20+10, and so on.

When you test the game, the scoreboard should display a value of "0" to start; this will then change to 10 when the Pachinko_Ball collides with the Pachinko_Bucket. Since you created these Behaviors in the Prototype (original) copy of the Actor, you can use that as a basis for new scoring systems. For example, you can drag a new copy of the Actor to the Scene, unlock the Instance (copy), and modify only the Instance to reflect different levels of score (e.g., +25 or -3)—depending on what you need for your game.

Readability

Research on the legibility of serifed vs. sans-serifed fonts has been inconclusive. Although serifed fonts (such as Times New Roman) are considered easier to read in print publications—and sans-serif fonts (such as Arial) are thought to be more legible on computer and television screens—the opposite (or no difference) has sometimes been found in various scientific studies by researchers such as Colin Wheildon and Alex Poole. Screen resolution constraints can cause serifed fonts to be difficult to read—but certain serifed fonts such as Georgia (with sturdier serifs and higher letters) are designed specifically for web readability.

Diagram courtesy of Per Olin.

Font Types

Arial™
sans serif

Times New Roman™
serif

Bauhaus 93™
stylized

Navigation

A game's *navigation* elements need to be accessible from the gameplay screen. With very few exceptions, it's possible for players in any game to pause and return to a menu system during gameplay. In some cases, players are able to save their places and quit; in others, players are simply given the chance to exit—with the option of re-starting that particular segment upon their return. When considering how you want your menus to work, be sure to take your hardware platform into account. The standards for desktop and web games are different from those on mobile devices. For games on Android devices, it is expected that the existing hardware "back" and "home" buttons will be integrated (rather than being built into the UI). In desktop games, the ESC (escape) key serves a similar function.

Image courtesy of Utopian Games.

Games such as *Running Wild* place the navigation buttons clearly on the unused portion of the screen, where they are difficult for the player to miss.

Being able to navigate into and out of a game is essential to encouraging players to come back. Feeling like you are "trapped" into playing a game without an easy way to reset the level or exit to the menu can be off-putting for many players. You can conceal your navigation—pushing your menus off to the side so that they expand or "pop up" when the player hovers over a particular icon or element—but it needs to be easily accessible to the player.

Consistency = Usability

It might seem like a "no brainer," but keeping the commands and controls consistent across all elements of the user interface is a key factor in building a *usable* interface. This is one of the reasons that hardware components such as the "back" button on Android systems are always integrated—so that all players know they can access the menu by clicking that button.

Smooth Navigation for Kids

I've designed game interfaces that make it easy for the user to navigate menus. With kids, it is especially important for them to navigate from page to page without difficulty. Buttons should also be labeled in such a way that reading is not required.

Jenny McGettigan (Owner, Beansprites LLC & Hamster Wheel Studios)

Instructions

Once upon a time, there was a widely held theory that a game should be as simple to play (or stick as closely to its genre tropes) as possible. First-person shooters (FPSs) should contain the same basic set of controls as most other FPS games. A "Match 3" puzzle game such as *Bejeweled* should allow players to swap two objects to make matching rows of three. With the huge influx of new players emerging from the meteoric rise of the casual game, the current wisdom is to instruct. Each and every new element that you introduce to the player should have matching *instructions* presented by the UI. This may be accomplished through slide-on boxes of text or actual gameplay illustrations where players cannot continue until they demonstrate that they understand the new rule. The latter is a bit more difficult to do because it requires a pre-planned interruption in gameplay with relevant text popping up when the appropriate conditions are met. With more "hardcore" games, it may be enough to simply call attention to the new feature without requiring the player to try it out. With casual games, though, gameplay stoppage is rapidly becoming a standard.

Source Apple Inc.

Games such as *Zombie Drop* walk the player through the first level— providing pop-up instructions at each moment of gameplay, rather than relying on a single page of "how-to" information.

GameSalad Creator is great for designing interfaces because you can easily test and move all Actors around the Scene and study how it can work best.

Nicolas Palacios
(Chief Executive Officer, ePig Games)

I'm a perfectionist, and I care about quality. I can sit moving one button up and down (even for one hour) to find the right place for it.

Marcin Makaj
(Chief Executive Officer, The Moonwalls)

:::::: Tutorial: Timed Instructions

Kimberly Unger (Chief Executive Officer, Bushi-go, Inc.)

For the purposes of this tutorial, you'll be placing your instructional popup text on a pre-rendered 2D image, rather than having Creator generate it on the fly. The most commonly found form of instructions appear at the beginning of a level and inform players of their tasks. The level opens on a text box, which then slides or shimmies or vanishes before the actual gameplay begins. Let's take a look at how to make a timed slider in Creator:

Image courtesy of GameSalad®.

In the Windows version of Creator, Images are assigned by either dragging them to into the Actor Attributes or selecting the image from the dropdown menu found to the right of "Image" under the Actor Attributes.

1. Create an Actor by going to the Actors tab and clicking ⊕.

2. Select the image you want to use with this Actor by either dragging an imported image into the Actor Attributes or selecting the image from the "Image" dropdown menu.

3. Set a timer that will cause this Actor to slide offscreen to the right after five seconds. Find the Actor in the Library and double-click on it to open it up in the Backstage window. Remember: If you double-click on it in the Scene, it will open both the Prototype (original) and the Instance (copy)— and you will need to be sure to select the Prototype tab for editing.

4. Note that there are two ways to add a timer to your Backstage in the Windows version of Creator. You can go to the Behavior Library by selecting the Behaviors tab on the left and add it from there, or you can click the Timer button at the top of the Backstage window. The three primary Behaviors (Group, Rule, and Timer) are all reflected here at the top of the Backstage for easy access.

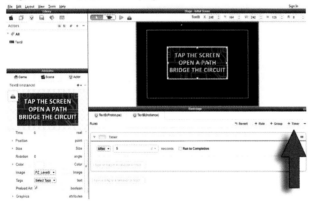

Image courtesy of GameSalad® and Kimberly Unger.

At the top of the Backstage window, you will also find a "Revert" button. This will revert any Instance of an Actor to the Prototype—so if you inadvertently add Rules or make changes to an Instance, you can restore it to the same state as the Prototype by clicking this button.

5. On the top right of the Backstage area, you'll find those little ⊕ icons that will allow you to add elements. For this object, add a Timer and set it to trigger "After" a certain period of time.

6. Go into the Library in the upper left portion of the Creator window and select the "Behaviors" tab. Select "Move to" and drag it into the Behavior box under the Timer you just added to your Actor. This will move your Actor to a specific location when the Timer finishes counting down.

7. Under the "Move to" Behavior you just added, be sure the dropdown box to the right is set to "Actor" rather than "Scene." We want the Actor to move away from its current location, directly to the right. In order to do this, it is simpler to have the game issue the Move command in relation to the Actor's current position.

Image courtesy of GameSalad®.

Movement and rotation Behaviors in Creator will allow you to choose whether their actions take place relative to the Actor (and the Actor's current location and rotation) or to the Scene in general.

8. The "Move to" will tell the game where to send your Actor. The numbers are always in X (horizontal) and Y (vertical) format. In this instance, you have told Creator that the Actor needs to be moved 500 pixels to the right after the five seconds have been counted down.

9. Since you never know when an extra object might cause trouble, you'll need to destroy this object as soon as it moves offscreen. (You could also forgo the "Move to" all together and just have your text box vanish, but the animation will give you a more polished look for your game.) Inside your existing Timer, place another Timer right after the "Move to" node.

Image courtesy of GameSalad®.

10. Set the new timer to one second. This will cause the new Behavior to occur one second after the text box has been moved.

11. Return to the Library and find "Destroy." Drag this into your new Timer. Your Actor will be destroyed one second after the text box finishes its move. Destroying the text box, rather than just leaving it offscreen, will help to free up memory that can be better used in-game.

There are few restrictions on stacking Behaviors, Rules, and Conditions. Creator allows you to nest Behaviors inside of others so that you can customize what you want your Actor to do.

Keep in mind that many players will be irritated if they have to be walked through the instructions every single time they play a level. If you can, set your instructions to run only the first time the game is played, or give players the chance to turn off the instructions in the options for your game.

It takes an average person around 3-5 seconds to read and understand a sentence. Keep your instructions short and sweet and allow them to remain onscreen for at least four seconds at a time.

Layers of Context

Creator provides the player with "Layers" much like in traditional still image editing software such as Photoshop CS5. These layers allow you to place non-interactive game elements on different layers of the game—giving you greater freedom to build, while at the same time keeping these components from accidentally interacting with the gameplay itself.

Image courtesy of GameSalad®.

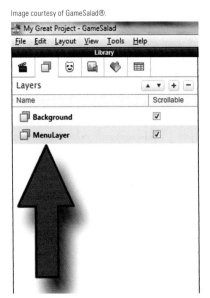

In the Windows version of Creator, the Layer tab is found alongside the Scenes tab—and the ⊕ button to create (or the ⊖ button to destroy) new layers can be found in the upper right corner.

When you create an Actor in the Mac version of GameSalad Creator, it is automatically placed at the top of the currently selected layer. In order to change it to another layer, you will need to select the "Scenes" tab and then click the "Layers" tab to open up the "Inspector" window. As in all of the Creator creation windows, you will see a ⊕ sign. (In the Mac version, this appears in the lower left of the "Inspector.") Once you click the ⊕ sign, you will be given a new layer that can be renamed as you see fit. Assigning objects to these players is a simple click-and-drag procedure.

Creating an Actor in the Windows version of Creator is slightly different than in the Mac version. "Layers" is the second tab in the top row of tabs (one to the right of the "Scene" tab). You can add new layers to the Scene in the same fashion by clicking ⊕—but in Windows, this button can be found in the top right corner of the Library window.

Invisible Controls

I've tried to make controls as 'invisible' or simple as possible. I've also taken great pains to give the player feedback on menu screens and in-game. Player feedback is absolutely key.

George Kotsiofides (The Head Sheep, Quantum Sheep)

Control Schemes

It is here that we begin to diverge from the more software-heavy components of UI design and move into the hardware elements. After all, the hardware is the player's first point of contact with any game—and perhaps more than anything else, the hardware will have the greatest impact on the way a player approaches your game. Let's take a closer look at hardware *control schemes* such as the keyboard, mouse, controllers, and touchscreens.

Source Games Press.

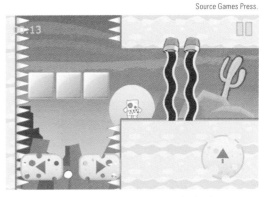

Keyboard

The *keyboard* of a desktop computer (whether Mac or Windows) is one of the most familiar control schemes out there—especially among the recent influx of new "casual" players brought in by the social gaming scene. There are a few control setups that are regarded as inviolate by players. Keyboard-only controls are most often found in action-adventure games, shooters, and beat-em-up or shoot-em-up games. These games also move very well into the console space, with the controller buttons serving as replacements for the keyboard keys (and vice-versa).

The WASD keyboard setup serves as the basic control scheme for a large number of desktop and web-based games—in particular, platformers such as *CheeseMan*. While these games may include custom keys for game-specific elements—such as using health-packs or picking up items—the basic movement and activation keys remain the same.

Mouse

The *mouse* is often used in conjunction with the keyboard interface for larger or more complex games. For shooters or RPG type adventure games, it is often used to direct the character through *point-and-click* movement (a control by which the character moves to the point on the ground that the player has clicked on with the mouse button). For social games, however, the mouse is often the *only* UI hardware used. Games such as *Monsters Melee*, a classic "Match 3" type puzzle game, use only the mouse for both gameplay and menu navigation. However, consistency is the key to a solid UI experience. If you choose to build your game so it is "mouse-only," then using the keyboard for any purpose—even accessing the main menu—becomes a consideration you must build into your design. Mouse-only games can translate well to mobile and touchscreen controls because of the single-action element. A single mouse click is all that's needed to activate a button, or a click-and-drag to place objects in a scene.

Source Apple Inc.

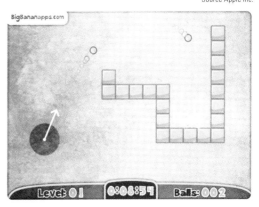

Casual games (*Tiny Balls*, shown)—particularly those found on popular social networking web sites—often employ a stripped down "mouse-only" interface. The entire UI, from menus to gameplay, is operated via mouse clicks—making these types of games a natural fit for touchscreen platforms as well.

Controller

The *controller* is most often used with consoles such as the current generation Xbox 360 or PlayStation 3, but the button controls also translate to handhelds such as the Nintendo DS or PS Vita. For the hardcore gamer, USB-based controllers are also available for desktop computers—but as UI components, these are becoming less common as consoles remain far less expensive than game-ready computers. Most controllers possess a movement control such as the *D-pad* (directional pad) that allows the player to move left, up, right, and down (an easy analog to the keyboard's AWSD)—and a set of four buttons that are most often mapped to in-game functions like weapons fire, jumping, object operation, and equipment swapping.

Image courtesy of Deep Blue Apps.

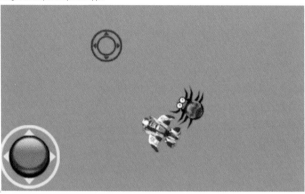

The four-axis controller is the most common control scheme for games on consoles, but virtual "joysticks" are also available on both touchscreen and desktop devices.

Touchscreen

Touchscreen controls currently require the most cleverness of the part of the designer. They make a quick and easy fit to mouse-only games—but when you move into genres that are a more natural fit for controllers or keyboards, a certain amount of innovation must take place. Some of the most popular games on touchscreen devices are those that have embraced the "touchiness" of the touchscreen—games that take full advantage of the tapping/swiping actions that work so well for non-game applications.

The most popular types of gameplay for the touchscreen come from games such as *Bamboo Forest* that have fully embraced the "touch" application. On a touchscreen device, tapping, stabbing, swiping, shaking, and tiling have all become viable methods of controlling the game.

Accelerometer controls comprise a subset of touchscreen controls. Most mobile (as opposed to console) handhelds have the ability to determine the orientation of the device—giving designers the opportunity to utilize actual physical elements such as moving, tilting, or shaking the device to help control the game. As a real-world example, many iOS applications use the "shake" to indicate when the user wants to clear all the information—much like shaking an Etch-a-Sketch will clear away anything drawn on it.

> I've developed swiping menu systems with inertia effects to simulate the common iOS feeling. There's basically no effect or UI approach that can't be created with GameSalad Creator.
>
> *Thomas Wagner (Owner, Gamesmold)*

Audio Feedback

Audio feedback is key to building out the UI. Players need some way to know when a button has been pressed or when the game is waiting for a process to finish running. Most game menus have different music than the game itself—a sure-fire way to remind players that they have stepped out of the gameplay. UI sound effects can often be purchased as sets—with different variations on the same sound being used to indicate whether a button has been pressed, a window has been closed, or a mouse has rolled over an active area. By working with sets of similar sounds, the UI sounds remain distinct and separate from the in-game sounds. Players will quickly (and unconsciously) memorize the UI sounds and will be able to tell immediately if something in the UI is not working as expected (e.g., if they hit the restart button rather than the save button).

Source Fire Maple Games. Image courtesy of Kimberly Unger.

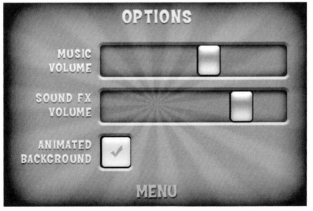

Being able to turn audio cues on and off (in games such as *Danger Cats!*, shown) not only allows players to avoid disturbing others—but gives a game the flexibility to be played in a wide variety of physical environments (e.g., office, bus, bathroom).

:::::: Case Study:
Audio Invaders

Image courtesy of
Stormy Studio.

I've built all the game interfaces using GameSalad Creator. With *Audio Invaders*, I'm currently working on a way to make the menu more accessible to the visually impaired after receiving some very positive emails from players who've requested more audio help. The game features "Audio Assistance" so that visually impaired players can navigate the main menu/options screen and understand the gameplay—while also hearing their game score and best high score.

Jon Draper (Director, Stormy Studio)

:::::: Case Study:
I, Killbot

Image courtesy of
Part12 Studios.

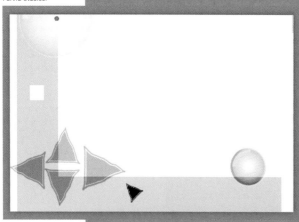

For *I, Killbot*—developed as part of the Peter Molyneux 48-hour game jam—I created a touchscreen directional pad interface. In order to ensure that the game would be playable on a number of devices and platforms (e.g., mobile, HTML5), I set up each move action to listen to both a keyboard input and touch event. The same approach was taken for the release action, which is a touch button—as well as listening for the space bar to be pressed for the same action. Since this was a 48-hour development cycle, I opted to not spend the time making a web- or mobile-only version—although I published it to both for testing.

Caleb Garner (Game Producer, Part12 Studios)

Menu Tree

Depending on the depth of the UI, it might be necessary to map out the *menu tree* beforehand—just to be sure you don't miss anything important. At the bare minimum, you will want a splashscreen (to promote your company and products), a title screen, and a place where people can go to check out the credits and other games you have developed. Other elements that are important might be different "viral" touchpoints, such as a place players can go (or must pass through) to link their Twitter or Facebook accounts to the game. These types of social prompts can go a long way toward getting players to promote your game to their own groups of friends and as such are now considered essential forms of advertising (especially for independent developers). Consider offering in-game rewards or perks to players who link their social media accounts to your game and promote it to their friends.

Even the simplest interface requires a certain amount of thought and pre-planning if it is going to provide the player with a great experience. Even when utilizing "standard" interfaces for a given game type or genre, the game's platform and the ways in which the player can interact with the game should be taken into consideration. The excitement and innovation of the gameplay will be significantly diminished if the player has a hard time getting into and operating the game in the first place.

Image courtesy of Kimberly Unger.

Constructing a menu tree can help to keep important elements (such as an options menu for turning music/sound effects on and off) from getting lost during the rush to get a product out the door.

True Immersion

As game hardware continues to evolve, the user interface will need to evolve along with it. *Augmented reality (AR)* games that overlay a game interface onto the real world have become ever more sophisticated—and with companies such as Google throwing their considerable talents behind products such as Google's Project Glass, we should be seeing different types of *overlay technology* hitting the market within the next few years. It will be up to the game developers to take these technologies and leverage them into new forms of gameplay. Initially, we might see straightforward translations of games and genres that already exist—and the tolerance of the players toward just how much "game" they prefer to have in their "real life" has yet to be tested. Once game designers put on their innovation hats, games that take full advantage of the new technology will start to emerge and will help push these emerging technologies into products will full and enthusiastic consumer support.

:::CHAPTER REVIEW EXERCISES:::

1. Describe and map out the most common control scheme for the type of game you want to make. Does this control scheme work particularly well for your game? Why or why not?

2. Will an integrated software interface work better for your game than a simple overly style interface? Why or why not?

3. What makes your game unique in terms of interface? Do you forsee challenges in breaking away from the genre's established interface canon?

4. How are you planning on depicting your player's progress through the game?

5. Is it possible for your game to be played on multiple platforms, or will it be necessary for you to redesign the controls for each platform?

6. Does your game's interface need to include social elements such as "bragging rights"? How do you plan to include these without interrupting the flow of the game?

7. Does your game need a multi-layered interface (e.g., menu systems, inventory items) or something simpler? Why or why not?

Prototyping
practice makes perfect

Key Chapter Questions

- At what point during the *production cycle* should prototyping take place?

- What *game elements* are best suited to prototyping?

- How does a tool such as *GameSalad Creator* enable rapid prototying in games?

- Is it possible to prototype a game with *incomplete* or *placeholder assets*?

- How can prototyping be used to *streamline* the entire production process?

Games don't spring, fully formed, from the fingertips of a developer like Athena from the head of Zeus. In fact, once a game is conceptualized, there is still a significant amount of back-and-forth tweaking and adjusting that occurs before it is ready to be seen by testers—let alone the broader gaming public. All the elements need to play out just right: interplay of characters and objects within a game; hits necessary to fell an enemy; jumps required to cross the screen; and speed at which the swinging axe of doom descends. Too difficult or unfair, and you lose a player—or worse, the player quits the game due to frustration and anger with the gameplay. Make too many players angry, and a snowball of negative criticism rolls over to anything else you develop. This can work with "positive" feelings as well; if like Rovio, your first game (*Angry Birds*) is a runaway hit, it's expected that the second (*Bad Piggies*) will follow suit! Tools such as GameSalad Creator can help you streamline your prototyping process and allow you to iterate on variations in your gameplay that can help to make or break your game.

In the Beginning, There Was . . .

For basic GameSalad Creator tutorials, see Appendix. For more information on prototyping, see *Game QA & Testing* (Levy/ Novak)—part of Delmar Cengage Learning's *Game Development Essentials* series.

Prototyping, the building of partial models for the purposes of testing and development, is hardly exclusive to game design. Each and every product created by humans, from USB drives to boxes of oatmeal, has gone through some type of prototyping—whether during initial development or further down the line as it became necessary to streamline production. In the 1960s and 1970s, software design followed a very different process than it does now—one that was very similar, in fact, to the way physical prototyping was conducted. Products were developed to completion, then iterated upon and adjusted until they were ready for use. This type of monolithic approach (also known as "Slaying the Dragon," in concert with the idea that a single developer was tasked with facing down a monolithic project) made it difficult to implement basic level changes—with whole sections of code becoming obsolete or needing to be replaced if a portion of the product didn't operate as required.

Image courtesy of Kimberly Unger.

The old-fashioned approach to software development was often referred to as "Slaying the Dragon" because it involved a developer facing a single, "fire-breathing" project.

In the 1970s, software development became more complex—not only due to the expansion of computing capability, but to the increased reliance on computers to handle automated tasks. As a result, the prototyping process formalized into several distinct types that depended on the needs of the design team. Software development evolved into a "back end" for interchange between designers, programmers, and consumers—helped along by evolving prototyping processes. As a component in the overall process of software and game design, prototyping is still rapidly evolving to suit the needs of development teams. Evolutionary prototyping systems such as "Systemscraft" (described by John Crinnion in *Evolutionary Systems Development*) were flexible processes that could work in a wide variety of situations by being molded and shaped to the environment in which they were used.

From Paper to Pixel

Prototyping is one of the best tools in a designer's arsenal. Being able to assemble a working prototype of a product—such as a game, app, or web site—goes a long way toward selling a producer or a publisher on it. Prototyping is also one of the best communication tools available to share a designer's vision with the rest of the team. A quick mockup can show everything from *user interface* (*UI*) functionality (discussed in Chapter 2) and player navigation to social media connections. Prototyping is a multi-step process—starting with conceptualization and data collection and finishing with the end of the prototype's lifespan (at which point the prototype has either evolved into something new or is discarded to begin the formal development process). A designer should clearly state a game's goals and how to achieve them. Part of the task is to research and detail all aspects of the game—from the UI to the credits. This might involve playing other games, lurking in player forums to determine common issues with existing games, and sketching possible layouts of a UI or level. You won't get everything right the first time—but after receiving input from other team members, you'll be able to work out the kinks. The end result of this process usually expresses itself in documentation form via a *concept*, *prototyping*, or short-form *game design document* (*GDD*)—depending on how much information and detail is included. Some developers use a prototype as part of a *proof of concept* during the concept development or pre-production phase—while others consider prototyping the first stage of the production process itself.

Style

There are two primary *styles* associated with game prototypes: *horizontal* and *vertical*. To determine which style meets your needs, it's important to consider whether the prototype should focus on *depth* or *breadth*. Let's take a closer look at these styles.

Horizontal

A *horizontal* prototype reflects all aspects of a certain design element across the board. In essence, it involves taking one element out of the game's documentation (concept, prototype, or GDD) and building it out to explore how it needs to be developed. The horizontal prototype tends to focus on higher-level (closer to the consumer) functional areas rather than basic, ground-level elements such as graphics rendering or processor threads. In game development, this might reflect the process by which players link the game to their favorite social media accounts.

Image courtesy of Kimberly Unger.

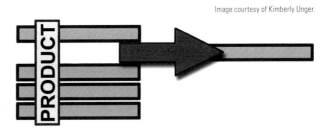

The horizonal prototype takes a single design element from the final product and builds it out so that it can be explored in full.

Vertical

The more complex *vertical* prototype often involves multiple layers of a project rather than just a single layer. This might include taking a slice of the game and drilling down more deeply to explore how different levels interact—from the consumer-facing UI to the rendering engines that underlie the programming. Working with a tool such as GameSalad Creator gives developers a leg up on vertical prototyping. Since the underlying game engine is already in place, it's possible to focus on any number of elements—including gameplay.

Image courtesy of Kimberly Unger.

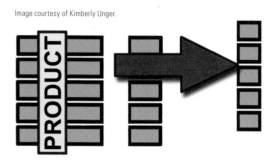

The vertical prototype takes a slice of the complete final product at all levels.

Proto "Oh-No"?

One key advantage to building a prototype, even it it's just a demo version of the interface, is that it can provide the opportunity to find issues and solicit feedback from the development team and even targeted users.

Classification

After considering the prototype's style (horizontal versus vertical), it's important to determine its *classification*—associated with a variety of functions. Some studios burn the prototype itself once its purpose has been fulfilled, while others prefer to turn it into the kernel of the final product.

Throwaway

Not surprisingly, *throwaway* prototypes are short-lived tools and are never intended to see the light of day. These tools are used as incubators for ideas and are usually put together with a minimum of visual assets and "Franken-code" cobbled together out of bits and bobs from company libraries or other projects. One of the key features of a throwaway prototype is functionality. The focus is not on longevity, attractive under-pinnings, or how well the code is commented because the prototype will be scrapped once it has outlived its usefulness.

Incremental

Incremental prototypes comprise a stack of mini-evolutionary prototypes. Distinct components of the final product are built separately and are combined at the end into a cohesive whole. Like the throwaway prototype, it has the advantage of involving a smaller subset (and any individual aspect that may be quick to build and test upon) while also sharing the presumed resource-saving features of the evolutionary prototype. However, the need to combine prototypes can cause delays and difficulties unless different team members have a clear understanding of how the pieces will need to fit together. There will invariably be issues with combining them all, so extra time and resources must be allocated to make the prototype a reality.

Evolutionary

In many game projects (particularly with smaller scale mobile and social game production teams), the *evolutionary* prototype is the most likely choice—primarily because many game studios license pre-existing platforms such as GameSalad Creator and thus can begin prototyping more broadly from the outset. Since the evolutionary prototype is designed from the beginning to serve as the core of a product, it needs to be robust; its code must be commented correctly, and bugs must be hunted down with impunity as they arise. Features should be developed as needed rather than because they might be "cool." As a result, evolutionary prototypes develop more slowly than throwaway prototypes—but they require constant testing and input from players to ensure they encompass all of the needed elements.

At Santa Monica College, we have been looking for the next industry solution for game prototyping. GameSalad Creator seems to fit the bill—not only due to its easy ramp-up and casual game approach, but also because it supports a number of target platforms.

—David Javelosa (Professor of Interactive Media, Santa Monica College – Design Technology)

GameSalad Creator is *made* for prototyping. You can test your game and layout right on the screen while dropping in Behaviors. This makes it easy to prototype and build levels and align objects visually—and it makes game creation fun!

—Jenny McGettigan (Owner, Beansprites LLC / Hamster Wheel Studios)

Prototyping Process

There are a number of prototyping tools used by producers at game studios to help better communicate their vision to development teams. As production schedules get tighter, particularly in mobile and social areas, being able to clearly describe the end product visually is essential in order to avoid wasted time and resources. Prototyping is particularly valuable for testing new game concepts or systems of use. Whether for games or applications, prototyping tends to follow a straightforward series of steps:

1. *Data gathering:* Collecting information on the project and determining which components (or even the entire project) require prototyping.

2. *Horizontal prototype:* Rough mock up of prototype—essentially a slideshow of the different screens involved.

3. *Review:* Work with development team to determine elements that should be explored more deeply.

4. *Vertical prototype:* Build more involved prototypes where needed to explore and develop new systems.

5. *Review:* Work with development team to determine which prototypes are successful and which should be tested on a user audience.

6. *Focus testing:* Expose chosen prototypes to a "cold" set of testers. Collect data to determine where additional modification and development are needed.

Image courtesy of GameSalad®.

Image courtesy of GameSalad®.

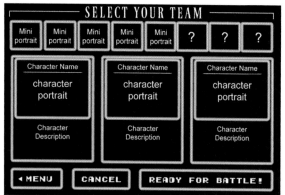

Battle Legend Infinity began with a limited paper prototype (left) before moving to a higher-fidelity prototype developed in Creator (right).

When working with a prototyping tool, it's important to stay on the "high level." With Creator, it's not necessary to prototype deeper aspects of a game but to simply show how the end result will look to the player. Prototyping of deeper elements (particularly if the final version of the product will not be developed on Creator) is up to the development team. Using Creator eliminates the need for core-level prototyping (such as a rendering engine). However, if Creator is only being used to do an initial mockup—and the final product will be done with in-house software—then prototyping on core elements is usually handled by a different part of the team.

Focus on Usability

Not all elements of a project need to be prototyped. An ideal use of a prototype is in *usability* testing—including elements and functions with which players will directly interact, rather than number crunching and other "behind-the-scenes" features.

Design & Data Collection

The first step in prototyping a project is to figure out exactly what needs to go into it. Part of this might involve taking a look at features and components of documentation (ultimately part of a GDD) that might require more depth and could benefit from a prototype to show the team. Some areas of a GDD will be a natural fit for prototyping—and some will not. Let's take a closer look at some relevant GDD components.

Overview

The *overview* or *description* of your game should include unique features that might "wow" the market. Let's face it: No one *ever* says, "Eh, we're just making an *Angry Birds* clone."

Competitive Analysis

A *competitive analysis* (including screenshots) of other similar projects is also recommended. When deciding which elements of your design might need prototyping while looking for other examples of products in the wild, consider carefully how your product differs from those examples. What are the key features that will set your game apart? These will be the elements that derive the most benefit from a design prototype.

Only Seven Original Ideas

Including screenshots from existing titles in your overview does not mean you are "copying" another game; rather, it's a part of the communication process. Showing examples of existing components makes it easier for a producer, publisher, or developer to understand the product you want to create.

Genre

The chosen *genre* for your game will clearly define some elements. There are several genre-specific conventions that players have come to expect. For example, players of role-playing games (RPGs) expect to be able to modify their characters over time—and strategy players expect to manage their resources. As you collect the information for your design, keep a close eye on any changes you make to these established conventions. Fiddling with these is a quick way to set your project apart in the minds of players—but if you take

Source Apple Inc.

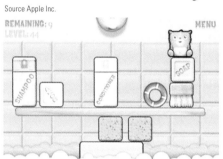

Source Apple Inc.

it too far, your audience will be put off by it. Prototyping and testing can help you determine whether your changes have crossed the line and explore ways to train players to understand these changes.

Physics puzzler *Danger Cats!* (left) has a different set of controls and UI interface elements than a point-and-click adventure game such as *The Secret of Grisly Manor* (right).

User Interface

Prototyping *physical interface* controls can be especially helpful to the team when you are blending genres. For example, an AAA title such as *Deus Ex: Human Revolution* contains the basic control set for a first-person shooter (FPS), but it also allows players to build out and modify their characters as they progress through the game—a feature most commonly associated with the RPG genre. One key breakaway in a game like *Deus Ex* from the "standard" FPS control set is that player characters cannot jump over obstacles. While this may seem like a minor change, it has a deep and lasting effect on the gameplay itself—allowing a much broader range of options for the player regarding routes taken through the environment and various solutions to missions.

Image courtesy of GameSalad®.　　　　Image courtesy of GameSalad®.　　　　Image courtesy of GameSalad®.

Multiple paper and slideshow-style prototypes are built for interface-oriented applications in order to test user reactions.

Games require *visual interfaces*, which can get complicated—featuring multiple sets of menus or monitoring game states. It is common practice when developing traditional interface components that are standard in apps as well as games (e.g., menu systems, social media interfaces, email solicitations) to prepare prototypes on paper or as non-working mockups of the application so that they can be tested out on focus groups (discussed below) and individuals outside of the development group. (See Chapter 2 for a more detailed discussion of interface design.)

Testing

Since UI setups need to be somewhat intuitive, building out a prototype so that it can be tested on live users is essential when it comes to software development. *Focus testing* (exposing an application to a set of standard users in order to gain insight) can be an invaluable part of trying out new controls schemes, or even just to determine whether a typical user is able to navigate through the game readily enough. Even if you don't have a formal "focus group" setup, having another person working hands-on with your prototype can show you things you never anticipated—and can help you avoid serious pitfalls along the way. (Let's face it: For most independent studios, the focus group is a handful of friends, family, or those five guys you ambushed at the pizza place at 2:00 a.m.!) It's one thing for the design team to be able to work with a *build* (a working prototype or "version" of a game), but it's something entirely different to hand that build off to consumers: They're known to push buttons; they try things you and your team won't have ever considered in a million years; they hold the phone upside down and shake it; and they hit the back button 27 times in a row. In short, your average consumer can be counted upon to raise a host of questions that can prove to be critical to improving your game.

During focus testing, it is very common to ask focus group members to examine several different versions of the same product—having them cross compare these versions and point out elements that are strong, intuitive, or confusing. Usually, focus groups are put together by larger scale companies—but a focus test can be conducted by a development house of any size as long as the personnel is available to manage the test, collate the information collected, and present the results to the development team.

External testing does not need to be conducted in person in the form of a traditional focus group, but it can be done as online *beta testing*—where players are solicited to participate in an *open beta*, which gives them early access to a game in exchange for a *non-disclosure agreement* (*NDA*) and written user feedback, usually in the form of an online user survey.

Image courtesy of Woo Games.

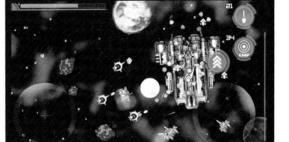

The open beta for retro space shooter *ErnCon* was announced on the popular social media site Reddit to attract testers.

Internal Prototyping

It's possible to prototype several different aspects of a game—and have several smaller throwaway prototypes that are used during the course of game development. Depending on the development team, you will need to evaluate their personal experience with a given game genre. If the team members are unfamiliar with that genre, be sure they become familiar with your chosen genre and its associated conventions. For example, individuals on the team might be professionally or personally familiar with FPS games—but this won't necessarily be helpful if you're building a collectible card game (CCG). It's one thing to simply hand your team a "to do" list—but teaching them the standard gameplay tropes associated with the project will give them an opportunity to innovate as well as develop.

Tutorial: Prototyping a Menu System

Kimberly Unger (Chief Executive Officer, Bushi-go, Inc.)

"Point and click" is the simplest way to create an interaction. It translates well to desktop, web, touchscreen—nearly every platform currently in use. A simple "button" interface can open menus, activate objects, and turn options on and off; it is one of the most used components built in GameSalad Creator.

Image courtesy of GameSalad®.

For a simple prototype of a menu system, create a set of buttons and their actions. Use them to spawn menu windows or even simply change the background from one image to another—depending on what aspect of the game you're prototyping (Windows Creator, shown).

To make a simple menu button in Windows Creator:

1. Create an Actor and name it appropriately (e.g., "Button01"). Please refer to Chapter 4 (Windows) or Chapter 5 (Mac) for the basics of creating Actors and importing art into Creator.

2. Select the image you want to associate with the Actor you created. (For a button, select button art in the dropdown menu under the Actor Attributes.)

3. Under the "Behaviors" tab at the bottom of the Creator screen, find the Attribute or Behavior you want to include.

4. Drag the "Mouse Button" Condition to the Rules for the new Actor and set the dropbox menu to "down." (This tells Creator that it should react when the mouse button is pressed.)

5. Your "Mouse Button" RULE should reflect:

   ▨ When "ALL" of the following are happening

   ▨ Mouse is "DOWN"

   ▨ Mouse position is "OVER ACTOR"

6. Under the "Behaviors" tab at the bottom of the Creator screen, select "Actions."

7. Drag the Action "Spawn Actor" into the Rules for your Actor. Position it over the word "do" in the Condition placed in Step 4. (This tells the Actor that "When the Mouse Button is pressed DOWN, DO Spawn Actor.")

8. Under the new "Spawn Actor" Action just placed, use the dropdown menu to select what Actor to *spawn* (create). In the example, we created "Actor02" and used a placeholder window graphic on it.

9. Under the new "Spawn Actor" Action, set the location where the Actor should spawn. You can choose to spawn an Actor relative to the Scene or to the Actor to which the Behavior is attached. (In the example, we chose to spawn at -100px vertically and 100px horizontally from the center of the Actor.)

10. Test the button by hitting the green "Preview" button at the top of the Scene Window in Creator. Your spawned Actor should appear when you click the button you created.

Image courtesy of GameSalad®.

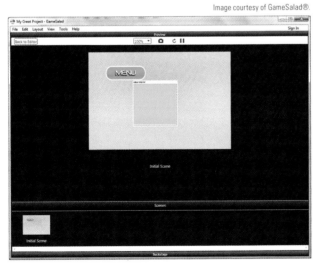

It's possible to test a prototype "on the fly" using Creator to see how the project may have been affected by modifications.

George Kotsiofides on Creator Prototyping Techniques :::::

George Kotsiofides
(The Head Sheep,
Quantum Sheep)

George Kotsiofides has been playing video games since they first arrived—from *Pong* and *Space Invaders* in the '70s, arcades and home computers/consoles in the '80s, and onward. In 1995, George began his career in the game industry—working in retail, marketing, journalism, and game design. He has worked for Microsoft, MCV, Monumental Games, Asylum, Headstrong, and Climax on a number of titles for the Wii, PSP, DS, PC, and GameBoy. George's days are spent daydreaming and making new games—as well as playing lots across all formats!

I always make a "generic" Actor (called "generic"!) that has no image attached, is non-moveable (to save on performance), and has four new Attributes attached to it (two boolean, two integer). I use this as an unlocked Actor in scenes for many different purposes (though I change the Actor's name to something more descriptive). Then I put in code for that particular Actor for the job I want it to do. This technique is useful for stuff like menus or buttons in general—and since you're only using one Actor (the generic one), it helps with memory management and loading times. Another technique is to avoid spawning things but instead move objects off-screen and bring them on-screen when needed. This helps, again, with performance. A big thing for me is getting a test scene done. I use this to prototype the idea and build one fully functioning level. I always try and stay on this screen for as long as possible—making sure it's as perfect as it can be before copying and pasting the entire scene to make new levels. This saves time in the long run to get it right from the start.

GameSalad Creator is by far the fastest tool for testing and developing. It is easier to use than Flash was, and it is much more powerful—and yet it's the fastest tool on the market.

—*Thomas Wagner*
(Owner, Gamesmold)

GameSalad Creator is incredibly fast for prototyping games. When you have an idea, you can start prototyping it very quickly—and in one day, you already have an idea of how the whole game could work.

—*Nicolas Palacios*
(Chief Executive Officer, ePig Games)

External Prototyping

GameSalad Creator offers game designers the chance to build and test a prototype that can be shown outside the team team to test usability and the "fun factor" of a title's gameplay. Prototyping for larger screens, such as those on laptops or desktops, is somewhat simple compared to smaller screens. Larger screens are ubiquitous— easy to access and impressive as showcasing devices. However, it's the handheld devices, the walled-garden of the iOS platform, and to a lesser extent the many devices sporting the Android operating system that bring trouble. For the designer working with any of these devices, knowing how the project should look on the device itself can be an issue. Even after running the math, determining the scale of the images on screen, and fiddling with the zoom, the final "look and feel" won't be clear until the images show up on those much smaller screens.

Image courtesy of GameSalad®.

GameSalad Creator gives developers several ways to test and showcase prototypes during the creation process. This ideally means that a prototype can be displayed anywhere, on any screen, without requiring special equipment.

GameSalad Creator gives the designer two advantages. The first is *cross-platform delivery*. A prototype can be shown off as an HTML5 document, a Mac game, or any leading handheld operating system. For anyone who has been caught in a case of "demo-itis" (a common disease where a demo that worked perfectly internally suddenly sprouts all sorts of issues when it is being showcased "in the wild"), having a stable, reliable prototype can make communicating your concepts a breeze. The second big advantage of using Creator as a prototyping tool is its iOS and Android *viewers*. Serving a similar function to publishing, these viewers can be used to see what a project might look like on a device—but they're geared toward working with Creator specifically for testing as opposed to distributing games to app stores.

Image courtesy of GameSalad®.

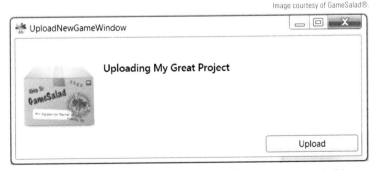

GameSalad Creator (Windows version, shown) allows developers to build working versions of prototypes (and final versions of projects) that can then be installed on devices as needed to demo and test.

Image courtesy of
Bharat Battu.

Bharat Battu, M. Ed.
(educational
multimedia developer)

Bharat Battu received a Masters of Education in Technology, Innovation, and Education in May 2012 from the Harvard Graduate School of Education. His professional work has included the production of dozens of online instructional videos for teachers of a nationally-disseminated engineering curriculum for elementary school students. While in graduate school, Bharat's learning focus has been on the effective and compelling design of educational interactive media—including web and mobile games. Through his coursework and related projects, Bharat has conceived, built, and tested working prototypes of four different educational games for mobile devices—including one prototype that was selected as a finalist for the Collegiate Prize for the 2011 National STEM Video Game Challenge hosted by the Joan Ganz Cooney Center.

GameSalad Creator is an excellent tool for quickly prototyping iterations of game levels. While it allows for quickly development of game-mechanics functionality without having to build a game engine from scratch, it's true power lies in its ability to lay out game elements visually in each scene simply by dragging and dropped objects where you want them. This allows for painless rapid creation of game levels. Different layouts and platforming challenges can be constructed and tested simply by moving objects around, without having to worry about X and Y positioning or layering in code. It fantastically makes game level design a WYSIWYG experience. Creator also has been helpful in easy playtesting. It's been great to be able to playtest a game project on both a MacBook (my development machine) and iOS devices. The pairing of GameSalad Creator and Viewer on my mobile devices has allowed me to effortlessly send over new builds of my game to the Viewer app on my iOS devices via Wi-Fi without having to worry about packaging .ipa apps and the headaches of provisioning profiles and App IDs for each prototype.

Bigger, Smarter, Faster, Stronger?

Nobody likes to do extra work if it can be avoided; at times, it may seem like the idea of developing a prototype of a project—even just a single component that is later going to be discarded—might be a waste of time. Nothing could be further from the truth: All of the work put into a prototype—even if the draft versions are discarded—is work *toward the final product*. All the test versions that didn't quite do what you thought they would—or the ones your focus testers rejected—will help you deliver a polished, final project.

Windows Game Development
every screen is a playground

Key Chapter Questions

■ How do *standalone Windows games* differ from downloadable or online products?

■ What are some art, design, and programming *restrictions* associated with developing games for desktop computing?

■ How are games designed for the broad range of *custom Windows devices* on the market?

■ How can *GameSalad Creator* be used to create and publish games for Windows?

■ How will Windows game development continue to evolve in the *future*?

For decades, the Windows PC has been the catch-all system for game development. With the ability to run a wide variety of software, Windows devices have a high level of flexibility—delivering games via Blu-ray disc, DVD, USB drive, digital download, and even Bluetooth file transfer. It's no surprise that game developers have traditionally worked with the Windows PC as their platform of choice. GameSalad Creator and Windows systems are a solid fit due to their broad compatibility: Games developed with Windows Creator may be distributed via download; they're compatible with a broad array of PC components (players won't need to purchase new hardware); and perhaps most importantly, players only need to install the game rather than an entire installation suite.

A Game Machine in Every Home

> For basic GameSalad Creator tutorials, see Appendix.

Windows game development—which descended from the introduction of *personal computers* (*PCs*)—experienced a fabulously muddy start. Games of one kind or another have existed on computers for almost as long as computers have used microprocessors—not home computers, but the massive room-sized mainframes of the past that were used to play comparatively simple games such as *Tic-Tac-Toe*. It wasn't until the first game console boom of the late 1970s and the rush to place a computer in every home that "PC gaming" really got its start.

Source Piga Software.

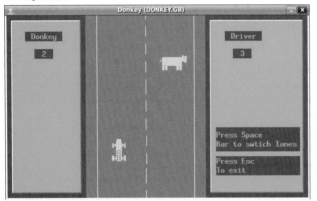

DONKEY.BAS, one of the very first "PC Games," was developed by Bill Gates and Neil Konzen—and it came pre-installed on early home computers manufactured by IBM. This image depicts *DONKEY.GB*, a free software remake developed by Piga Software.

Today, we're used to the Big Three *operating systems* (*OSs*)—OSX, Windows, and Linux—dominating the market. However, when the home computing market first took off, the shelves were full of companies all vying for attention. Some, such as Commodore, delivered a computer/console hybrid—the Amiga, a computer that was optimized for playing games, while still being a general purpose computer. Others, such as the computers manufactured by IBM, focused solely on being business machines; the ability to play games was an afterthought.

The changeover from text-based computing to *graphical user interface* (*GUI*) systems occurred in the early 1980s. In 1983, Apple introduced the Macintosh—which relied heavily on the use of now common elements such as windows and icons; Microsoft followed suit with the first version of Windows in 1985.

Source Will Crowther.

```
.RUN ADV11

WELCOME TO ADVENTURE!!  WOULD YOU LIKE INSTRUCTIONS?


YES
SOMEWHERE NEARBY IS COLOSSAL CAVE, WHERE OTHERS HAVE FOUND
FORTUNES IN TREASURE AND GOLD, THOUGH IT IS RUMORED
THAT SOME WHO ENTER ARE NEVER SEEN AGAIN. MAGIC IS SAID
TO WORK IN THE CAVE.  I WILL BE YOUR EYES AND HANDS. DIRECT
ME WITH COMMANDS OF 1 OR 2 WORDS.
(ERRORS, SUGGESTIONS, COMPLAINTS TO CROWTHER)
(IF STUCK TYPE HELP FOR SOME HINTS)


YOU ARE STANDING AT THE END OF A ROAD BEFORE A SMALL BRICK
BUILDING . AROUND YOU IS A FOREST. A SMALL
STREAM FLOWS OUT OF THE BUILDING AND DOWN A GULLY.


GO IN
YOU ARE INSIDE A BUILDING, A WELL HOUSE FOR A LARGE SPRING.


THERE ARE SOME KEYS ON THE GROUND HERE.


THERE IS A SHINY BRASS LAMP NEARBY.


THERE IS FOOD HERE.


THERE IS A BOTTLE OF WATER HERE.
```

Text adventures such as Will Crowther's *Colossal Cave Adventure* initially dominated the PC game market.

As home computing transitioned from text-based interfaces such as *MS-DOS* (*Microsoft Disk Operating System*) to GUIs, PC gaming entered its Golden Age. The market had previously been dominated by games that had little to no graphics requirements, text-based adventures such as *Colossal Cave Adventure* and *Zork*, or games repurposed from arcade platforms and modified to fit the lower end graphics available on home PCs. Once graphics became an integral part of the OS, higher quality video processing became common—and game developers began to push the boundaries of household PCs.

By 1996, Microsoft Windows had established itself as the top player in the world of personal computing—and the drive of PC-focused game developers sparked a revolution in the way graphics were handled by home computers. Hardware-accelerated 3D graphics and video cards that held their own, dedicated memory allowed the 3D graphics in computer games to quickly surpass what was available on consoles. In fact, players for the first time were updating and customizing the hardware in their computers to be able to handle the more sophisticated graphics found in games such as *Unreal* and *Quake II*.

Source id Software. Image courtesy of Jeannie Novak.

For the first time, players updated and customized their own PCs to handle graphics found in games such as *Quake II*.

Not to be left out, adventure and role-playing games (RPGs)—genres that had traditionally been text-based—began taking advantage of the greater depth of color and higher resolutions made available by new advances in graphics technology. Games such as *Myst* and *The 7th Guest* relied on richly detailed, memory heavy artwork and video to pull players into their worlds. These games pushed graphics (and storage) technology just as aggressively as processor-heavy 3D games.

Source Games Press.

Adventure games such as *Myst* contained rich graphics and video that pulled players into immersive environments.

OS Wars

Windows OS has many functional similarities to Mac OS (discussed in Chapter 5). Visual content for both is organized into boxes of graphics and text; data is stored in a system of metaphorical files and folders; and a mouse is used to access programs, move sliders, and drag elements around the screen. However, both systems handle things very differently beyond the "screen" level—and because of these differences, it's necessary to discuss Windows Creator and Mac Creator separately.

Source Microsoft Corporation.

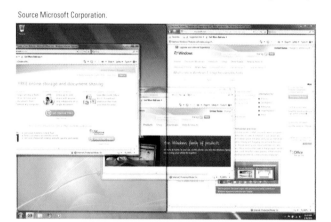

The look and feel may be different, but the underlying structure is common across both Windows and Mac operating systems (Windows desktop, shown).

Graphic Considerations

For the purposes of this chapter, we are going to start with the big picture: those elements that everybody sees before the first menu. Windows Creator works exclusively with raster graphics (those that are drawn pixel by pixel and have a fixed size), which are distinct from vector graphics (common in Flash-based games those that are programmatically generated so they can scale to suit the players screen). Raster or pixel graphics require a fixed size—but as such, they allow a greater degree of control over the player experience. It's important to determine the game's playable screen size early on in the development process.

Raster vs. Vector Graphics

Raster (or *bitmap*) graphics are created on a pixel-by-pixel basis. When the art is scaled up, the new space has to be filled by a (somewhat sophisticated) guess: The program takes the existing pixels (e.g., a black and white pixel side by side) and averages out the color in a technique known as *anti-aliasing* to create the new pixels. The larger a bitmap image is scaled up, the blurrier it gets. However, this technique works well for reducing graphics down to their smallest possible size; manipulating the image on the pixel level, choosing which pixel to cut, and determining whether to make the pixel 80% black or 60% black will provide the greatest degree of control while minimizing the size of the game. Raster graphics also allow detailed images to be created very quickly. In contrast, vector graphics need to be created a single shape at a time—much like working with construction paper cutouts. Although it's possible to create highly detailed images with vector graphics, the process is significantly more time-consuming—requiring a specialized skillset that is found more often in illustration or advertising than in games.

Vector graphics comprise entirely different types of images. In layman's terms, vector graphics are generated by a mathematical function or series of functions. Since the images are created by the program on the fly, based on a set of numbers, they can be scaled up and down with only a minimum of loss. Programs such as Flash and Illustrator use vector graphics to great effect for clean, easily scaled graphics for web and print use. Web-based games use vector graphics so heavily in part because the image file size is based on the vector file—not the size of the end graphic. This is a key component in many games developed using Flash for delivery on web and mobile platforms.

Due to being generated by the program on the fly, vector graphics can scale cleanly as a game is being run. Raster or bitmap graphics, on the other hand, will blur as they are scaled up and down—so different versions of these images need to be created at multiple sizes.

How big should a game be in terms of actual screen real estate? How many pixels wide, and how many pixels high? It's possible to design around this limitation for many game types. RPGs and racing games do this particularly well. Consider the edges of the screen as frames of a window—with the ability for game elements to move out of sight off screen. A game's screen real estate size reflects the edges of its visible area, but this does not have to be a hard edge. Backgrounds can be scrolled and adjusted—allowing the game to be as large as needed.

There are some standard sizes that depend on the game's target platform. Computer monitors were once at a 4 x 3 ratio (derived from the 640 x 480 pixel size of a standard television screen)—and even now, with the increasing domination of larger format screens, 4 x 3 remains a popular standard format. With web-based delivery (discussed further in Chapter 7), many online portals will restrict the game to a 640 x 480 window, which can be trimmed to 640 x 360 for a widescreen effect.

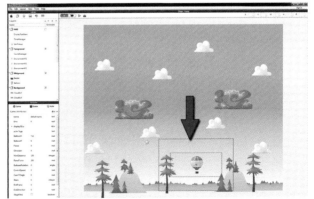

The thin white border in this image represents the edge of the visible area in this Scene, but the background and game elements are brought in from off camera.

Image courtesy of GameSalad®.

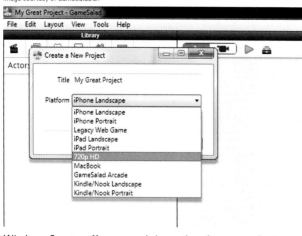

Windows Creator offers several size options for new projects—giving developers a head start.

Creator provides preset sizes—each tailored to a different platform or device. For developing a downloadable product for Windows machines, consider how 720P HD (widescreen) or a more traditional 6:4 ratio such as 1024 x 768 might enhance a game—depending on its design. When publishing to GameSalad Arcade, Creator clearly presents size as an option during project setup. Many online portals have set guidelines for screen and file size of a product. Creator also allows for the ability to choose a custom size and layout.

Screen	Dimensions (pixels)
iPhone Landscape	480 x 320
iPhone Portrait	320 x 480
Legacy Web Game	720 x 480
iPad Landscape	1024 x 768
iPad Portrait	768 x 1024
720P HD	1280 x 720
MacBook	1280 x 800
GameSalad Arcade	480 x 320
Kindle/Nook Landscape	1024 x 600
Kindle/Nook Portrait	600 x 1024

The number of pixels per side may vary, but most games follow either the 6:4 standard or 16:9 widescreen ratio.

Asset Hoarding & Other Habits

Over time, we all collect things—such as papers, photos, art, and music. Assets for games should fall into this same category; even if you're finished with a product, keep your assets handy so they can be used as more complete forms of "dummy art" for the next project. Simple moveable blocks and circles provide a good start—but having something that can more closely represent elements such as actions and reactions of animated characters can make development easier.

Importing Art Assets

It might be preferable to begin a project with temporary art assets and refine the visuals later once the gameplay has been polished. Simple placeholders—such as circles instead of boulders, rectangles instead of platforms, and line art instead of painted backgrounds—may be used to move your project forward. Game-ready art assets may also be acquired for free or at a low cost online or through GameSalad's asset store. It's often simpler to develop with a visual rough—similar to an outline—so that you can perfect your gameplay before worrying about the look.

When importing an asset into Windows Creator, there are a few things to consider. First, take a look at the pixel size of the game's main visual component or character. When the visual elements for a game are pulled into memory, the processor stacks them together, side by side—so in order for a game to run cleanly and quickly, the images will need to be cropped down as much as possible. Creator will work with almost any asset provided, but it will make the game more efficient and will help to keep the final file size smaller.

Second, what *type* of asset is it? Is it a still asset, such as a tree or a rock—or does it need to be animated? Is it a background, window, or splash screen? Windows Creator makes no distinction between them, but each type requires slightly different handling. For example, in order to bring in a set of animations for a single character, name the frames in sequence (e.g., Bob_Run_001.png, Bob_Run_002.png, Bob_Run_003.png) to lay the groundwork for the animation.

Import . . . with a Click of a Button

Importing images is a fairly simple task in Windows Creator. Simply go to the "Images" tab, click ➕, and select the images that should be imported. Creator allows importing multiple images at once by selecting them in the dialogue box.

Memory Issues

Having a vast amount of *memory* was once the "be-all, end-all" for PC games. The faster the processor, the more *RAM* (*random-access memory*) was available; this guaranteed the rich experience all hardcore players wanted—whether they were playing a 3D-rendered game or a richly detailed 2D title. Gaming rigs have topped off for the moment, and many players of casual games will have access to laptops or desktops equipped with programs suiting their lifestyles—with games being an added bonus. Unless a game's target market consists of hardcore players, a rich 2D gaming experience can be delivered without pushing the limits of what an average PC can handle.

Windows Creator automatically compresses art and sound assets to the smallest possible size as they are imported—but if more compression is needed, assets should be designed with speed and efficiency in mind. Simple ways to bring file sizes under control include using large areas of flat color (one reason why the "toon" look is so popular) and limiting the use of gradients.

Workflow

When it comes to assets, it's possible to break most games down into a few simple sets. It's best to first plot out the visual and sound assets needed to build the game—filling this asset list with temporary files (sprites from other projects, scanned sketches, and doodles). Final files can be swapped in later with ease.

- *Player Assets*: Arguably, the player is the most important part of the game. Assets can vary depending on the type of game. For example, a first-person shooter (FPS) might need to show a pair of hands and a weapon, or an RPG might show the character class selected—but having something ready to work with is essential.

- *Background Images*: Even with a rough pencil sketch in place, it's possible to position assets, determine gameplay flow, and attach behaviors without needing final art in place.

- *Environmental Assets*: Non-interactive assets that inhabit the game world (such as clouds that float through the sky or trees that shift in the wind) can add detail and variation that might allow a developer to build a dozen unique levels on top of a single background image.

- *In-Game Assets*: Interactive components are often referred to as "in-game" assets—including animated sprites and sound effects. Maintaining a list of these assets (even if there's only a single still image at the outset) will prevent a developer from losing track of tasks that need to be completed.

The *Bill & Ted* Problem

In the cult film, *Bill & Ted's Excellent Adventure*, a circular problem arises when the main characters determine that in order for their band (Wyld Stallyns) to be a "super band," they need to have Eddie Van Halen on guitar. However, they realize that they won't be able to get Van Halen until they have a "triumphant video"—and that it's pointless to have a triumphant video before they have "decent instruments." Finally, they conclude that they can't have decent instruments when they don't know how to play them—and *that's* why they need Van Halen! The term "*Bill & Ted* Problem" has been used internally in some game development studios: The programmers need art to work with, and the artists need programming to work with their art. Who goes first? Since Windows Creator takes the programming out of the equation, the answer is straight-forward for a change: Start with the art!

Setting Up an Animated Sprite

Setting up an animated sequence is a fairly straightforward process. Once animation frames have been imported, it will be necessary to create an Actor. This is accomplished by clicking under the "Actor" tab. An empty Actor is something like an empty box; now that it's there, it can be filled with the images and instructions needed to create an animated sprite.

After creating an Actor, select the "Behaviors" tab at the top of the screen. Scroll down to find and select the "Animate" behavior and drag it to the Backstage window to the right. Within the new box that opens up to reflect the Behavior, animation frames can be dragged and dropped into the box.

In the bottom half of the Behavior box, right under where the animation frames have been placed, set the specifics of the animation. Traditional cartoon animation runs at 30 *frames per second* (*fps*), but animation in games can vary depending on needs and number of frames available. (Once the animation frames are in place, it will be necessary to add Behaviors to tell the game how to use them. This will be covered further in the "Adding Behaviors" section below.)

Behaviors, Attributes, and Functions are all customizable elements that can be used to set up the rules that govern an Actor's actions and reactions.

Image courtesy of GameSalad®.

Windows Creator will play the frames in the sequence provided, and frames can be duplicated or swapped around as needed.

Larger static images such as single backgrounds, splash screens, or environmental elements will need to be compressed as much as possible without losing quality. Specific Behaviors may need to be added to these objects as well. For example, a scrolling background image for a racing game might need Behaviors indicating when to loop itself—or middle ground elements like those seen in *Bumps* might need Behaviors allowing reactions to player contact.

Image courtesy of Utopian Games.

Higher resolution visual assets may be used in Windows development than in mobile or online games (discussed in Chapters 6 and 7, respectively). When the game is stored locally on the player's computer, download time and network lag aren't as much of a problem (*Bumps* shown).

Layers

Like many popular art programs, Windows Creator allows developers to work in layers. When working with game assets—particularly where a drag-and-drop interface is concerned—being able to organize and access objects quickly and efficiently is a key part of the development process. Place your far background objects on one layer; include an animated middle layer for your game objects; and then add a far forward layer for UI elements. This simplifies the task of game creation by allowing you to focus on one layer at a time. If you're working with dummy art or mockups that need to be closely matched (e.g., in a hidden-object game), use the layer system to build on top of the existing mockups—and then cleanly delete the dummy art by removing the mockup layers. For Windows development, the inclusion of multiple layers of movement can help add:

Image courtesy of GameSalad®.

Objects that can collide with one another, such as the protagonist and the velociraptor in *Raptor Storm*, should be kept on the same layer in Creator. (Objects that are there for appearances only or that are not yet interactable, such as the pterosaurs, should be kept on a separate layer to avoid unnecessary complications.)

- significant depth to a game
- more traditionally painted backgrounds blended with simpler, cleaner animated characters
- visual effects layers
- easier rotation of gameplay elements in and out of the Scene

With online and mobile games, the number of layers needs to be limited to keep from bogging down performance—but the desktop provides a greater degree of freedom.

Adding Behaviors

Once the art assets are imported—whether they're dummy or full-blown final assets—attaching them to Actors and assigning Behaviors is the next logical step. Behaviors and Attributes allow you to tell an Actor just what to do given a certain set of conditions. In Creator, the Behaviors are broken down into the following sets:

- Blocks
- Conditions
- Persistent
- Actions
- Custom

Let's take a closer look at each of these sets.

Blocks

Blocks comprise a Behavior set within Creator that allows you to group sets of instructions together so that they can be easily triggered by the game. There may be several different sets of instructions for any given object, but you may not need use them all at the same time—or even in any particular order. Blocks are, essentially, used to create smaller containers within the larger container of the Actor (much like Tupperware containers keep leftovers fresh and accessible within the larger confines of your refrigerator).

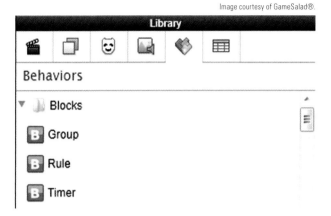
Image courtesy of GameSalad®.

Blocks allow Behaviors to be grouped—ensuring that they all act in the correct order.

Components of Blocks include:

- *Group*: A Group is a set of instructions that are executed together. Groups will not affect the order in which your commands are executed. Creator processes commands from top to bottom, so Groups serve mainly as organizational tools.

- *Rule*: A Rule is a type of "conditional" statement (e.g., WHEN the D key is pressed, THEN move the character to the right).

- *Timer*: A Timer is used to trigger Behaviors based on specified intervals (e.g., "After 5 seconds, destroy this Actor" or "Every 60 seconds, spawn another enemy"). The Timer groups this "time" component with a dialog box that allows the developer to define what happens when the time runs out.

Image courtesy of GameSalad®.

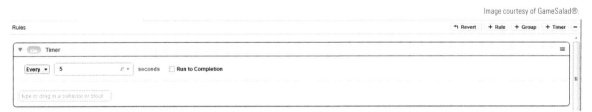

Sets of instructions can be grouped within a Behavior, allowing the developer to tailor them to specific actions or responses within the game.

Order of Operations

Behaviors and Attributes within an Actor are executed in order—from top to bottom and left to right, just like reading a book.

Conditions

Conditions are sets of Behaviors that can be used to trigger actions in the game. Each of the seven Conditions made available to the player allows Rules to be set based on different qualifications being met.

Components of Conditions include:

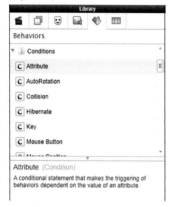

Image courtesy of GameSalad®.

Conditions help the developer tell the game what needs to happen before it can execute a Behavior.

- *Attribute*: An Attribute is an element of a character. This condition allows the developer to define the state of any given Attribute, along with the Behavior that happens when that state is achieved.

- *AutoRotation*: AutoRotation allows the developer to set the rotation of an Actor and define what happens when it's rotating. For example, if the Actor is a boulder, AutoRotation can define what happens when the boulder is rolling. The game could create a puff of smoke when it begins to rotate, or an explosion when it stops.

- *Key*: The "Key" Behavior allows the developer to map game actions such as character movement to different keyboard keys.

- *Mouse Button*: Mouse Button is similar to Key, but it draws its input from the clicks of the mouse button.

- *Mouse Position*: Mouse Position is more subtle—creating a rule based on where the mouse is on the screen at any given point in time. This is particularly useful for elements such as menus that slide on and off the page when the mouse hovers over them.

- *Collision*: Collision is perhaps the most often used condition in any game. It allows the developer to define just what happens when two objects collide with one another. This can include anything that has an action or reaction when it touches anything else. For example, do the NPCs turn into zombies when touched by the player?

- *Touch*: Touch describes what happens when the screen is touched. This is useful for games that will be deployed on Windows as well as touchscreen devices because Creator automatically interprets a mouse click as a "touch." (Touch is also used extensively for mobile game development—discussed in Chapter 6.)

"Button Button, Who's Got the Button?"

Windows computers usually ship with a mouse that has two buttons, but Mac computers ship with a mouse that has only one. To support both platforms, it's necessary to rethink the button controls.

Persistent

Persistent Behaviors cover rules that always apply. No conditions need to be met in order to execute an action; these rules apply all the time (such as, "When the Actor 'ball' hits Actor 'ground,' it bounces"). These rules are much more specific—such as defining the acceleration of an Actor toward a specific point, or moving an Actor from Point A to B.

Deep Thought

For a deeper look at individual Persistent Behaviors, see "Behaviors in GameSalad" (part of GameSalad's online Cookbook at http://cookbook.gamesalad.com).

Actions

Actions are clear and straightforward—such as "Stop Music," "Play Sound," or "Change Image." These are one-off Actions that need to be executed, rather than being held in a state of readiness as with Conditions.

Custom

Initially empty, the *Custom* tab is where any reuseable Behaviors that have been created are held in readiness. Included might be a link to the associated purchase account or advertisement display trigger.

Image courtesy of GameSalad®.

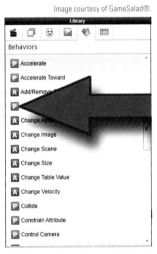

Persistent Behaviors are often used for setting game rules and conditions.

Image courtesy of GameSalad®.

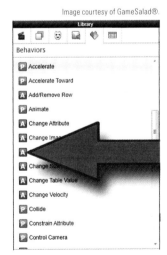

Actions are all about "doing" things: growing bigger, moving sideways, exploding, making noise—you name it.

Image courtesy of GameSalad®.

Custom behaviors allow you to store the kinds of behaviors you use most often, with your own tweaks already included. Examples might be links to external URLs to drive social media.

Attributes

The *Attributes* tab gives the developer control over the broader aspects of a game—such as setting the name or Actor size. It also shows (and allows the developer to access) the available devices. For Windows games, the primary device will be the mouse—but as market penetration gains speed on touchscreen displays for the PC, there will be more use for touch-related games.

Animated Characters

The Behaviors added to Actors control every aspect of their actions. As an example of how to link Behaviors together, let's look at the setup for an animated character—starting with the three components to a moving actor: Art, Behaviors, and Sounds.

Image courtesy of GameSalad®.

Behaviors are built to be nested inside one another, allowing the designer the freedom to create multiple scenarios within a single Rule.

The art of the character itself includes any and all animations that might be needed. A full sequence of motions can be created (e.g., one set of frames of the Actor turned to the right, and another set of the Actor turned to the left). Creator can also rotate and invert art assets using Behaviors and Attributes, so a single set of frames may be all you need. For this example, we'll use a single shape (a circle) so that we can highlight the translation (movement along an axis).

Instances & Prototypes

The *Prototype* is the name for an original version of an object in a game. (Several game engines also use the term "Prefab.") Usually, the Prototype is set up with the most "common" elements (e.g., motion, collisions) built in. Once it has been set within a Scene, it becomes an *Instance* (a copy that links back to the original Prototype)—so that any changes to the Prototype are also copied over to the Instance.

Behaviors are the instructions that tell an Actor what to do and when to do it. Create an empty Actor and be sure the art has already been imported. The first step is to tell this Actor how to react to the player's actions. Since we are working with a Windows-based game, it is unlikely that players will be using a D-pad or joystick. Movement is often handled with either the arrow or WASD keys—so let's tell the actor that the player character needs to move to the right when the D key is pressed. Here is how this is handled:

1) *Select Behaviors/Conditions/Key and drag it to the Rules window associated with the Actor.* Notice there is an option of choosing "All" or "Any," which allows multiple conditions to be set for an action. For example, if the character should do something different when Ctrl-D is pressed, that value can be set here. For a simple forward motion, let's leave leave it at "All."

2) *Type "D" in the key press dialog box.* Again, note that a dropdown menu allows different settings to be chosen. For example, the action could only be executed when the key is released.

3) *The rest of the dialog box is set up with a dropdown for "do" and "else." Set it for "do," since the Behavior should occur when the key is pressed.* Since this will be a basic control for your animated figure, grab the "Move" behavior from under Behaviors/Persistent and drag it to this space in the Rule. The movement parameters will then be visible. The "move in direction" tells the program at which angle to move the character. For example, "0" moves the character directly to the player's right—and "180" moves the character in the opposite direction to the left. The movement (e.g., direction) can be changed so that it's relative to the Actor rather than the player. Leave the "additive" dropdown and speed as they are for the moment. These elements will allow adjustments to be made with regard to character movement—including manner and speed (including fluctuations over time). It is often easier, when first starting out, to have the basics of the character working on screen, so that these components can be adjusted later to see how they affect the end result (rather than having to guess at setup).

4) *Click and drag the new Actor to the game screen.* Referring to the image below, notice how the Rules have been greyed out and there is text near the bottom of the screen referring to clicking the lock to modify the Actor. By clicking and dragging the Actor, an instance of the Actor is created. To make changes to just *this* copy of the Actor, click the lock on the screen. Changes made will not affect the original. To reverse any changes, click the "Revert to Prototype" button just above the Rules box on the right.

Image courtesy of GameSalad®.

Once all the Behaviors have been included, adding an Actor to the Scene is a simple as clicking and dragging it to the game space.

5) *To test the Behavior, click on the green, right-facing arrow just above the game layout to access a Preview stage.* After a few seconds, press the "D" button. The Actor should then slide off the stage toward the right. To make the Actor wrap around or slide off the screen to the right (magically reappearing on the left), it will be necessary to turn to the characteristics of the Scene—the basic state of the game environment that affects all the components within it.

Like art, character sounds should already be imported into the game. After the import, take a look through the Behaviors that have already been assigned to the Actor and think about where those sounds are best placed. For example, if the character should have squeaky footsteps, add a Behavior into the same group that will play a sound when the walk sequence is being triggered. If a clanking sound should be played when the character runs into a light post, the Behavior could be attached to the light post (how it reacts when bumped into) or the character (how it reacts when it bumps into something).

Scene Characteristics

Every game world has rules; remembering their specifics and enacting them as Behaviors on every single object place in the world will become tedious when all is said and done. Universal rules that apply across the board (such as gravity and wind, or whether or not Actors can slide off the edges of the world) will be set in the Scene itself. Of course, each Scene may have a completely different set of Rules (e.g., each planet in the solar system has an entirely different gravitational pull).

Image courtesy of GameSalad®.

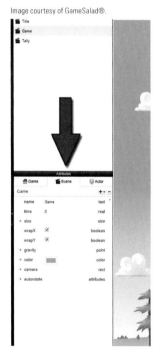

Selecting the correct tab under Attributes allows the developer to access and modify any local Attributes (such as gravity) within a Scene.

Clicking the "Scenes" tab at the top of the Windows Creator workspace will reveal an area for a list—similar to the area available for images or Actors. In this area, new Scenes may be created by clicking. Creator provides an "Initial Scene," but additional Scenes may be added. (For example, the splash screen and menus are usually couched in their own, individual Scenes—and each level within the game will have its own Scene as well. Once all local elements have been set up within a Scene, it's possible to make a copy of it—reducing the need to build each and every Scene from scratch.

Don't Bring Me Down

Gravity, despite being a key force on the planet, may not be entirely necessary in a game. In fact, the inclusion of physics (such as gravity) was a later development in the history of video games. While it might be nice to just let things fall where they may, there's a risk of not having a fine enough level of control—and with gravity affecting *every* moveable object in a Scene, this might cause more trouble than it's worth. (Setting the gravity in a Scene will cause everything that is marked as "moveable" to fall in the direction that's chosen, but this doesn't mean objects will automatically collide. It will be necessary to add Behaviors that define what happens when two objects meet.)

Scene Attribute	Description
name	Covers the name of the current Scene (and how it will be referred to throughout Creator), so make sure it's easy to remember.
time	Can be called upon but not actually set here (so you can read it, but you can't change it in any way); it's a counter that reflects the amount of time the Scene has been active.
size	Provides the height and width of the current Scene in pixels; it can be adjusted at any time after setting up the Project initially.
wrapX	Allows the developer to set what happens when objects hit the edge of the screen; if this box is checked, an object that disappears off the X axis (left or right side of the screen) will reappear on the other.
wrapY	Provides the same function as "wrapX," but it refers to the Y axis (top and bottom of the screen); when both "wrapX" and "wrapY" are checked, an object that disappears off any side of the screen will reappear on the opposite side.
gravity	Sets the gravity in a Scene; this is one of the most used options, but it's important to think carefully before working with it due to being processor-intensive. Setting the gravity number to around 100 will provide close to "normal" gravity, but using negative numbers will result in objects tending to move up (going against gravity)—while setting the Y (up/down) or X (left/right) value in the attribute will set the direction in which the gravity pulls.
color	Sets background color, which is especially useful because it is procedurally generated (by the program, rather than being an imported .bmp or .jpg); if a specific background image is not needed, go with a plain color and save the memory.
camera	Allows the adjustment of how the camera reacts to an Actor with the "control camera" Behavior set; sub-areas include: *size* is adjustable and refers to the camera's viewable area; the playfield can be larger than the screen, and the view of the camera can move about—which can be adjusted in order to zoom in on an Actor. *tracking area* sets the boundaries of a camera's motion when it is following an Actor. *rotation* determines how the camera reacts if the game is on a mobile device with an autorotation function; it cannot be set manually and is exposed so that it can be easily accessed through the Behaviors if needed.
autorotate	Is most often used for mobile and sets whether or not the screen automatically rotates to match the direction the user is holding the device.

Publishing to Windows

When a Windows game is published on Creator, it isn't "published to Windows," per se; instead, Creator sends the game to the GameSalad servers, where it is turned into a binary file. This binary is then uploaded to the Windows 8 App Store, where Windows 8 users can download the game

Image courtesy of GameSalad®.

Uploading your game to the GameSalad servers allows you build a binary for all platforms from a single original file. Each platform will have different sets of information requirements that will need to be filled out in order to complete the publishing process.

Fate of Windows Development

There's no way to deny it: The rise of the "next-gen" consoles took a big bite out of the Windows game market. AAA titles that formerly relied on the dedicated memory and hardware acceleration of gaming PCs found a new home on consoles that provided a stable, single configuration platform and an HD screen that could make you feel almost like you were playing your game in a movie theater. However, rather than dry up and blow away, the PC game market has moved beyond pretty graphics and has become the home to innovation. PC gaming has reclaimed its right as the birthplace of new gameplay ideas and methods of engagement.

Scene Attribute	Description
name	Covers the name of the current Scene (and how it will be referred to throughout Creator), so make sure it's easy to remember.
time	Can be called upon but not actually set here (so you can read it, but you can't change it in any way); it's a counter that reflects the amount of time the Scene has been active.
size	Provides the height and width of the current Scene in pixels; it can be adjusted at any time after setting up the Project initially.
wrapX	Allows the developer to set what happens when objects hit the edge of the screen; if this box is checked, an object that disappears off the X axis (left or right side of the screen) will reappear on the other.
wrapY	Provides the same function as "wrapX," but it refers to the Y axis (top and bottom of the screen); when both "wrapX" and "wrapY" are checked, an object that disappears off any side of the screen will reappear on the opposite side.
gravity	Sets the gravity in a Scene; this is one of the most used options, but it's important to think carefully before working with it due to being processor-intensive. Setting the gravity number to around 100 will provide close to "normal" gravity, but using negative numbers will result in objects tending to move up (going against gravity)—while setting the Y (up/down) or X (left/right) value in the attribute will set the direction in which the gravity pulls.
color	Sets background color, which is especially useful because it is procedurally generated (by the program, rather than being an imported .bmp or .jpg); if a specific background image is not needed, go with a plain color and save the memory.
camera	Allows the adjustment of how the camera reacts to an Actor with the "control camera" Behavior set; sub-areas include: *size* is adjustable and refers to the camera's viewable area; the playfield can be larger than the screen, and the view of the camera can move about—which can be adjusted in order to zoom in on an Actor. *tracking area* sets the boundaries of a camera's motion when it is following an Actor. *rotation* determines how the camera reacts if the game is on a mobile device with an autorotation function; it cannot be set manually and is exposed so that it can be easily accessed through the Behaviors if needed.
autorotate	Is most often used for mobile and sets whether or not the screen automatically rotates to match the direction the user is holding the device.

Tags & Types

One Attribute of an Actor is denoted as a *tag*, which allows the developer to broadly categorize objects (e.g., "platform," "bouncy platform," "insta-kill"). This allows Rules that apply to every object to be set with that tag rather than a long list of objects—such as setting a collision Behavior to "explode" for any objects tagged with "insta-kill" rather than setting the collision Behavior "explode for Object01, Object02, Object27, Green Meanie, The Box," etc. This can greatly streamline the production process—allowing multiple objects to be covered by set of Attributes and allowing new objects to be included with the correct tags without having to find every individual Block and change the components manually.

Image courtesy of GameSalad®.

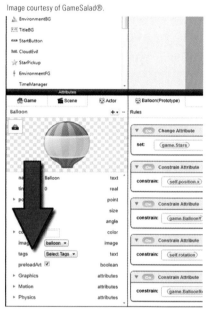

An Actor has a basic set of characteristics that can be modified as needed—such as changing the associated art image or denoting whether or not the object is moveable.

Particle Effects

Particles can be thought of as the "icing on the cake" for so many games. They can be used to great effect as alerts when the player succeeds at a task—and to create smoke trails, explosions, sparkles, fireworks, dust, and even in-game critters such as snakes or bugs. They are commonly seen when a player picks up a power-up or passes a checkpoint. A particle is essentially an object within a game with actions, reactions, and lifespans that are controlled by a set of mathematical equations. One of the benefits to Windows Creator is that it's not necessary for the developer to figure out and encode those equations. Creator allows for the creation of 2D particles through the use of the particle Behavior. Keep in mind that it will be necessary to create 2D sprites for particle shapes; otherwise, only default white squares will appear in the game. Windows Creator will provide these as "instances" within the game in order to minimize the impact on frame rate.

Testing as You Go

One great feature for developers is the "test as you go" capability in Creator. A game may be tested at any point during the development process without having to wait for long compile times or exporting to one platform or another.

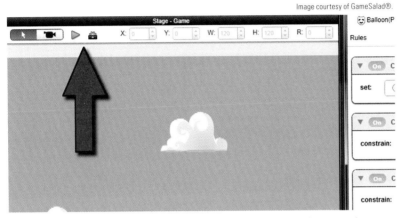

Image courtesy of GameSalad®.

Selecting the green, right-facing arrow will access a test screen where any elements added to the game may be played through.

In the "Preview" area, all existing Scenes are laid out along the bottom of the screen. Double-clicking on any of these Scenes will open them in the Preview, which will have full functionality—allowing the developer to switch Scenes in-game (e.g., using the menu buttons from the start screen). When finished, select the "Back to Editor" button to resume editing Scenes.

While in the Preview area, the game cannot be affected or edited in any way—other than to play through it. In order to facilitate bug hunting, Creator has provided two very helpful buttons: "restart" and "pause." When making notes on an error, it is often helpful to take a screenshot to record exactly what happened. The pause button allows for this—pausing the game just as the error occurs so that a screenshot can be taken before moving on.

Screenshots

The Preview screen is an easy place to grab good, high-quality screenshots. Just click the camera icon in the top center of the screen.

Publishing to Windows

When a Windows game is published on Creator, it isn't "published to Windows," per se; instead, Creator sends the game to the GameSalad servers, where it is turned into a binary file. This binary is then uploaded to the Windows 8 App Store, where Windows 8 users can download the game

Image courtesy of GameSalad®.

Uploading your game to the GameSalad servers allows you build a binary for all platforms from a single original file. Each platform will have different sets of information requirements that will need to be filled out in order to complete the publishing process.

Fate of Windows Development

There's no way to deny it: The rise of the "next-gen" consoles took a big bite out of the Windows game market. AAA titles that formerly relied on the dedicated memory and hardware acceleration of gaming PCs found a new home on consoles that provided a stable, single configuration platform and an HD screen that could make you feel almost like you were playing your game in a movie theater. However, rather than dry up and blow away, the PC game market has moved beyond pretty graphics and has become the home to innovation. PC gaming has reclaimed its right as the birthplace of new gameplay ideas and methods of engagement.

Additional material based on these exercises and chapter topics is available as part of the Instructor Resources package.

91

:::CHAPTER REVIEW EXERCISES:::

1. Write up a one-paragraph description of an original Windows desktop game. What gameplay style will you focus on? Are there other games developed using GameSalad Creator that have similar elements?

2. Take a stroll through the Windows 8 App Store, paying special attention to the games that use the gameplay style you chose in Exercise 1. Which genres are suitable for your game?

3. Create a rough sketch of your game in both 4:6 and 10:16 formats. Will one of the formats in particular enhance the way your game is played?

4. Examine the overall size of your game on screen (pixel by pixel). What percentage of your screen real estate should be dedicated to your user interface?

5. Take another look at the games you reviewed for Exercise 2 and compare the art styles. What visual style do you want your game to reflect? Photoreal? Toon? Pixel-painted?

6. Think about the mood you want to invoke in your players and how this might affect the audio elements you choose in your design. Using the music program of your choice, locate a song or two that sets the proper mood for your game.

7. Using the storyboard templates provided as online resources, sketch out a few moments of gameplay. Include arrows to indicate directions of motion. Now, rotate the storyboard template 90 degrees and redo your storyboard sketches. How does the gameplay need to change to fit the new format?

CHAPTER

5

Mac Game Development
garden of digital delights

Key Chapter Questions

- How do *standalone* Mac games differ from online or Windows games?

- How do *art* requirements for games change when working on higher resolutions available with the Mac's Retina screen?

- How can *GameSalad Creator* be used to develop and publish games for Mac?

- How do the *distribution* paths differ for Mac versus Windows games?

- How will Mac game development continue to evolve in the *future*?

It has often been said that developing for the Mac operating system requires more finesse and patience on the part of the designer. Since the advent of the original Macintosh back in 1984, Apple has provided developers with a structured experience and a clearly defined set of guidelines with regard to the consumer experience. Working within the "walled garden" of Apple's App Store means a tighter set of restrictions—but also a cleaner delivery path and more direct access to players. Applications developed for Apple's mobile operating system (iOS) are making an easier transition to Mac than PC games—bringing a whole new source of game content into the arena. Working with tools such as GameSalad Creator can take the mystery out of publishing to the app stores and provide non-programmers with a much smoother route to their audience.

Is There an App for That? Not Yet!

For basic GameSalad Creator tutorials, see Appendix.

It's been an interesting run for Apple devices as game hardware. A broad range of games were available on early models Apple II and IIe before the advent of color screens—and Steve Wozniak showed an early focus on games by modifying the BASIC programming language into "GameBASIC." Early educational games, arcade ports, and dungeon crawlers—such as *Lemonade Stand*, *Zaxxon*, and *Wizardry*, respectively—made the first generation or two of the upstart personal computer an excellent gaming machine, as opposed to the strictly business models available from competitors at the time.

Image courtesy of Kimberly Unger.

```
HI!  WELCOME TO LEMONSVILLE, CALIFORNIA!

IN THIS SMALL TOWN, YOU ARE IN CHARGE OF
RUNNING YOUR OWN LEMONADE STAND. YOU CAN
COMPETE WITH AS MANY OTHER PEOPLE AS YOU
WISH, BUT HOW MUCH PROFIT YOU MAKE IS UP
TO YOU (THE OTHER STANDS' SALES WILL NOT
AFFECT YOUR BUSINESS IN ANY WAY). IF YOU
MAKE THE MOST MONEY, YOU'RE THE WINNER!!

ARE YOU STARTING A NEW GAME? (YES OR NO)
TYPE YOUR ANSWER AND HIT RETURN ==> *
```

Despite the initial lack of a color screen, the first few generations of Apple computers (Apple 2, shown) proved to be popular for games such as *Lemonade Stand*.

When Apple changed format in 1984 with the release of the original Macintosh, the company was most interested in pursuing the lucrative business market that had been dominated up until then by IBM. Despite the original Apple's popularity as a more universal machine—good for programming, playing games, and word processing—the Macintosh shipped with a single "accessory" product called *Puzzle*.

Gamers, however, were not to be denied. Despite Apple's insistence that the Macintosh was a productivity machine—with a monocolor screen (a seemingly backwards step from the color screens that were available for the Apple IIe and IIc) and a new "closed box" operating system—games for the new machine began to emerge almost immediately. First came text-based adventure games that had no need for fancy graphics or color screens; these were followed up by ports of popular games from the Apple II generation. Despite this persistence, though, the market for games on the Macintosh was too small to attract serious attention—so it missed out on versions of the most popular console titles published by companies such as Sega.

As the Macintosh evolved away from its business-oriented roots, newer versions began to add game-friendly elements such as a color screen and more memory—but ports of popular games still had to go through a complete programmatic reboot in order to appear on the increasingly popular personal computer. In 1987, everything changed when Apple released HyperCard as part of the *original equipment manufacturer* (*OEM*) toolset for the Macintosh. HyperCard allowed designers to blend varying types of multimedia, programming, art, and sound with a graphical interface. This addition allowed games to blossom on Macintosh systems, and it gave a new generation of game designers easy access to a market that was hungry for new content.

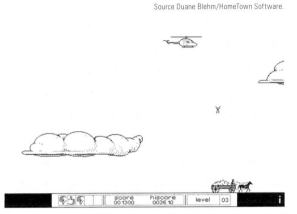
Source Duane Blehm/HomeTown Software.

Source Silicon Beach Software, Inc.

Examples of early Macintosh games include *Stunt Copter* (left) and *Dark Castle* (right).

Macintosh games comprised a "niche" market through the late 1990s and into the early 2000s—with fewer than 30 games released for the OS in 1998 and fewer than 40 in 1999. With the release of the iMac, there was an upsurge in the number of "gamers" on the Mac platform. Where publishers had previously refused to fund development of Mac titles (or only backed ports of already successful Windows titles), the gradual—but reliable—rise in the number of Mac users reopened the possibility of original titles being developed for the Mac.

Interestingly enough, it was the release of the iPod back in 2007 that seems to have opened up the Mac gaming market for good. As independent development studios rushed to work with the handheld platform, many smaller "casual" games were an easy transfer from the mobile version of the OS to the desktop version. Concurrent with this, a number of the independent AAA game studios (most notably id Software and Epic Games) made it clear that they would be supporting the Mac with their own game engines; Bethesda Softworks (publishers of the hugely popular *Elder Scrolls* series) and Telltale Games have also both established themselves as developers for the Mac as well as the Windows platform.

With the successful release of Steam (Valve's online game delivery service) and Apple's revamp of its online App Store for Mac OS (not to be confused with iTunes, though they share some similarities), the market for Mac gaming was wide open and ready for new development. The question remains whether traditional game publishers will back the platform with the same enthusiasm as Windows (PC) or console markets—but this means that independent developers now have a clear field of play.

OS Wars

The Mac *operating system* (*OS*) contains many functional similarities to that of Windows (discussed in Chapter 4). Visual content for both is organized into boxes of graphics and text; data is stored in a system of metaphorical files and folders; and a mouse is used to access programs, move sliders, and drag elements around the screen. However, both systems handle things very differently once we move beyond the "screen" level; due to these differences, Mac Creator is discussed separately.

Source Apple Inc. Image courtesy of Kimberly Unger.

Source Microsoft Corporation.

The Mac desktop (left; Mac OSX Lion, shown) is dramatically different in look and feel from the Windows desktop (right; Windows 8, shown), but both operating systems share many similarities.

Graphic Considerations

One key difference between Mac and Windows off the shelf is the screen resolution available. The installed base for Mac laptops and notebooks (e.g., MacBook Pro) is higher than that of Mac desktops (e.g., iMac). With the Mac desktop platform, there are a broad range of monitors available to the user—and there's no real way to control pixel resolution. However, the *Retina Display* available on the MacBook can provide a figure for the highest possible resolution—and we can see how other applications, not optimized for the Retina display, handle the differences. At this time, Mac Creator includes Retina Display support for the iPad 3, but not for Mac desktop, so mobile game developers are able to take advantage of this higher resolution. This means that it will be necessary to tweak the graphics a bit. However, building a "one-size-fits-all" set of art assets will allow for the option to set the game to open at a lower resolution.

Source Apple Inc. Image courtesy of Kimberly Unger.

Not all applications are currently compatible with the extremely high resolution of Apple's Retina Display. Certain applications can be set to work at distinct resolution settings, and many are being updated to accommodate the higher resolution.

Retina Displays arrive in what is called a "pixel-double" configuration. This means that for every pixel on an older style screen, there are four doing the same job on a Retina screen.

When building a game project, make sure that the "Resolution Independence" option is switched on. This will cause Mac Creator to provide multiple versions of the visual assets for the game; the lower resolution assets will be swapped in on systems that don't have Retina Displays.

Image courtesy of Utopian Games and Kimberly Unger.

Working with a 4x6 ratio screen size will allow players with any monitor to enjoy your game the way you want it to be played. *Bumps* (shown) fits nicely into the available screen space on any monitor without distortion.

Since the variation in available screen resolutions is up for grabs on the Mac, how big should a game be in terms of pixels? It's easy to think that there's as much space as you could possibly want when designing for more pixels—but sticking to a size that fits comfortably on an average computer monitor (regardless of resolution) will allow you to greatly simplify design tasks. While the edges of the playfield may seem to be a barrier to design, many gameplay styles take advantage of scrolling backgrounds that effectively allow an unlimited playfield even on a small, low-res monitor. Role-playing games (RPGs) and racing games do this particularly well. Consider the edges of the screen as frames of a window—with game elements able to move out of sight off screen.

When it comes to monitor sizes and resolutions, there are some legacy standards to be considered. The 4x3 ratio (derived from the 640x480 pixel size of a standard television screen) remains a common standard format, but widescreen formats are becoming increasingly popular—especially since users have the option to set the resolution of their monitors to best suit their needs. The 4x6 ratio also provides the best available solution: working on all different types of screens with minimum adjustment.

Even when planning or working with high-resolution images, it's possible to begin work on gameplay design with smaller resolution objects and placeholder art. New game designers may start with a much smaller pool of assets—but after creating a few games, it will be possible to reuse assets (e.g., character animations, background images) to develop the gameplay and then replace them once the final art is complete.

Image courtesy of GameSalad®.

Mac Creator links directly to GameSalad's online Marketplace, where developers may purchase a variety of game assets to help flesh out a project or serve as asset placeholders.

Mac Creator is designed to handle a broad range of art formats—but for small file-sizes with a limited loss in quality, .png is probably the most popular (particularly for sprites and other in-game assets that require transparency).

Systems of Information

The way players access and "control" a game or app can have a huge impact on how long they stay—and how they feel about the experience. Building these *systems of information*, such as the *user interface* (discussed in Chapter 2) can easily be as important as the playability of the game itself. Be sure to create a mockup of your game screen with an emphasis on the necessary interface elements. Although these will vary by designer and genre, nearly every game genre has clear visual representations of key gameplay components. At the very least, a block-breaker title such as *Gem Buster* will display the player's health/number of lives, current score, and high score to beat. The key here is *screen real estate*, which is much larger on desktop computers (Mac or Windows)—allowing developers to convey significantly more information to the player than on a smartphone, for example. Interface elements are resolution-dependent; it will be necessary to consider how these elements scale down for lower resolution devices, and an additional set of assets may need to be created to ensure they're clear and easy to understand no matter what screen your game is played on.

When designing for a particular platform (e.g., computer, tablet, smartphone), it's important to consider hardware specifics (e.g., buttons, touchscreen) and the way games have traditionally been played on that platform. This means that a player who habitually uses a Mac will have slightly different interface expectations than a player who habitually uses a console, Windows system, handheld, or mobile device for games.

The best user interfaces tend to be minimal and stay out of the way (*Gem Breaker,* shown). There is nothing more frustrating than an interface element covering a key piece of gameplay.

Core Components

A simple game contains a few core components and concepts that are almost universal across all game types. Let's take a look at the key components of a *Pachinko* game using Mac Creator and how those components can be used in other game types. *Pachinko* consists of a board covered with tiny pegs. The player drops a ball or a disk at the top of the board with the goal of it landing in one of several slots at the bottom of the board. Important components include gravity/movement (causing the balls to drop), collisions (how the balls react when they hit the pegs), and scorekeeping.

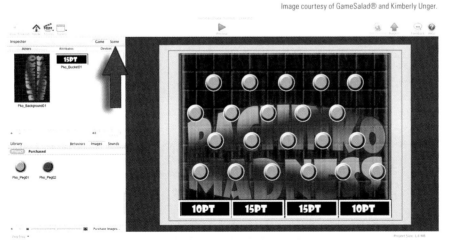

The sample game *Pachinko Madness* demonstrates how to work with collisions using Mac Creator.

Setting the Scene

Setting up a Scene in Mac Creator allows the developer to set worldwide parameters such as *gravity*—or how an object slides off the left side of the screen and then reappears on the right. Clicking the "Scenes" tab at the top of the Mac Creator

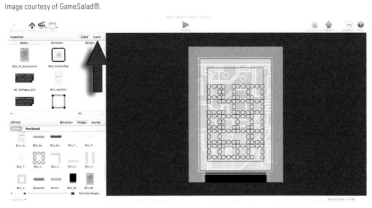

Image courtesy of GameSalad®.

workspace will reveal an area for a list—similar to the area available for Images or Actors. In this area, new scenes may be created by clicking ⊕. Creator provides an "Initial Scene," but additional scenes may be added. Each level within the game will have its own Scene as well. Once all local elements have been set up within a Scene, it's possible to make a copy of it—reducing the need to build each and every Scene from scratch.

Selecting the "Scene" button allows developers to work with the broader-based scene characteristics such as gravity.

For *Pachinko Madness*, the Scene Attribute for "gravity" should be set to 100 ("Earth-normal"), and the direction should be set to pull downward; setting the values in the X and Y coordinates of the "gravity" Attribute determines which direction objects will move.

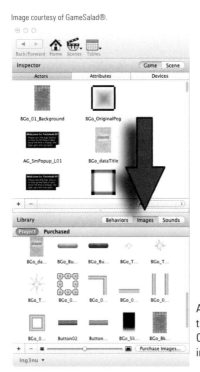

Image courtesy of GameSalad®.

To import images, access the "Images" tab at the bottom of the Mac Creator screen and click ⊕. This will open up the dialogue box that allows the background image to be imported. This same procedure should be used to import all of image assets.

Once the images have been imported, each of them will need to be made into an Actor within Mac Creator. Keep in mind that although the background is only a still image, it serves as a useful Actor to collect many Scene Behaviors.

After selecting the "Images" tab at the bottom of the Mac Creator screen, all game images may be imported.

Scene Attribute	Description
name	Covers the name of the current Scene (and how it will be referred to throughout Creator), so make sure it's easy to remember.
time	Can be called upon but not actually set here (so you can read it, but you can't change it in any way); it's a counter that reflects the amount of time the Scene has been active.
size	Provides the height and width of the current Scene in pixels; it can be adjusted at any time after setting up the Project initially.
wrapX	Allows the developer to set what happens when objects hit the edge of the screen; if this box is checked, an object that disappears off the X axis (left or right side of the screen) will reappear on the other.
wrapY	Provides the same function as "wrapX," but it refers to the Y axis (top and bottom of the screen); when both "wrapX" and "wrapY" are checked, an object that disappears off any side of the screen will reappear on the opposite side.
gravity	Sets the gravity in a Scene; this is one of the most used options, but it's important to think carefully before working with it due to being processor-intensive. Setting the gravity number to around 100 will provide close to "normal" gravity, but using negative numbers will result in objects tending to move up (going against gravity)—while setting the Y (up/down) or X (left/right) value in the attribute will set the direction in which the gravity pulls.
color	Sets background color, which is especially useful because it is procedurally generated (by the program, rather than being an imported .bmp or .jpg); if a specific background image is not needed, go with a plain color and save the memory.
camera	Allows the adjustment of how the camera reacts to an Actor with the "control camera" Behavior set; sub-areas include: *size* is adjustable and refers to the camera's viewable area; the playfield can be larger than the screen, and the view of the camera can move about—which can be adjusted in order to zoom in on an Actor. *tracking area* sets the boundaries of a camera's motion when it is following an Actor. *rotation* determines how the camera reacts if the game is on a mobile device with an autorotation function; it cannot be set manually and is exposed so that it can be easily accessed through the Behaviors if needed.
autorotate	Is most often used for mobile and sets whether or not the screen automatically rotates to match the direction the user is holding the device; it doesn't apply to Mac.

Building with Nodes

After the art assets (whether placeholder or final) are imported, the next step is to attach them to Actors and assign nodes to them. Instruction nodes such as Behaviors and Attributes inform an Actor of its function, given a certain set of conditions. In Mac Creator, these are broken down into the following sets:

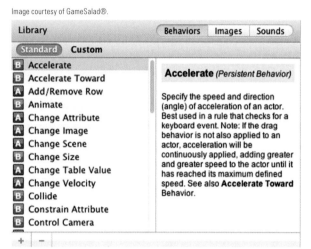

Image courtesy of GameSalad®.

Within the Behaviors list, different instruction nodes can be determined by the icons to their left.

B Behaviors **N** Notes

A Attributes **G** Groups

Standard Behavior nodes are designed to allow developers to string together a series of instructions for any given Actor without any programming required. In order to attach one Behavior (or series) to any given Actor, it's necessary to first decide which elements will be necessary. Selecting a Behavior will display its definition and function.

Tags

The *tags* Actor Attribute allows the developer to broadly categorize objects (e.g., "platform," "bouncy platform," "insta-kill") and to set Rules that apply to every object with that tag rather than for a long list of objects. For example, it's possible to set a collision behavior to "explode" for any objects tagged with "insta-kill" rather than having to set the collision behavior "explode" for Object01, Object02, Object27, Green Meanie, The Box," etc. This greatly streamlines the production process—allowing the developer to cover multiple objects with one set of Attributes and have the freedom to bring in new objects with the correct tag without locating every individual Block and changing the components manually.

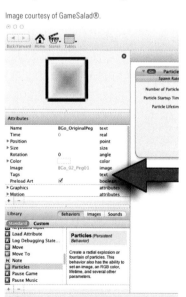

Image courtesy of GameSalad®.

Behaviors can be set to work with designated tags rather than specific objects. This allows the developer to change the actions associated with a single tag, and it will cascade to affect all objects that have that tag.

Assigning Behaviors

Once all images are loaded, it will be necessary to attach them to an Actor. In Mac Creator, the Actor is best thought of as a container that houses all of your pieces—including art assets, sound assets, and Behaviors that tell the game just how that Actor acts and reacts. An Actor is created by accessing the Actor tab in Mac Creator and clicking ⊞—similar to accessing the Images tab to import images. When creating an Actor, be sure to give it a distinctive name to avoid confusion later on. Images automatically become Actors upon import, so they're already under the Actors tab—ready for Behaviors to be assigned to them.

For *Pachinko Madness*, let's work with collisions—both on the bumps on the backdrop and the "ball" itself. To assign Behaviors to any object, begin by selecting the Actor in question, and then move down to select the "Behaviors" tab at the bottom half of the screen.

Since we're first working with bumps—which are static objects in the world (so we don't have to worry about how they move)—we will be looking for the "Persistent" tab. Select the "Collision" behavior under the "Persistent" tab and drag it to the "rules" box on the right. This will cause a new box to appear that reflects the attached Behavior.

This is where tags can come into play. Mac Creator allows one or more tags to be assigned to any given Actor in a game. Rather than setting the collision to react to every single ball that gets dropped, set it to react to objects that are "tagged."

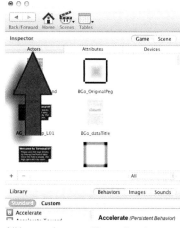

Image courtesy of GameSalad®.

All images become "Actors" on import and show up under the Actors tab. However, these images will also appear under the "Images" tab and can be assigned to new Actors as needed.

Image courtesy of GameSalad®.

The collision can be set to work with any object by name or with a particular tag. It's important to check the collision shape—getting it as close a match to the actual in-game object as possible.

Naming Conventions

Most game studios use a custom "naming convention" for each game created to avoid confusion. These conventions tend to follow a setup something like this: GameInitials_AssetType_AssetName_Number. For example, a tree in a game called *Buster Rocket* might be named: "BR_S_LgTree_001.bmp" (BusterRocket_StaticAsset_LgTree_001.bmp).

Layers

Like many popular art programs, Mac Creator allows developers to work in *layers*. This is particularly helpful when it comes to separating a game out into interactable and non-interactable areas. It's possible to place a far background, animated middle ground, and in-game elements on separate layers. Actors that interact with one another (game assets) should be placed on the same layer for ease of development. Actors can interact with other Actors on different layers, but it is easy to lose track if you have multiple layers of objects. This means that while we might choose to use one layer for the background image, we should ensure that the pegs on which we have just set the collision *and* the ball dropped by the player both use the same layer in the game.

For Mac development, the inclusion of multiple layers of movement can help do the following:

- add significant depth to a game
- blend more traditionally painted backgrounds with simpler, cleaner animated characters
- layer visual effects or rotate gameplay elements in and out of the scene more easily

On mobile or web platforms, it's important to limit the number of layers to keep from bogging down a game's performance—but on a desktop, there's a greater degree of freedom.

Leapfrogging Layers

Using Behaviors, it is possible to cause a game object to change layers at some predefined point in the game. Ideally, all interactable game objects would be built into the same layer—but there are special circumstances that might make it necessary for them to be built onto separate layers. For example, a second layer of game objects might be activated when a player receives a powerup—or there might be development issues caused by the depth and richness of the game's environments that require the number of objects to be limited to a single layer. From a game design standpoint, being able to leapfrog from one layer to another provides another "layer" of interactivity that can be put to good use.

Physics

Now that we've discussed setting up a static object with collision properties, let's take a quick look at how to get an object to fall. In this case, we'll refer to the falling balls for our mythical *Pachinko Madness* game. First, to set the ball-dropping physics, go to the Scene Attributes and hunt up the "gravity" parameter discussed earlier. There are two options: X and Y. "X" sets the gravity or amount of pull from side to side (negative numbers pull left, and positive numbers pull right), and "Y" sets the gravity from top to bottom (negative numbers pull up toward the top, and positive numbers pull down toward the bottom). Set Y to 100 to start. This value may need to be adjusted later (while testing the ball's gravity), but 100 should provide an "Earth-normal" pull of gravity in the Scene. Without the "Y" setting, the object won't move at all.

The Weight of the World

Despite being a key force on the planet, gravity may not be entirely necessary in a game. In fact, including physics such as gravity was a recent development in games. While it might be nice to just let things fall where they may, there's a risk of not having a fine enough level of control—and with gravity affecting *every* moveable object in a scene, this might cause more trouble than it's worth. (Setting the gravity in a scene will cause everything that is marked as "moveable" to fall in the direction that's chosen, but this doesn't mean objects will collide in a certain way. It's necessary to add Behaviors that define what happens when two objects collide.)

Scoring Systems

Keeping score is an inevitable part of games—even in those that don't keep score in the traditional sense; it's always necessary to track counters of varying kinds—such as the number of times a character jumps, breaks something, or dies. The developer needs to keep score, even if players don't see it. In *Pachinko Madness*, there's a series of buckets along the bottom of the screen. Behaviors should be attached to the buckets so that they destroy the ball when it hits and count the proper number of points when they destroy the ball. Setting up a scoring system requires creating a global attribute and access to an Actor (in this case, one of the buckets at the bottom of the *Pachinko* board).

Image courtesy of GameSalad®.

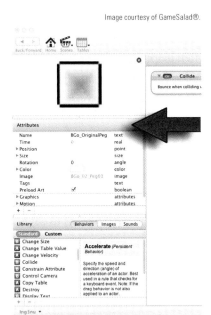

Within each Actor, a set of characteristics may be modified as needed—such as changing the associated image or denoting whether or not it's moveable.

Additional material based on these exercises and chapter topics is available as part of the Instructor Resources package.

:::CHAPTER REVIEW EXERCISES:::

1. Write up a one-paragraph description of an original Mac desktop game. What genre will you focus on? Are there other games developed using GameSalad Creator that have similar elements?

2. Take a stroll through the Mac App Store, paying special attention to the genre you have chosen for your game in Exercise 1. How saturated is your genre? Which other genres are suitable for your game?

3. Create a rough sketch of your game in both 4:6 and 10:16 formats. Will one of the formats in particular enhance the way your game is played?

4. Examine the overall size of your game (pixel by pixel). What percentage of your screen real estate could be dedicated to your controls?

5. Standardize a naming convention for your game assets. Discuss how you'll differentiate between sound, animation, static art, and other assets.

6. Think about the mood you want to invoke in your players and how this might affect the colors you choose in your design. Using Photoshop (or another graphics program), put together a color scheme that might reflect this mood.

7. Using the storyboard templates provided as online resources, sketch out a few moments of gameplay. Include arrows to indicate directions of motion. Now, rotate the storyboard template 90 degrees and redo your storyboard sketches. How does the gameplay need to change to fit the new format?

Physics

Now that we've discussed setting up a static object with collision properties, let's take a quick look at how to get an object to fall. In this case, we'll refer to the falling balls for our mythical *Pachinko Madness* game. First, to set the ball-dropping physics, go to the Scene Attributes and hunt up the "gravity" parameter discussed earlier. There are two options: X and Y. "X" sets the gravity or amount of pull from side to side (negative numbers pull left, and positive numbers pull right), and "Y" sets the gravity from top to bottom (negative numbers pull up toward the top, and positive numbers pull down toward the bottom). Set Y to 100 to start. This value may need to be adjusted later (while testing the ball's gravity), but 100 should provide an "Earth-normal" pull of gravity in the Scene. Without the "Y" setting, the object won't move at all.

The Weight of the World

Despite being a key force on the planet, gravity may not be entirely necessary in a game. In fact, including physics such as gravity was a recent development in games. While it might be nice to just let things fall where they may, there's a risk of not having a fine enough level of control—and with gravity affecting *every* moveable object in a scene, this might cause more trouble than it's worth. (Setting the gravity in a scene will cause everything that is marked as "moveable" to fall in the direction that's chosen, but this doesn't mean objects will collide in a certain way. It's necessary to add Behaviors that define what happens when two objects collide.)

Scoring Systems

Keeping score is an inevitable part of games—even in those that don't keep score in the traditional sense; it's always necessary to track counters of varying kinds—such as the number of times a character jumps, breaks something, or dies. The developer needs to keep score, even if players don't see it. In *Pachinko Madness*, there's a series of buckets along the bottom of the screen. Behaviors should be attached to the buckets so that they destroy the ball when it hits and count the proper number of points when they destroy the ball. Setting up a scoring system requires creating a global attribute and access to an Actor (in this case, one of the buckets at the bottom of the *Pachinko* board).

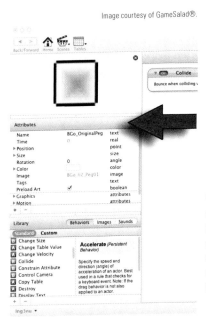

Image courtesy of GameSalad®.

Within each Actor, a set of characteristics may be modified as needed—such as changing the associated image or denoting whether or not it's moveable.

:::CHAPTER REVIEW EXERCISES:::

1. Write up a one-paragraph description of an original Mac desktop game. What genre will you focus on? Are there other games developed using GameSalad Creator that have similar elements?

2. Take a stroll through the Mac App Store, paying special attention to the genre you have chosen for your game in Exercise 1. How saturated is your genre? Which other genres are suitable for your game?

3. Create a rough sketch of your game in both 4:6 and 10:16 formats. Will one of the formats in particular enhance the way your game is played?

4. Examine the overall size of your game (pixel by pixel). What percentage of your screen real estate could be dedicated to your controls?

5. Standardize a naming convention for your game assets. Discuss how you'll differentiate between sound, animation, static art, and other assets.

6. Think about the mood you want to invoke in your players and how this might affect the colors you choose in your design. Using Photoshop (or another graphics program), put together a color scheme that might reflect this mood.

7. Using the storyboard templates provided as online resources, sketch out a few moments of gameplay. Include arrows to indicate directions of motion. Now, rotate the storyboard template 90 degrees and redo your storyboard sketches. How does the gameplay need to change to fit the new format?

Physics

Now that we've discussed setting up a static object with collision properties, let's take a quick look at how to get an object to fall. In this case, we'll refer to the falling balls for our mythical *Pachinko Madness* game. First, to set the ball-dropping physics, go to the Scene Attributes and hunt up the "gravity" parameter discussed earlier. There are two options: X and Y. "X" sets the gravity or amount of pull from side to side (negative numbers pull left, and positive numbers pull right), and "Y" sets the gravity from top to bottom (negative numbers pull up toward the top, and positive numbers pull down toward the bottom). Set Y to 100 to start. This value may need to be adjusted later (while testing the ball's gravity), but 100 should provide an "Earth-normal" pull of gravity in the Scene. Without the "Y" setting, the object won't move at all.

The Weight of the World

Despite being a key force on the planet, gravity may not be entirely necessary in a game. In fact, including physics such as gravity was a recent development in games. While it might be nice to just let things fall where they may, there's a risk of not having a fine enough level of control—and with gravity affecting *every* moveable object in a scene, this might cause more trouble than it's worth. (Setting the gravity in a scene will cause everything that is marked as "moveable" to fall in the direction that's chosen, but this doesn't mean objects will collide in a certain way. It's necessary to add Behaviors that define what happens when two objects collide.)

Scoring Systems

Keeping score is an inevitable part of games—even in those that don't keep score in the traditional sense; it's always necessary to track counters of varying kinds—such as the number of times a character jumps, breaks something, or dies. The developer needs to keep score, even if players don't see it. In *Pachinko Madness*, there's a series of buckets along the bottom of the screen. Behaviors should be attached to the buckets so that they destroy the ball when it hits and count the proper number of points when they destroy the ball. Setting up a scoring system requires creating a global attribute and access to an Actor (in this case, one of the buckets at the bottom of the *Pachinko* board).

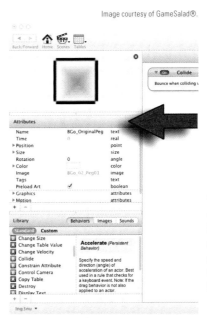
Image courtesy of GameSalad®.

Within each Actor, a set of characteristics may be modified as needed—such as changing the associated image or denoting whether or not it's moveable.

Testing as You Go

One great feature for developers is the "test as you go" capability in GameSalad Creator. A game may be tested at any point during the development process without having to wait for long compile times or exporting to one platform or another. For desktop games especially, it's possible to test a true version of how the game will play out when it goes live—and players will expect a minimum of updates or patches needed to ensure that the game runs smoothly.

Image courtesy of GameSalad®.

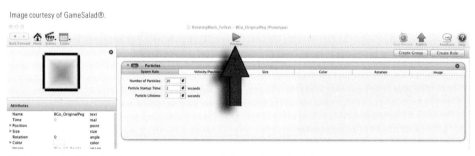

Clicking on the "Preview" arrow generates a quick playthrough of the Scene.

In the "Preview" area, all existing Scenes are laid out along the bottom of the screen. Double-clicking on any of these Scenes will open them in the Preview, which has full functionality—allowing the developer to switch Scenes in game (e.g., using menu buttons from the start screen). To resume editing Scenes when finished, select the "Back to Editor" button.

While in the Preview area, the game cannot be affected or edited in any way—other than to play through it. In order to facilitate bug hunting, Creator has provided two very helpful buttons: "restart" and "pause." When making notes on an error, it is often helpful to take a screenshot to record exactly what happened. The pause button allows for this—pausing the game just as the error occurs so that a screenshot can be taken before moving on.

Screenshots

The Preview screen is an easy place to grab good, high-quality screenshots. Just click the camera icon in the top left of the screen.

Publishing for Mac

GameSalad Creator does a nice job of streamlining the publishing process. All it takes is the press of a button (in this case the big orange button at the top of the Mac Creator screen). Creator will then push the game to the GameSalad servers, where a binary will be created based on the requested settings. While you cannot control the size or resolution of the screen your game will be displayed on, working toward higher-resolution settings will help ensure that it will look great at all screen sizes and resolutions. You'll note that the "Retina Display" checkbox that shows up when you publish to iOS (discussed in Chapter 6) isn't available to you here. This is because the file Creator produces will automatically use the highest setting you have chosen.

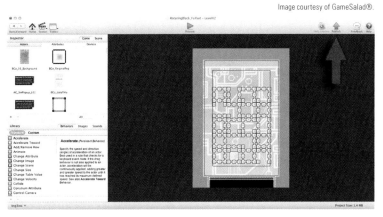

Image courtesy of GameSalad®.

The "Publish" button at the top of the screen in Mac Creator allows the game to be sent to the GameSalad servers.

Gatekeeper is Apple's newest user protection technique—embedded in the current update to the MacOS Mountain Lion. The official goal of Gatekeeper is to is to prevent users from running software that might be riddled with malware; as such, it requires a two-step permission process (click to open, click again to verify) to run any software not purchased from the Mac App Store. Games built with GameSalad Creator can be published quickly and easily to the Mac App Store—ultimately allowing developers to bypass this multi-step process while providing an additional level of legitimacy to their apps and games.

A Brighter Future?

Mac has had a rocky history when it comes to game development due to a combination of factors: Apple's resolve to be considered a "serious" tool; the trickiness of developing for the Mac platform; and the reluctance of publishers to back AAA titles for the Mac (other than ports). However, the advent of iOS and the casual gaming market has opened up a vast new world that has proved to be a perfect fit for the stylish personal computer. It remains to be seen if changes in these new markets, and in Apple's business strategies, will encourage this new influx of games—or stifle it again before it can grow.

:::CHAPTER REVIEW EXERCISES:::

1. Write up a one-paragraph description of an original Mac desktop game. What genre will you focus on? Are there other games developed using GameSalad Creator that have similar elements?

2. Take a stroll through the Mac App Store, paying special attention to the genre you have chosen for your game in Exercise 1. How saturated is your genre? Which other genres are suitable for your game?

3. Create a rough sketch of your game in both 4:6 and 10:16 formats. Will one of the formats in particular enhance the way your game is played?

4. Examine the overall size of your game (pixel by pixel). What percentage of your screen real estate could be dedicated to your controls?

5. Standardize a naming convention for your game assets. Discuss how you'll differentiate between sound, animation, static art, and other assets.

6. Think about the mood you want to invoke in your players and how this might affect the colors you choose in your design. Using Photoshop (or another graphics program), put together a color scheme that might reflect this mood.

7. Using the storyboard templates provided as online resources, sketch out a few moments of gameplay. Include arrows to indicate directions of motion. Now, rotate the storyboard template 90 degrees and redo your storyboard sketches. How does the gameplay need to change to fit the new format?

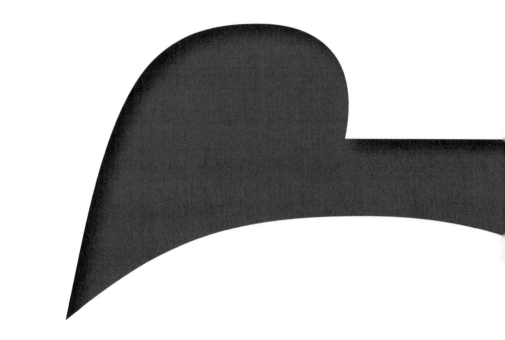

CHAPTER
6

Mobile Game Development

play as you go

Key Chapter Questions

- How have mobile devices *evolved over time* to become major game development hardware platforms?

- What are some art, design, and programming *restrictions* associated with developing games for mobile devices?

- What are some *hardware specifications* associated with different smartphone and tablet devices?

- What are some popular game *genres* played on mobile devices, and how are mobile hardware features contributing to the development of brand new genres?

- How can *GameSalad Creator* be used to create and publish mobile games for both iOS and Android devices?

- How will mobile game development continue to evolve in the *future*?

Mobile game development is tempting. From the seasoned developer tired of spending 3-5 years polishing and revamping the look-and-feel of an AAA game, to the bright-eyed bushy-tailed game designer itching to delve into a dream—mobile games offer a wealth of opportunity. As the mobile industry continues to change the way games are played and produced, throngs of developers are jumping on the bandwagon and releasing games for mobile devices—particularly those running either iOS or Android operating systems. GameSalad Creator is the perfect tool for this growing segment of the industry; let's take a look at how it can be used to develop and publish mobile games on smartphones and tablets using the iOS and Android native operating systems.

History in Brief

For basic GameSalad Creator tutorials, see Appendix. For more information on mobile game development, see *Mobile Game Development* (Unger/Novak)—part of Delmar Cengage Learning's *Game Development Essentials* series.

Games that could be carried around and played "on the go" have been popular throughout history. Well before electronic games were ever developed, we relied on cards, dice, checkers, chess pieces, boards, and other "analog" materials whenever there was a need for fun. As technology began to advance enough during the later 20th century, dedicated electronic toys emerged—and handheld electronic systems such as Mattel's *Electronic Quarterback*, *Merlin*, and Atari *Touch Me* quickly rose in popularity. This marked the dawn of the mobile game industry.

Early Handheld Systems

Early handheld games were very simple and relied more on custom-built circuit boards than on the software commonly used today. In fact, single-game electronic devices such as the successful *Tamagotchi* keychain virtual pets still exist. However, these devices were soon overshadowed by handheld systems that allowed users to play multiple games—often using some form of solid-state storage, which most know as cartridges.

Source Milton Bradley Company.
Photo by Robert Entrekin.

Some early handheld devices such as Milton Bradley's Microvision (*Block Buster*, shown)—which used interchangeable cartridges—paved the way for handheld game development.

In 1989, Nintendo released the original Game Boy, which was followed shortly afterward by the Atari Lynx and Sega Game Gear. Although the other devices had color screens, it was the Game Boy that survived through multiple versions and is still popular to this day—eventually evolving into the dual-screen Nintendo DS. The DS's lower touchscreen changed the way handheld games were played—and its successor, the DSi, added cameras and the ability to download games from an online store. The most recent model, the 3DS, supports 3D on the top screen using *autostereoscopy* (without requiring special glasses). Sony has also been a player in the handheld market, entering the field with the PSP (PlayStation Portable) in 2006 and most recently launching both the PlayStation Vita (dedicated handheld game console) and the Xperia Play (phone/game hybrid). Early handhelds all relied on variations of classic analog controls: buttons, joysticks, D-pads, and similar options. The newest generations of these handhelds (PS Vita, 3DS) have incorporated reliable touchscreen technology as well—allowing for an even broader range of gameplay styles.

Source Sony Computer Entertainment America.

Source Nintendo.

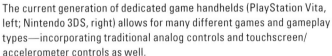

The current generation of dedicated game handhelds (PlayStation Vita, left; Nintendo 3DS, right) allows for many different games and gameplay types—incorporating traditional analog controls and touchscreen/ accelerometer controls as well.

Personal Digital Assistants

While the handheld segment of the mobile industry continued to advance—and well-before wireless Internet access—*personal digital assistants* (*PDAs*) positioned as productivity tools were developed in parallel by electronics giants Sony, Casio, Palm, and Hewlett-Packard. The earliest PDAs didn't do much more than store an address book—not unlike Casio Databank watches. However, they improved as technology continued to advance—and devices running Palm OS and Microsoft's Pocket PC OS eventually became very popular. These devices supported many downloadable programs and games found in early app stores that sported larger screens and greater depth of functionality that would later emerge in the first generation of "smartphones."

At the same time, cell phone technology was also advancing. Although the earliest cell phones were "just phones," games began to show up just as the technology advanced enough to accommodate them. Nokia included *Snake* on its phones as early as 1997. *Snake*-style games were first introduced during the arcade era—and as such, the gameplay style was immediately familiar to the general public. Couple this familiarity with the ease of converting the control scheme to a mobile phone, and the game became a runaway hit on mobile devices. Color screens and other advances caused a surge in game development for cell phones in the early 2000s, but each game had to be purchased directly from the associated "carrier deck." Many consumers were unaware that these games existed—and those who did often didn't know to purchase them! Development was also extremely difficult due to the wide variety of phone hardware available and was primarily done using either Java ME or Qualcomm's Brew (C++).

:::::N-Gage: A Handheld Hybrid Misstep

Source Nokia. Photo by Robert Entrekin.

Nokia's N-Gage was one of the first handhelds to focus on downloadable content over the air rather than on bulky and expensive cartridges.

In an attempt to create a hybrid game/phone system, Nokia released the N-Gage (2003) and the N-Gage QD (2004). Despite a widely anticipated release, the N-Gage didn't meet sales expectations—in part because it didn't work well as a phone; its uncomfortable "taco" shape forced it to protrude out from the ear at an odd angle, and changing games required removing the plastic cover and battery compartment. Nokia later used the "N-Gage" brand to offer downloadable games, instead of the cartridges used by previous systems. Despite its shortcomings, the N-Gage proved to be a somewhat prophetic development—being the first to market with a number of developments that were perfected in today's crop of cutting-edge smartphones.

In 2003, Palm released the Treo 600—the first real attempt to combine PDAs with cell phones. This kick-started the development of smartphones—but it was Apple's iPhone, with its readily available and heavily marketed app store, that successfully convinced consumers to start downloading multiple apps (including games) to their phones. Smartphones available today include models running Windows Phone, BlackBerry, and Nokia's Symbian OS—but iOS and Android devices are at the top of the heap.

iOS & Android Development

The iPod, released in 2001, was primarily a music player—but since it was a handheld device based on a microchip, its engineers just *had* to include some games. (For as long as the game industry has been in existence, games as "Easter eggs" have been included in hardware and software!) The first iPod included the game, *Brick* (originally created by Steve Wozniak), as an Easter egg—and more games were featured on later iPods. The addition of color and the creation of the iPhone and iPod touch in 2007 (a touchscreen version with a much larger screen; an iPhone without the phone functionality) resulted in the iPod gradually becoming as much of a game device as a music system. A year after Apple launched the first iOS devices, Google released its open source OS—Android. With its own app store, Android is quickly catching up to Apple as far as the number of available apps and games.

In early 2010, Apple introduced the iPad—a larger tablet running iOS. Tablet devices had been around for years running Microsoft Windows but never had a very large following. However, the iPad was such a success that it triggered the development of many other tablets running Android OS. Even major book retailers now have their own Android-based tablets, such as Amazon's Kindle Fire and Barnes & Noble's Nook.

Operating Systems: iOS vs. Android

Understanding the differences between the iOS and Android operating systems might help you decide which one to initially focus on. One difference involves hardware. Keep in mind that iOS only runs on a limited number of iPhone, iPad, and iPod touch models. Due to this, you are also guaranteed a certain amount of compatibility. Android runs on a much wider range of hardware, making it much harder to guarantee that your program will run on all of them. Applications using iOS and Android are developed very differently from one another. Consider that iOS applications are generally built using Objective C—a deceptively named language, since "C" is for "Cocoa" and there is very little resemblance to C/C++. Objective C was designed by Apple to be easier for non-programmers and those unfamiliar with the C syntax of most other languages. Android applications are built using Java, which is more familiar to most programmers. This means that unless you're generating a game through a third-party program such as Creator, developing a cross-platform app means writing the same app twice in different languages.

Source Apple Inc.

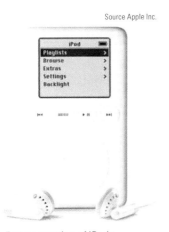

The first generation of iPods contained only a few games—but as the product evolved, game designers were encouraged to seriously consider the device.

Source Apple Inc.

The iPad was not the first tablet device on the market, but it allowed iOS developers a larger visual format and direct access to a large and already interested user base.

Mac or PC?

Since any iOS game has to be run through Xcode on its way to the Apple App Store, iOS titles will need to be published with the Mac version of Creator. The Windows version of Creator can be used for development, but it will be necessary to export to the Mac version to actually publish the game for iOS.

Although there are development differences between iOS and Android, it can be argued that the biggest distinction between them is actually the way each of their associated marketplaces functions. Apple maintains tight control of all apps that are released on the iTunes store. Adult content, for example, is not allowed in an iOS app—and neither are products that might contain "hate speech." This is reminiscent of the rules developed by Nintendo in the early days of console gaming to make its Nintendo Entertainment System (NES) platform more family-friendly.

Most Android app stores have no such restrictions. This has practical consequences beyond simply the game's rating. The vetting process for iOS apps can be long and frustrating. Since time is money, it can be expensive for a small developer to wait for Apple's approval process. Quick, nimble development houses may be more attracted to the more straightforward release process for Android apps. Although there are some "walled garden" Android stores popping up (most notably Amazon's Appstore), they do not yet represent a significant percentage of the market.

Multiple Platforms . . . and More!

I use Creator to make a number of games from the ground up, and I always design my games for both iOS and Android. I usually start with iOS and then build an Android version. The power I see with Creator is the cross platform ability; it also allows me to get my ideas made and out there quickly so that I can move on to my next idea or client gig.

Caleb Garner (Game Producer, Part12 Studios)

With Creator, you can make one game and publish it to both iOS/Mac and Android (including Kindle Fire, Nook, and Android marketplace). It's wonderful and easy to use—and it allows you to publish to all the latest platforms and monetize your app in more than one store.

Jenny McGettigan (Owner, Beansprites LLC and Hamster Wheel Studios)

I've been developing and publishing for iOS (iPhone and iPad) as well as MacOS. For both platforms, Creator is an easy to use but powerful tool for extremely fast app creation.

Thomas Wagner (Owner, Gamesmold)

Programming: Xcode vs. Eclipse

If you are not using a separate tool such as Creator to develop your games, you will generally be developing with either Xcode or Eclipse. Even if you are already working with a licensed set of programming tools, you may need to use either Xcode or Eclipse as the final step before publishing if you want to include new features (e.g., analytics, third-party add-ons).

Xcode is an *integrated development environment* (*IDE*) that was developed by Apple specifically for iOS and Mac development. It's free for OSX users and includes an *emulator*—a tool that simulates what the game will look like on the actual device. This emulator will load automatically when you run your game from Xcode.

Xcode for Android

Although Xcode's main function is as an iOS development platform, some have had success using Xcode for Android platform development. See David Janes' Code Weblog at http://code.davidjanes.com/blog/2009/11/20/how-to-use-xcode-for-android-projects/ for more information.

Source Apple Inc.   Source Apple Inc. Photo by Kimberly Unger.

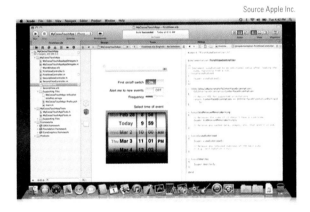

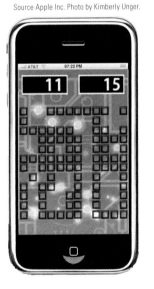

Xcode (above) is an integrated development environment provided for free by Apple for the development of iOS and Mac applications. In order to simplify development for the iOS platform, an iPhone emulator (right) has been made available to developers through the Xcode development environment.

Eclipse is a free, open-source IDE that can be used with a number of programming languages—including Java, C++, Ruby, Python, and Perl. Based on plug-ins (and relying on them for most of its functions), Eclipse is often used for Java programming. The number of plug-ins available makes it possible to create software for a huge variety of environments and architectures. The Android plug-ins mesh well with Eclipse and install an emulator that will run automatically for testing.

Source The Eclipse Foundation.

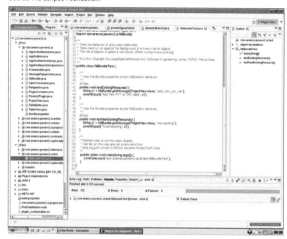

Eclipse, which can be downloaded for free through the Android Developers site, is a well-supported integrated development environment (IDE) that can be used for the Android platform.

IDEs such as Xcode and Eclipse will form the basis of your toolset when developing programs for mobile devices; being familiar with them will give you much more flexibility as a designer and developer—even if you choose to use pre-fabricated tools for prototyping. These IDEs are by no means exclusive to mobile development; they are commonly used in both Windows and Mac development processes and to develop a broad range of non-mobile products.

Source The Eclipse Foundation.

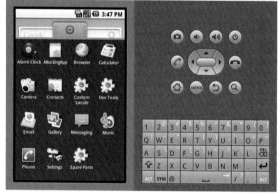

Android emulators provide the functionality of multiple devices with the same operating system, but with different processor specifications or hardware.

Eclipse Game Development Community

For every tool, you will find a community of developers who dedicate their time and resources to expanding and improving on it. Often, the strength of a tool lies more in the support it receives from its community contributions (tutorials, discussion groups, forums, upgrades and improvements) than in the technology behind the tool itself. The Eclipse community can be found at http://www.touchofdeathforums.com/eclipse/

Case Study:
Zen Hopper

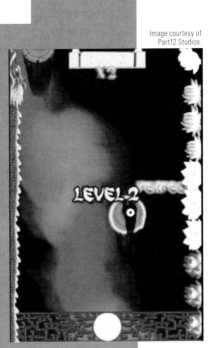

When I first got into GameSalad, I wanted to create a simple game that I could develop quickly—and familiarize myself not only with Creator but with the entire process of mobile app development. *Zen Hopper* was a game that my partner (a programmer) and I (*not* a programmer) tinkered with a year before we got serious about mobile development. We were experimenting via traditional programming using tools such as Unity3d and Cocoa 2d. However, we were soon neck deep in programming intensive client work—making it impossible to develop any of our backlog of game ideas. So I decided to resume *Zen Hopper* development alone using Creator and was empowered to do what otherwise wouldn't have been possible until the planets aligned to make it happen!

Caleb Garner (Game Producer, Part12 Studios)

Game Engines & Drag-and-Drop Tools

One of the key differences between the previous and current generation of mobile phones and handhelds is the availability of pre-written game software. Until the iPhone hit the market in the early 2000s, all programming for mobile devices was custom (specific to the studio that worked on the title). The functionality of a particular studio's code—and the speed and agility with which they could adapt it for new titles—was often a deciding factor when development contracts were handed out. This meant that small or even one-person studios were extremely rare, and the core of any team had to be centered around the programmer. However, drag-and-drop tools such as GameSalad Creator give designers and artists with limited programing skills the ability to prototype, design, and release their own products. This serves the dual purpose of allowing designers to experiment with new gameplay styles and ideas, as well as keeping a steady stream of new content flooding into the app store for all platforms.

Smartphones vs. Tablets

If you want to create a game that will work on both smartphones and tablets, you'll need to focus heavily on the marked difference in screen size. It will be necessary to either offer an alternate graphical layout for the larger screen or create the graphics so that they still look good when stretched out on a larger screen. The best practice is to test the game extensively on different emulators or other devices. It's also possible to develop different versions of the game for each type of device. Games for iPad only are available through the Apple App Store, and there are many Kindle Fire apps available through the Amazon Appstore.

Source Apple Inc.

Source Apple Inc.

The iPad screen is much larger than the iPhone 5 screen —with a resolution as large as 2048 x 1536 (iPad) vs 1136 x 640 (iPhone 5).

Community Love: Templates & Tools for Creator

GameSalad is supported by a very active and engaged community of developers. Many community members provide examples of their projects in progress—showing exactly how they have solved problems like object creation on the fly, or scoring and saving examples. They have built some very helpful Creator templates for shoot-em-ups, platformers, vertical shooters, tower defense games, and more.

Case Study: *The Secret of Moonwall Palace – Magic Can Be a Crime*

My first game, *The Secret of Moonwall Palace – Magic Can Be a Crime*, was inspired by *Half-Life 2*—with the totalitarian atmosphere, cops on every corner, and pervasive fear. I worked almost 12 hours a day to finish the game as quick as possible, but it still took me more than seven months. I didn't have any templates or tutorials how to make adventure games with Creator—primarily because my game was one of the first adventure games made with the software. (*The Secret of Grisly Manor* by Fire Maple Games was the first, but my game was released just one week afterward.) After many hours, days, and months, my first game was finished. After launch, I decided to make an iPad version—but I knew it would probably a huge amount of work and time. Fortunately, I discovered that Deep Blue Apps released its amazing software, GS Project Resizer—a tool that helped me make an iPad version of my game in just two days! Both versions are my top-selling games, even to this day.

Marcin Makaj (Chief Executive Officer, The Moonwalls)

Image courtesy of
The Secret of Moonwall Palace.

Image courtesy of
The Secret of Moonwall Palace.

Dimensions: 2D vs. 3D

Two dimensions are still much more popular than three in mobile applications, in contrast to games on non-mobile platforms. This is in part because the platforms are less powerful and don't have the storage space for large 3D graphics (which means that 3D games run much more slowly). However, the rise of mobile games has inspired a rash of 2D games (including remakes of many old arcade- and early console-era 2D games); mobile players are not all "hardcore" gamers who demand 3D. In addition, older Android phones may not support OpenGL ES 2.0—a common platform for 3D on mobile devices.

There are tricks to prevent 2D art from seeming flat. Layered backgrounds, parallax motion, "2.5 dimensions," and looping/tiling are all old-school game development tricks that help the developer get more use out of limited file storage space. Creator contains tools that add graphic complexity to a game project—making it ideal for a one- or two-person team.

Currently, 3D for mobile is gaining hold—and tools such as Unity are being used to specifically handle 3D development for mobile games. However, developing 3D mobile games requires the creation of 3D models in software such as 3ds Max or Maya—making the development process much more involved and time consuming.

Necessity is the Mother of Invention

The problems framed by the limited processing power of mobile devices are not new by any means. As the available processing power for desktop computers and game consoles increased, the need for developers of more traditional games to adhere to tight space constraints began to fall off. ("Best practices" still dictate clean and efficient use of resources, but the consequences of some "bit bloat" were often overlooked because they didn't affect the final outcome as drastically.) With extremely limited download sizes and smaller development cycles (compared to desktops and consoles), mobile games required a re-imagining, and occasional reinvention, of older tricks—such as using a palette animation to give the appearance of motion to water in a scene or the flapping of a flag.

:::::Interface: Native iOS vs. Android

Both iOS and Android have built-in user interface elements that can be used to easily create simple interfaces. Standard user interface elements such as buttons, text fields, checkboxes, and drop down lists are handled natively by the operating system to maintain a consistent look and feel without having to write them from scratch. Interface Builder, a program that comes with Xcode, can be used to develop interfaces for iOS. Screens are generated by visually placing elements on the screen—and the tool generates an .xib file (essentially an .xml file that tells Xcode which objects to put where). Eclipse offers similar capabilities using .xml files. Interfaces can be created visually within Eclipse—or the .xml file can be manually edited to create the desired screen.

Source Apple Inc.

Source Google.

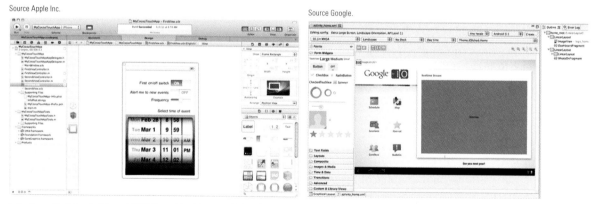

Interface Builder (left) and ADT Graphical Layout Editor (right) are used to develop interfaces for iOS and Android, respectively.

Case Study:
Bumps

Creator has several strengths—including being fast and easy to use. I remember when I first looked into iOS for our hit PC game *Bumps* (we wanted a conversion from PC to iOS), some of the quotes we got back were in excess of $85k. I found Creator and made it myself within 6 weeks! The physics in *Bumps* was something we were really pleased with, and changing them on the bumps was only a click away—so during testing, we used a variety of different settings in density, friction and "bounciness" until it felt right. Using only a small number of actors, we could create realistic curved platforms for the bumps to roll over—which was a really nice change from flat, boring rectangular platforms.

Darren Spencer (Owner, Utopian Games & Deep Blue Apps)

Image courtesy of Utopian Games.

Project Setup

When you first set up your project, be sure to select the appropriate platform (in this case, Mobile). See Appendix for a tutorial on how to set up a project, and more!

Using the iOS/Android Viewers

Xcode can be used to install the Creator viewer onto iOS devices—allowing you to view your game on the actual device. This requires you to be registered as an iPhone developer and to generate a provisioning profile with Apple. A tutorial on how to install the Creator viewer is available at http://cookbook.gamesalad. com. This will allow you to easily test your game project on your mobile device. The Android viewer requires you to be a little more familiar with the command line. The process is subject to change, but full up-to-date instructions for installing both versions can be found at http://cookbook. gamesalad.com/.

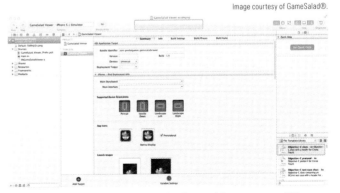

Image courtesy of GameSalad®.

Using Xcode, it's possible to install the Creator Viewer onto an iOS or Android device for testing.

Marcin Makaj on Guidelines for Mobile Developers :::::

Image courtesy of Marcin Makaj.

Marcin Makaj
(Chief Executive
Officer, The
Moonwalls)

Marcin Makaj might be one of the first GameSalad developers in Poland. Before discovering GameSalad Creator, Marcin didn't have any experience in games and high technology. He has always been creative—enjoying drawing and building structures with Legos. He's interested in computer games, economy, law, marketing, movies, and meditation. Marcin has a Master's degree in Economics and is currently a law student. It has always been Marcin's dream to make a game. His favorite game genre is the classic point-and-click adventures—first on an Amiga 600 and later on PC, Game Boy Color, iPhone, and iPad—which led to his adventure game series, *The Moonwalls*, developed with Creator.

Here are my guidelines for mobile developers:

1) Make one big game and one small game so that players have something to play while waiting for your next big title.

2) Try to keep your project and files organized. For example, use consistent naming systems for attributes, scenes, images, etc.

3) Make only games that you want to play.

4) Don't expect to make a lot of money; just create and have fun!

5) There are great games with low sales; it all depends on good marketing.

6) Respect your players and customers; make the best games possible, answer their emails, and provide support.

7) Listen to feedback, read reviews, and always make improvements; it's never too late to create a bestseller.

8) Don't be afraid to invest money; if you treat development as a business, you will eventually make money.

9) Don't rip off other games, steal ideas, or cheat Apple's review policy; you will get sued or banned sooner or later.

10) Test, test, and test your game before releasing each update.

11) If you think that you have "the best idea ever" for a game, stop it! There are tens of thousands of other developers who think the same about their ideas—and most of them can be thrown in the trash.

12) Games with simple ideas are the best.

13) Love your work—and your players will love your work, too.

What's So Different about Mobile?

The mindset behind the design of most mobile games is different than with traditional desktop or console games. Mobile titles are not only designed for the "quick fix," but they are generally much more permissive when it comes to gameplay styles and innovations. Advertising is permitted, even encouraged, by players who are more willing to download and play a free application that supports the developers through advertising than they are to pay for a product up front. So while the techniques of game design and development used in more traditional products still holds, the developers have a much broader range to play in. This is resulting in new and innovative gameplay types and control schemes, as well as creative advertising and marketing.

Mobile Design

Many different types of games are available in the app stores. Many older games from other platforms have been ported to mobile devices. Games such as *Angry Birds* are very popular—since people on the go like to play short, simple games for 3-5 minutes while waiting in line or otherwise passing the time. However, all types of games are available— from text adventures to full 3D first-person shooters to puzzle games … and everything in between!

Image courtesy of GameSalad®.

In addition to complete games, the GameSalad online community offers solutions such as how to encourage players to rate your app.

Case Study: Quake Builder

The first game I made with Creator, *Quake Builder* was the first of many "Eureka!" moments. I learned my first bit of trigonometry (which I hadn't touched in about 10 years) and made a platform rotate back and forth—with a lot of help from the GameSalad community. *Quake Builder* took around three months and two hours a day to develop. I made it available on the App Store for free; it received over 250,000 downloads in a week and was one of the US top 100 free games. I promptly added iAds to the game using Creator and started reaping the rewards!

Image courtesy of Stormy Studio.

Jon Draper (Director, Stormy Studio)

Mobile Programming

Mobile platforms are more limited and have less memory than most consoles or PCs. When programming for mobile devices, be aware of the limitations and make sure to optimize your game with this in mind. Best practices insist that any unused or unseen game elements be removed from memory. This prevents obvious issues like lag within the game and more insidious things like memory leaks or unusual conflicts between objects that are hard to debug later on.

Mobile Art

Games require assets—all of which will increase a game's total size. Since mobile games need to be downloaded before running, the space taken up by art needs to be as small as possible. Some mobile carriers even place limits on the size of apps that can be downloaded over their 3G/4G networks—and larger apps require a Wi-Fi connection. A game requires a number of art assets—including scrolling backgrounds, levels, particle effects, and sprite graphics. The small size of mobile screens is a major restriction on the types of art used in these games. The most successful mobile developers have been inspired by these limitations to incorporate vibrant, iconic graphics into their games.

::::: Powers of Two

To avoid ugly artifacts in the final game, all artwork for an iOS device should be sized so that the pixel width and height are even numbers (i.e., divisible by two). This might seem like a strange rule, but it's an important one! It is also generally better to use graphics loaded into memory at sizes that are powers of two: 8 x 8, 16 x 16, 32 x 32, etc. If a graphic's width and height are even, the graphic will still be loaded into memory at the size of the next power of two. Therefore, a 20 x 20 image will be loaded as a 32 x 32 image—using more memory than you might have planned on. A 30 x 66 image will be treated as 32 x 128—which uses almost twice as much memory as it should! Note that images cannot exceed 2048 x 2048. It is also better to use .png files (although GameSalad Creator will convert images to this format automatically) at a resolution of 72—while maintaining aesthetic appearance.

Diagram courtesy of Per Olin.

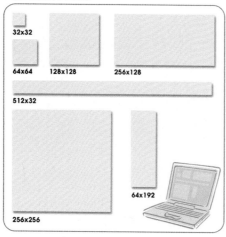

32x32
64x64   128x128   256x128
512x32
256x256
64x192

Case Study:
Spooky Hoofs

Spooky Hoofs was my second endless runner game made with GameSalad Creator. Designed for a Halloween release, the player controls a stagecoach—dashing through eerie woods and spooky landscapes. To permanently have smooth, physically correct movements throughout the game, I tried to move the coach only by Creator's physics engine. In order to do so, I couldn't use some kind of pseudo scrolling; instead, I had to use a single, very large scene where there was enough room to really race around. The ground consists of seven blocks that keep on placing themselves outside the right border of the camera. This way, the coach can actually travel to the right and have the real physics working (with the camera smoothly following). Once the carriage has reached somewhat around x=10000 or so, I set everything (ground, coach, enemies, background, camera etc.) back to x minus 9000. This happens within a single frame and isn't noticeable; this way, you get the feeling you are traveling endlessly. Another challenging task was the creation of the carriage itself. With the horses, the coach-

Image courtesy of Thomas Wagner
© 2011 Gamesmold.

Image courtesy of Thomas Wagner
© 2011 Gamesmold.

man, the passenger, the shaking lantern, the wheels and all the other animated details, it consists of over 20 single actors (some visible and some not) that manage a very realistic, physically convincing real-time movement of the whole carriage. Most of the time, when it gets to detailed or complex animation, it is much more efficient to assemble an object of many separate actors rather than trying to create all animation simply by linear image sequences. *Spooky Hoofs* was "New and Noteworthy" worldwide on the iPhone and in the Mac App Store—and it is still is one of my best selling game apps so far.

Thomas Wagner (Owner, Gamesmold)

New Control Schemes

Smartphones have very different interfaces from most other devices. When accommodating control schemes for touchscreens, note that buttons need to be large enough to touch with a finger without accidentally hitting the buttons surrounding it—so it's necessary to experiment with button sizes until you "get it right." Creator was designed as a multi-platform product, so it includes the option to have an actor react to a finger touch, mouse click, or even a dramatic change in the orientation of the player's smartphone using the built-in *accelerometer* (the sensor that tells the phone which end of the device is pointing up and whether it's being rotated, shaken, etc.).

The touchscreen has developed new ways of interfacing, such as *swiping* a finger across the screen to scroll left or right. It is also common to use a two-finger interface for pinch-to-zoom, stretch-to-zoom, or pinch/stretch functionality: Many mobile apps allow *stretch* (moving fingers apart) to zoom in and *pinch* (moving fingers together) to zoom out.

Mobile games often take advantage of the accelerometer functionality, and Creator has a full suite of acceleration-based functions that you can use. Many games such as *Pocket Labyrinth* and *Zombie Games!* use the accelerometer as the main control scheme; by tilting the phone, it's possible to control the direction you move in a game. Some games use the *microphone* as a controller—with players humming or blowing into it to navigate or control other actions. Other smartphone capabilities that can be used as control schemes include the *camera*, *global positioning system* (*GPS*), and *gyroscope*.

chapter 6   Mobile Game Development: play as you go

Image courtesy of GameSalad®.

In the Creator Scene Attributes, it is possible to check the orientation of the game (Windows Creator, shown).

::::: Tutorial: Up, Down & Sideways

Kimberly Unger (Chief Executive Officer, Bushi-go, Inc.)

Setting up a game to automatically flip over when the player's smartphone is turned over—so that it will always be right-side up—is very simple in Creator. Inside the scene, select Scene/Attributes and expand Auto-rotate. For a Landscape game, check both "Landscape Left" and "Landscape Right." For Portrait, check both "Portrait" and "Portrait Upside Down." Creator will then flip the game automatically. Causing an object to move when the mobile device is tilted is a little more complicated:

1. Inside the Actor settings create a rule for each direction in Creator by clicking the "Create Rule" button on the top right. Then, choose "Attribute" and "Devices/Accelerometer" from the dropdown menu next to it. The attributes can be accessed via the "Attributes" tab in the browser at the bottom of the screen. Select and set an attribute after creating the rule and before adding the specifics of how the accelerometer reacts.

Image courtesy of GameSalad®.

Accelerometer menu selection

2. For a Landscape mode game, check "y" for left and right and "x" for up and down. For portrait, reverse this. To check for tilt, the first rule should check if this is greater than some small number (such as 0.01). If so, add a behavior inside the rule to handle this by finding "Accelerate" in the behavior library and dragging it inside the rule you have set up. Set the direction to 180 and acceleration to 200. In addition, set the dropdown for "Relative To: to scene."

Image courtesy of GameSalad®.

Creating a rule for using the accelerometer to move an object

3. After creating one rule, a copy of it can be created by holding down [Alt][Shift] and dragging the rule underneath it. Once this is done, the next rule can be created by changing "greater than" (>) to "less than" (<) and 0.01 to -0.01. You also need to change the acceleration behavior: Change "180°" to "0°" to reverse direction.

4. To move up and down, create new rules—but check the accelerometer "x" instead of "y." The direction to accelerate will now be 90 and 270. (Consider basic geometry, where a circle is 360°—which will help you remember why the directions are 0, 90, 180, and 270!)

Image courtesy of GameSalad®.

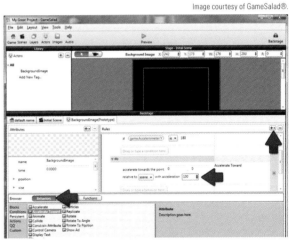

Adding the second rule, allowing it to move right and left

5. If you have implemented the automatic switching for "Landscape Left" and "Landscape Right": After creating rules for all four directions, put them inside another rule that checks the Devices/Screen/Interface Orientation. Set this for "Landscape Left" and then copy the new rule and all its contents to create another one for "Landscape Right." Switch the "Acceleration" directions for all the rules inside that one by 180°.

Case Study:
Z is for Zombie

Image courtesy of Jonathan Mulcahy.

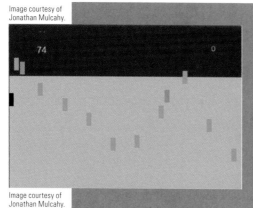

Image courtesy of Jonathan Mulcahy.

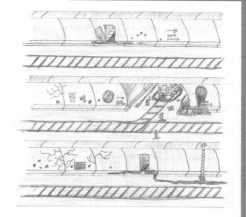

Z is for Zombie was my first dive into GameSalad Creator. I started working on the game before Creator even supported publishing to the iPhone. I had a working prototype of the game finished in 45 minutes, in which I had player-controlled hero fighting green zombies shooting black bullets. Everything was just squares—but it worked. After that it was just a matter of tweaking—drawing the artwork and putting it all together. I went from not knowing anything about GameSalad to submitting my first game in under two months. The game featured multiple weapons the player could find, a story and survival mode—and even a way to recalibrate the accelerometer during playback.

Jonathan Mulcahy
(Developer, How I Hate the Night)

Z is for Zombie prototype (top) and final "sketch style" game art (bottom).

Making Mobile Development Fun

Creator makes mobile development not only a fast, robust experience, but one that is really enjoyable. Coding is not fun for me, I don't enjoy typing out line after line of code. I'm a creative person by nature and enjoy seeing things that I'm creating happen visually. The development side of mobile gaming is notoriously tricky—with provisioning profiles, developer certificates, keystores, and other endless obstacles to overcome (besides learning the programming language). However, Creator takes that complicated process and makes it as easy as possible for beginners and advanced users alike.

Ace Connell (Managing Director, Mynameisace Ltd)

Publishing

Before beginning to develop an iOS game, check to make sure it fits Apple's guidelines to maximize its chances of being accepted. To publish a game to the iTunes store, you must be an Apple Developer. Membership in the Developer community currently costs $99/year. Once an app has been submitted, it will go through a review process; it's necessary to wait for approval and make any requested changes or fixes. Note: If your game is rejected, you can appeal that rejection to the App Review Board—a group of Apple employees who handle such appeals. The Android publication process is a bit complex, but it does not involve submission to a board for approval. If you want to publish your game for the Kindle Fire, you will need to upload your game to the Amazon Appstore. Membership is $99 a year.

Source Google.

With so many app stores available to consumers, publishers are in a rush to ensure that developers have all the necessary tools to serve up their content.

Apple & Android Instructions

Detailed instructions for iTunes publishing for GameSalad users can be found at http://cookbook.gamesalad.com and Apple App Store Review Guidelines are available at http://developer.apple.com/appstore/guidelines.html. Detailed instructions for Android publishing for GameSalad users can be found at http://cookbook. gamesalad.com and Amazon Appstore membership details are available at https:// developer.amazon.com/welcome.html.

Discoverability

Once your game is published, it is very important for people to be able to find it. The first days and weeks that your game is available to the public are critical. Sales of any given title can drop off quickly, and the speed of that drop partially depends on how many people know about the title. The people who want to download or buy your game need to know about it before they can do so. Prior to release, spend some time thinking about how to market your game. When uploading to the iTunes store, you'll have an option to include a link to a YouTube video with your game listing. That's free marketing—and you'd be silly not to take advantage of it by having a short, punchy video of your gameplay ready for linking by the time you get to this step.

Source Apple Inc.

The "walled garden" of the Apple App Store can offer preferred placement to apps that show superior quality or innovative content.

Luis Levy on Creating a Successful Mobile Game Trailer:::::

Photo by Jeannie Novak.

Luis Levy
(Co-Founder,
Novy Unlimited, Inc.)

Luis Levy is the co-founder of Novy Unlimited and the director of Novy PR—a public relations firm specializing in high-technology, mobile, and indie developers with clients such as Appy Entertainment, SRRN Games, PlayScreen, Swarm, Greenpeace, Shadegrown Games, and Woo Games. At Novy, Luis manages strategy, planning, media placement, speaking opportunities, and trade show bookings. Prior to Novy, Luis was an account executive at The Bohle Company—where he represented game and high-technology clients such as Spacetime Studios, The Voxel Agents, Muzzy Lane, and TimeGate Studios. Luis has also worked in advertising, sales, film and television editing, and as a game tester at Activision and Treyarch. He co-authored *Play the Game: The Parent's Guide to Video Games* and *Game QA & Testing* with Jeannie Novak. Luis was born in São Paulo, Brazil and attended Fundação Armando Álvares Penteado (FAAP), where he received a B.A. in Film & Television.

Step 1: Make the Trailer

It's hard to believe that some developers choose *not* to make a trailer. But it happens. While screenshots are easy and straightforward, trailers sound terribly complicated and time-intensive. Don't let the extra workload deprive your game of a proper trailer. The consequences are often dire, starting with less coverage and ending with non-existing sales.

Step 2: Make Every Second Count

The only thing worse than not having a trailer is having a three-minute one. *No one* will watch a three-minute trailer for a mobile game. The ideal length is 45 seconds to a full minute.

Step 3: Make It Dynamic

We like trailers that show off different gameplay mechanics, characters, locations and atmosphere. You can't have a minute of the same exact gameplay, over and over again. Think of the joy of driving on the Pacific Coast Highway versus the mind-numbing boredom of the Interstate.

Step 4: Make It Descriptive

Text-less trailers might look stunning but will often leave viewers with a big question mark. Is it a sequel or an update? Is it for Android or iOS? Is this a new feature? Is it free? This information must be in there. If the best you can do is list the most important information at the very end, with bullets, that's still better than leaving everyone in the dark.

Step 5: Make It Real

Killzone 2 is famous for trying to pass CGI for actual gameplay. Don't be tempted to make the same mistake. I know it's easier to re-purpose the intro CGI or cut-scenes in the trailer, but you will lose your target audience in the process. Gamers watch trailers on YouTube and GameTrailers in order to evaluate a future purchase. They need to see how the game *plays*, not how great the cut-scenes are.

Step 6: Make Your Mark

Lush trailers can cost a lot of money. They usually have sweeping 3D art, post-processing, sharp HD visuals and booming soundtrack. This is awesome if you can pay for it, but it doesn't mean a more "indie" trailer can't compete. Be creative. Make the trailer an extension of your game. Give it an attitude. That's the only way to fight the big boys, with their over-produced trailers and licensed music.

[This material originally appeared on the Novy PR web site at http://novypr.com/post/21939549035/trailers-win-the-youtube-wars-get-ink-make-it-a-hit]

Affinity Marketing

A good way of marketing your game is to find the people who will be most interested in purchasing it. If your game is about a train, for instance, there are dozens of train enthusiast web sites and online forums. Why not find out who's in charge of those communities and let them know about your game? If you're polite and succinct, you may get a mention on the web site's home page; this puts your game in front of a large number of potential customers. Be considerate; don't overdo it by being one of those overzealous developers that spam people weekly (or daily)!

Future Possibilities

Mobile games have changed drastically over the years and are sure to change even more in the future. What possibilities lie in store? One area that seems to be gaining popularity is *augmented reality (AR)*, which attempts to meld what is happening in the real world into the game. At this point, it is difficult to find a phone that doesn't have a camera in it, and mobile games are able to take advantage of the camera to bring the outside world into the game. For example, *Star Wars Arcade: Falcon Gunner* has an AR mode that lets you shoot Tie Fighters in your own living room. Another area that is currently expanding is voice recognition/personal assistant software such as Siri (iPhone). At this point, voice recognition is being adopted for a small number of titles such as *Scribblenauts Remix* on iPhone 4S.

Augmented Reality: Camera, Gyroscope & GPS

Augmented reality (AR) games use the camera to bring the real world into the game. The gyroscope is used to aid in navigation—and even the global positioning system (GPS), now built into most phones, is being used to map real-world places onto the game experience.

Going Mobile

Your first mobile game will be a blend of your own innovative ideas and old "hat tricks" that have produced quality gameplay through several generations of consoles. Just because a game type has been used before does not mean there isn't a way to give it a fresh feel, a new twist. That blend of new and nifty and old and comfortable has carried a great many games to success. In the best "garage" spirit of the 1970s and 1980s, mobile games have re-opened the world of game development to solo agents and small teams. Tools such as GameSalad Creator are giving both budding and experienced game designers the chance to develop and sell games that might not find a home at a larger studio—or might be too daring to fit in with a publisher's current lineup. The pre-coded elements and the drag-and-drop nature of Creator's interface are designed to give you the power to release a game across multiple platforms—thus reaching the widest possible audience.

:::CHAPTER REVIEW EXERCISES:::

1. Create an idea for a mobile game. Consider theme, goals and target market. Don't worry about fleshing things out too much at this stage. Your goal is to create a concept in 1-3 paragraphs.

2. Odds are, your game fits cleanly into one of the more common game genres (platformer, puzzler, etc.). As you look through the different sample games that Creator has to offer, make a list of the genres. Are there any missing?

3. Will your game work better on a tablet or phone? Can you play it with one hand? Will the extra screen real estate on a tablet be a plus—or do you need to figure out a clever way to make use of the extra space?

4. Create some art assets for your game—a background, foreground elements, and a player character (which could be as simple as a steel ball or as elaborate as a fully armored knight). Be sure to size the artwork properly for use in your target platform.

5. Find a Creator template that is similar to the type of game you have been working on and open it. Look at the scenes, and go inside the actors—seeing what behaviors are attached. How do the pieces fit together to create the game?

6. Mobile games often take far fewer art assets than you might think. Between clever re-use, procedural elements such as particles, and coded-in elements such as palette stitching, you can make just a few images go a long way. Create a new project and import your images into it. Drag some actors onto the screen and start developing your game! When you have something you like, preview it. If it works, try installing one of the viewers onto a device (if one is available) and try playing your new game!

7. Think about ways you can promote your finished game. Come up with a few unique ways you might be able to promote your game based on its content. How could you make AR or Siri-like technology work in your game?

Online Game Development
deploy everywhere

Key Chapter Questions

■ How is *online* game development distinct from other forms of game development?

■ What sets *HTML5* apart from other online and web-based development platforms?

■ How does *GameSalad Creator* export to HTML5?

■ How are online games *distributed and marketed*?

■ What *delivery platforms* are ideal for HTML5?

In 1999, when HTML4.01 was the web development standard, web pages were still the focus—and social networks had not yet come into play. In the intervening decade, *everything* about online development and deployment changed. While HTML4.01 was designed for web pages and was used for web-based games and animation, third-party tools such as Flash, Wildstorm, and Unity3D proved to be far more effective for the task and were used for the majority of web-based game development and distribution. However, iOS was incompatible with Flash, and the far more versatile HTML5 was released—causing the marketplace to take a dramatic turn. New game-oriented tools such as GameSalad Creator have stepped to the fore—delivering cross-compatible games that not only take full advantage of the new HTML5 web standard, but that can be deployed without relying on "walled-garden" type app stores.

Everything is Connected

For basic GameSalad Creator tutorials, see Appendix.

The World Wide Web started with a brilliant but simple idea that researchers working together on a topic could link their documents together over a network. This would allow them to directly reference and immediately view other relevant documents that would be updated as soon as they were edited. However, as with most clever ideas, it took some time before this could truly blossom. When *hypertext* (linking text from one document to another on the same computer) became mainstream with the development of HyperCard and similar programs such as Guide for UNIX and DOS based computers, the groundwork for the eventual development of the web had been laid.

By the mid-1980s, the *distributed name service* (*DNS*) was created to map common names onto the long and complicated numbers that specified network addresses. (For example, 207.241.148.80 is mapped to www.about.com.) This simple innovation—allowing common names to be assigned to networks—gave us a crucial second piece in the evolution of the web. As the DNS system changed the way networks were accessed, protocols such as email and *Finger* (allowing for the exchange of status and user information) suddenly got much easier for the layperson to use.

In order to extend the hypertext idea of cross-linking files from network to network (as opposed to solely within a computer), something simple was needed. *Hypertext Transfer Protocol* (*HTTP*) was developed for the purpose of retrieving other documents via the linked text in an original document (which is very common today). The language for this was called *HyperText Markup Language* (*HTML*) and was built to an international standard. Rather than keep this development private, it was opened up to the community at large allowing for feedback and ideas.

Source Bitstorm.org. Image courtesy of Jeannie Novak.

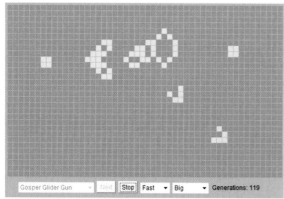

Gosper Glider Gun ▾ | Next | Stop | Fast ▾ | Big ▾ | Generations: 119

Some games (such as a version of *Conway's Game of Life*) worked equally well in the older version of HTML. Some camps favored scrapping everything and working on a new standard, while others wanted to upgrade and properly document what had gone before.

As it evolved over time, each variation of HTML was slowly adopted by engines that were designed to read it—such as Mosaic (later Netscape), Internet Explorer, Opera, and Mozilla (later Firefox); these tools lived and died by their ability to properly interpret HTML, but integrations could only be done so quickly. Backwards compatibility became essential as development moved forward.

It Goes with Everything

Keep in mind that *HTML5* is not a game engine, a development tool, or a programming language such as C# or Javascript; rather, it's a *markup language*—similar to a sophisticated set of homework instructions that tell a web browser where to place images, what font to use for the text, and how to handle links for email or embedded video. After the release of HTML5, multiple projects moved forward simultaneously and changed quite dramatically over time.

Every new system begins with competing viewpoints. Every new way of doing things starts with a half a dozen smaller groups trying to make "their" idea the new standard. When HTML4.01 started to get a little long in the tooth, there were several groups trying to develop the latest and greatest version of the language. HTML4.01 worked, but it was not able to keep up with the rapid pace at which the web was evolving. As broadband worked its way into every home and business on the planet, and smartphones took the world by storm, the needs of the Internet grew faster than anyone had anticipated.

HTML5 vs XHTML: Fight!

The redevelopment of HTML began almost as soon as HTML4.01 was broadly released. In 1998, the *World Wide Web Consortium* (*W3C*)—a community focused on the development of web standards—began to work toward the new standard that would be the successor to HTML4.01.

XTML (*Extensible HyperText Markup Language*) merged HTML and *XML* (*Extensible Markup Language*). HTML was designed to display information, while XML was designed to transport information. It seems like they should be a natural fit, two halves of the same whole—but while the mashing together of the two languages may have seemed like a good idea, the rest of the web (particularly the browsers such as Internet Explorer and Opera) didn't hold to the standard; they still read pages in the HTML4.01 format—so the extra work done to ensure that new web content met the far stricter standards of XHTML was misplaced.

Source Andrew Kirmse & Chris Kirmse. Image courtesy of Jeannie Novak.

Early online games such as *Meridian 59* pushed the HTML envelope. Without possessing the full 3D visual capabilities of console and desktop games of the time, they cleverly blended text and images to create a compelling user experience.

Soon after, the *Web Hypertext Application Technology Working Group* (*WHATWG*) began working on upgrades and changes to HTML that would eventually become the core of HTML5. They enforced two core principles:

1. Backwards compatibility (i.e., don't ignore the web that exists *now*)
2. Specifications (glossary or index of everything) and implementations (actual usage) *must* match one another

This meant that the WHATWG undertook the huge task of figuring out just how HTML is being used "in-situ" (in real-life). After five years, they produced a massive document that set the specifications for just how browsers need to read, understand, and react to HTML. This specification is now referred to as the HTML5 parser.

In 2005, the W3C and the WHATWG came together to work on wha was called "Web Apps 1.0" but was later renamed "HTML5." After ab of collaboration, WHATWG's Ian Hickson assembled and published t HTML5—but there were still many changes that needed to be incorp

Ever Forward

Currently, HTML5 is still not "finished." It is considered by experts to be system—one that will continue to change and grow as the needs of the community evolve to meet the desires of the consumers.

With all new technology releases, adoption takes time—and to a certain degree, incentive. Early adopters of HTML5 include Apple's Safari browser, YouTube, and Firefox—all companies who live and breathe by the seamless user experience the web offers. Other companies were slow to follow suit; after all, Flash had done an excellent job of filling the hole in interactivity left by the older, less nimble HTML4.01. There were already thousands of Flash designers and development companies out there, while HTML5 was still new and untested. Flash worked well on every web browser published, and it was cross compatible with every stem on the market … except *one*.

In April 2010, CEO of Apple and larger-than-life personality, Steve Jobs, made it absolutely clear that Flash would *not* be allowed to function on Apple's line of iPads, iPhones, and other portable devices; among other reasons, he was concerned that the development rate by third-party developers would be too slow. Flash websites and games simply would not be allowed to run on the iOS platform. Clever developers stepped up to the challenge, building workarounds—but each and every one eventually ceased to function or was pulled from the Apple App Store. It was possible to run Flash-based software on an iOS system that was *jailbroken* (where the device and operating system are hacked to allow complete software access), but the vast majority of Apple's user base stayed true to their contracts and avoided this risky procedure:

> *"If developers grow dependent on third-party development libraries and tools, they can only take advantage of platform enhancements if and when the third party chooses to adopt the new features. We cannot be at the mercy of a third party deciding if and when they will make our enhancements available to our developers."*

With developers unable to showcase Flash projects on what was, at the time, the premiere platform for games and multimedia, HTML5 got a huge bump in interest. Android devices (which *could* access Flash games and websites) had not quite gained enough market share to offset the loss of iOS as a delivery platform. This was coupled with the fact that HTML5 would allow developers to build a single app or website and then deploy it across *all* platforms without having to create a series of *ports*. The potential reduction in development costs alone gave many small developers plenty of reasons to change from coding platform specific apps to the broader based HTML5.

As HTML5 has gained speed, more companies have redeveloped everything to match the new standard. Popular sites and networks such as LinkedIn and Twitter adopted HTML5 for development of their apps on iOS and Android devices. Multibillion dollar corporations have torn down their old websites and updated to the new standard—resulting, in many cases, in a double-whammy of a new user experience on the graphics side coupled with cleaner more responsive programming under the skin. In mid-2011 (just over a year after Steve Jobs delivered his commentary), over 34% of the top 100 trafficked websites were using HTML5.

With over one billion smartphones on the market that are capable of using HTML5, what remains to be seen is how the discoverability and marketing of HTML5 products plays out. For many small game designers, the lower cost of development can be offset by a more difficult path to discovery and the necessity of a larger marketing budget. While HTML5 is proving to be very effective as a development platform, it remains to be seen whether the existing roads to monetization—such as publication in the Apple App Store or in an aggregation community like Kongregate—will allow developers make enough money back on their investment to continue developing exclusively in HTML5.

Design Differences

So just what *is* different about designing for HTML5 versus designing for an iPhone or a standalone desktop system? Shinier buttons? Bigger bad guys? More ammo? Perhaps not so much. Remember, HTML5 was developed (like its predecessors) for use on the web. That means it's going to run within a web browser. Even if an HTML5-based game is being played on a smartphone, it will need to be developed within the structure of that device's native browser—whether it's Safari (iOS), Chrome (Android), or Windows (Windows Phone, Surface). The speed of your game *may* be an issue. Currently, HTML5 is expected to reach parity with natively developed apps. This means that an HTML5 app should run just as well and as fast as an Xcode (iOS) or a Java (Android) app. However, when it comes to game design, building a clean and efficient product is always the best way to go.

::::: Efficiency in One . . . Two . . . Three . . .

There are a couple of universal truths to making a game more efficient. You can spend your time tweaking individual elements and settings—but your life will be much easier if you plan ahead and follow just a few suggestions:

Image courtesy of Kimberly Unger.

As nice and smooth as it may be, the gradient on the left tops out at around 30 KB as a .png file without optimization. In contrast, the flat black image to the right is around 3.8 KB—which is a huge difference in memory, especially where web-based and mobile games are concerned.

- *Optimize graphics*: If you want pretty game sprites that don't take up too much memory, optimize them beforehand; don't trust the machine to do this for you. This means taking out any unnecessary blending or dithering. If you don't need that edge anti-aliased, trim it down. Think twice before you blow all those pixels on a nice smooth gradient.

- *Reduce, reuse, recycle*: Use elements more than once. If you have a bouncing beach ball in only one room of one level out of 25, think twice. Is there another pre-existing in-game element that will serve the same purpose? Keep unique elements at a minimum without harming your gameplay.

- *Trim audio*: Do you really need that five-minute electronica/dubstep mashup? Can you edit it down to a shorter looping audio file? Next to graphics, audio has the potential to take up the most memory. If you do the work up front to optimize your audio, then you will spend less time trying to trim down and replace each little piece as you move forward with your game.

While broadband certainly has made huge inroads, you will still need to design with the idea that players are going to have different setups. Some may have high-end gaming machines—and others will try to play your game on a middle-grade netbook (or on their outdated first-gen Android tablet). While it can be exciting to develop for the latest and greatest, keep in mind that only a small percentage of your player base will have access to the newest technology.

"Down Low" on the Download

Due to the broad variation in systems, Creator renders all HTML5 browser games at a lower resolution of 480 x 320 pixels (landscape). The first-generation iPhone resolution of 320 x 480 pixels (portrait) is the standard import resolution for YouTube videos and many Flash-based browser games, so it serves as a safe "baseline." Designing at this level will ensure that everyone will be able to access and play your game.

Clicks & Touches

Designing for HTML5 is, first and foremost, designing for the web. This means that you should first take best web practices into account and *then* make adjustments for touchscreen devices. A large percentage of players will have a mouse and keyboard at their disposal, rather than a touchscreen. Due to this, there are a few design elements to consider.

Visual and audio cues

Traditionally, there are all kinds of nifty things that happen when you place your mouse cursor over a button on a web browser—such as animations, color shifts, expanding text, and sound effects that might indicate whether a button is "awake" or has been clicked. You can get a lot of value out of these elements when deploying solely on the web—but if your game will be delivered to mobile devices as well, those elements will be lost. There is no "rollover" on a touchscreen; there is only a touch.

Players may be particular about sound options—such as the ability to play their own music files in the background or toggle annoying sound effects on and off. Allowing the player to customize these elements can be an element in your favor.

Source GameSalad®. Image courtesy of Jeannie Novak.

Sound assets can add a level of polish to a game (*Bamboo Forest*, shown)—but avoid overloading an online game with large files that can increase load times.

Keyboard controls

Web-based players will have keyboards at their fingertips (literally), and using the virtual keyboard that is included with touchscreen devices and tablets will make absolute hash of your game design. Many cross-platform designers get around this

Image courtesy of Utopian Games.

by simply designing all controls to be operated with the mouse. This means that instead of hitting the keyboard's space button to "jump," a player would have to click a button on the game screen. Fortunately for developers, this has already been somewhat established by the current state of web-based gaming. This trick is already used on communities and web sites that collect *thousands* of rookie, free, and experimental games to ensure that players can access particular games from anywhere and on any system.

Many HTML5-based games such as *Running Wild ARCADE* might be deployed on mobile web browsers. This means that controls otherwise mapped to the desktop keyboard are instead re-imagined as clickable buttons that will work with the mouse as well as the touchscreen interface.

Specials

Let's face it: Your average desktop will not have an accelerometer, vibration setting, or global positioning system (GPS). (See Chapter 6 for a discussion of these and other mobile-specific features.) While these elements may be great to use on a smartphone, they will not be viable on an HTML5 product. The tactile feedback that makes games using console controllers and touchscreens so much fun is, for the most part, not going to be available to players. It's best to design more toward audio and visual feedback in order to keep players engaged.

Image courtesy of Gamesmold.

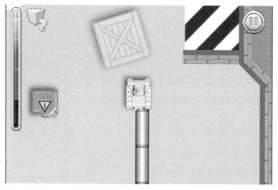

HTML5 games such as *Puzzle Dozer Lite* do not make use of "specials" such as accelerometer, vibration, or GPS.

Procedural Components

Procedural components (bits of visuals that are generated on the fly by the program, rather than taking up memory as textures or sprites) are normally very good elements to include in a game. One of the key restrictions on consoles and standalone desktops is the amount of available memory space (a key design factor when designing for those platforms). However, HTML5 is web-delivered content—and web browsers are optimized for pretty pictures, not for running complex math on the fly. These components, such as *palette animations* (animating or changing the color of a sprite or object by tinting it in the object's attributes), can cause an uncomfortable amount of lag during online gameplay. It is better for the initial load to take an extra second (to bring in more art assets) than for your game to lag at a crucial point. Nothing brings on a *ragequit* (quitting a game in frustration—usually vocal and physical [e.g., throwing things at the screen]) faster than a game lag causing problems with the gameplay.

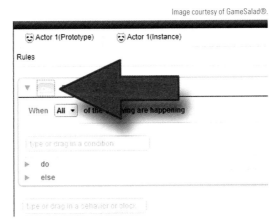

Image courtesy of GameSalad®.

Nodes can be temporarily disabled in Creator to test whether or not they are causing game-affecting lag.

This is a place where testing will come into play. (See Chapter 3 for a detailed discussion of protoyping.) Creator allows you to comment out Nodes and Behaviors within Actors. This may cause some occasional hitches in gameplay during testing—but with many procedural elements, these are add-ons (e.g., particles) that involve visual feedback rather than critical elements in the basic functioning of the gameplay.

One File to Rule Them All

By pushing your game to GameSalad Arcade in order to handle turning it into a binary, Creator simplifies the publication process by allowing you to have a single project file that can then be published in multiple formats. That said, GameSalad's server is only going to process the code for you; if you've designed a game that has buttons running off the screen or you forgot to include your touch controls, you're on your own.

:::::Tutorial: Publishing to GameSalad Arcade

Kimberly Unger (Chief Executive Officer, Bushi-go, Inc.)

The first step in publishing an HTML5 game is to upload it to the GameSalad Arcade servers. For the purposes of illustration, let's take a look at the hypothetical game, *Pachinko Madness*. The first step is to upload the game to the GameSalad Arcade. (In this tutorial, we are using Windows Creator.)

1. Access "File/Publish" to open. This will open a dialogue box informing you that your file is being uploaded to GameSalad Arcade. (*Don't panic!* Nothing will actually be done to the file without your express permission.)

2. Creator will open a default web browser and your *personal portfolio* (game files you have already uploaded). If you are not logged into the GameSalad web site yet, Creator will ask you to do so.

Image courtesy of GameSalad®.

Creator requires that you first upload your game to the GameSalad web site. From there, select the specifics of publishing your title before the binary is put together. This allows you to upload a single version of your game and then publish it in multiple formats.

3. You will see a dialogue box that asks you to choose "Create New Game" or "Update Existing Game." Select the "Create New Game" button. You will now be taken to the publishing options page.

4. To your left, you will see a list of options—each of which will contain information that has to be filled out in order to publish your game on various platforms. Be sure you begin with the icon and game title so that you can easily distinguish this game from the others you will be publishing. (GameSalad has created a simple percentage system that tracks how much information you have completed vs. how much more needs to be filled in before your game can go live.)

5. Select HTML5 from the list of options on the left and fill in your information. You will need to complete at least 78% of the form and requirements before you will be allowed to publish your game. (You can save your place and exit the setup at any time, so don't worry if you're not quite ready to publish; you can make adjustments and come back later.)

6. Note the checkbox by "Allow Game Embed." Leaving this checked will allow you to embed your game in a wide variety of web sites, simply by using the link provided once the game has been published. Also, when the game is "embedded," any changes made to it on GameSalad Arcade will be propagated across all copies of the game that use this link.

7. Once you have completed filling in the information and uploading the icon, you will be bumped to the "Arcade" segment of the questionnaire (if you haven't already filled it out). It is here that you include your screenshots and other essential pieces of distribution information.

8. Fill out everything and *be sure* to include screenshots of your game. Players tend to be visually driven and will often try out a game that "looks" cool before checking to see how the gameplay works.

Image courtesy of GameSalad®.

9. Once you have uploaded your screenshots and filled in as many of the required fields as you can, you are ready to publish your game to HTML5. If you return to the HTML5 tab from the list on the left, click the "Publish" button in the top right corner (which should now be active).

Creator does a comprehensive job of keeping developers alerted to what remains to be done when it comes to required tasks. In the sidebar to the left, note the red "Alert" icons that will let you know if there are issues that need to be addressed during the publishing process.

10. Once the GameSalad server has finished processing your file, it will be necessary to wait a few minutes before the new *binary* (compressed and packaged) file is ready.

11. Once the binary is ready, look near the bottom of the HTML5 screen. If you wish to make your game visible to the public, select the appropriate radio button. If not, select the "Work in Progress" button.

12. Next to the "Publish" button, you will see that the "Play Game" button has become active. When you click this button, it will take you to your game's GameSalad Arcade site. (Depending on the radio button you selected in Step #11, it may or may not be visible to the public.) At the bottom of the site, you will find an "Embed" code; you will need this code to link to your game from other HTML5 sites.

Patching As You Go

When you use the "embed" link, you are giving web providers with a "living" link to your game. Any "bug fixes," updates, and changes to your game will be included in *every* version of the game that is attached to this link. This also means that "wild" versions of your game (those that have been propagated to other aggregate sites without your knowledge) will also get those updates.

Distribution & Discovery

Distribution and discoverability are the cornerstones of successful game design. Open up any aggregation community's website and you will see hundreds of *Angry Birds* clones, dress-up games, "mow down the zombie" shooters, or other variations on almost every type of 2D game that has ever been created. It is supremely easy for your game, as excellent a product as it may be, to get lost in this sea of content. It even happens to professional game publishers with actual marketing budgets. Eyeballs are everything, but GameSalad Creator will make it as easy as possible for you to distribute your game to a wide range of outlets, including Facebook.

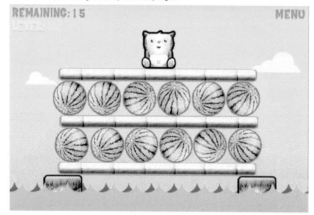

Source GameSalad®. Image courtesy of Kimberly Unger.

Games such as *Danger Cats!* with a distinctive look and feel, along with clearly identifiable, even "mascot-like" characters, can stand out from the crowd on games delivered via social media portals.

The first and least expensive way to help players discover your game is to choose an appropriate set of *tags* (keywords that are exposed to search engines, such as Google and Bing, that help them to find and rank your game in the search results). Most web sites, blog posts, and product lines use tags to help users find their websites and products. When deciding on your game's tags, choose between 5-10 good descriptors. Choosing a bunch of "controversial" tags in that have nothing to do with your game may get you to pop up in search rankings, but this has the strong potential to backfire. This practice is usually referred to as *keyword spamming* and, with most players being reasonably computer savvy, it can result in a negative response. Here are a few tips for good tag practice:

1. *Title*: Use the name of your game as one of the keywords so that when people recommend it to their friends while standing around the water cooler (or soccer field), they can go search for it online later.

2. *Genre*: Is your game a shooter, puzzle, or role-playing game (RPG)? Players tend to gravitate toward a certain genre—so when they search online, they often include the genre as one of the keywords.

3. *Setting*: Is your game set in the past, present, or future? Is it in Medieval Paris, on Mars, or in the Amazon Rainforest? Is it historically accurate, or in a fantasy universe? Some genre-type descriptions such as Steampunk, Cyberpunk, Dieselpunk, and Noir might also suggest certain settings.

4. *Platform*: It may seem like an odd choice—but if your game is created specifically for iOS, Android or HTML5, you will want to add a tag so that it will show up in platform searches.

5. *Descriptors*: Nouns such as props, vehicles, and other entities (e.g., robot, zombie, sword, spaceship) are also relevant—especially if they play an important part in your game.

6. *Qualifiers*: Adjectives such as "fun," "exciting" and "challenging" are less effective because they're too generic; many games are "fun," but not all of them have "lasercats"!

Once your game is published and ready to send out into the wider world, it will be essential to investigate as many options for exposure as possible. The goal, of course, is to have your game go "viral" and become wildly popular via word of mouth. *Virality* is tricky to master, however. There is a *ton* of free content available on the web: games, blogs, cat videos, and funny GIFs of people doing embarrassing things. How can you cut through all the noise?

Review Sites

Review sites such as Kotaku, Joystiq, DIY Gamer, and Rock Paper Shotgun can give you a good start. Bloggers are always looking for new content, so don't just send them a link to your game and ask "pretty please …?" Tell them a story—not just about the game itself, or why it is the niftiest thing since the invention of the mouse. Tell them a bit about your team and perhaps relate the story about the really cool discovery you made when you added particles. This doesn't have to consist of pages and pages; in fact, a paragraph will probably do the trick.

Video

A *video* is almost a "must have." Note that the publishing options in Creator allow you to include a URL for a YouTube video. That video can be a short, 30-second teaser such as a movie trailer or an assembled handful of the finest moments of gameplay you can muster. Many online game developers even go so far as to provide a full video walkthrough of their game—particularly where more difficult puzzle games are concerned. Video can sell a game that might be hard to explain in a simple batch of screenshots. Many online games now provide walk-through or tutorial videos as a way to not only reach out to potential players and showcase their product—but also to connect to the online community by offering walk-throughs or informational videos about the game, developers, and production process.

Image courtesy of Quantum Sheep.

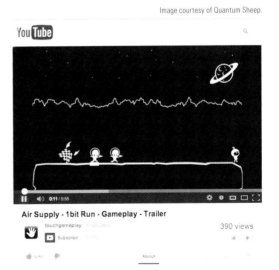

Online game developers often provide promotional video trailers encouraging prospective players to try out a game—or gameplay walkthroughs so that players who get stuck can find a solution without getting overly frustrated (*Air Supply - 1 bit Run,* shown).

Social Media

Social media should be a given, but no one ever mentions how hard it can be for developers to plug their own products to their Twitter, Facebook, and Google+ followings. Keep in mind that people follow you for a reason—whether they're friends, family, colleagues, or interested acquaintances.

Image courtesy of GameSalad®.

Image courtesy of GameSalad®.

Encouraging players to interact by contacting friends and inviting them to play—or asking them for game-related help—can help your game grow its audience and go viral (*Too Fat to Fly*, shown).

As long as you don't overdo it (i.e., don't post "buy my game" on a regular basis), you'll avoid alienating others most of the time. Deliver a "call to action": Let others know what you'd like them to do (e.g., download and review your game, "like" your Facebook page, attend your game release party). Be sure to ask *clearly*.

::::: Tutorial: Publishing to Facebook

Kimberly Unger (Chief Executive Officer, Bushi-go, Inc.)

For our purposes, Facebook is a good example of how app publication to a social media site can be handled. Every web site is, of course, going to have its differences—but some core elements (e.g., sign up as a developer, acquire tokens and keys) will be similar. Ideally, each site will provide potential developers with a proper set of instructions to publish a game on their site; not all of them will take third-party development software such as GameSalad Creator into account. Here are the steps you should take to publish your online game to Facebook:

1. Go to https://developers.facebook.com and register as a developer. Select "Create New App."

2. Add your game title and agree to the terms and conditions.

3. This will take you to the "Setup" page for your soon-to-be-published game. Look familiar? You will need to enter pretty much the same information you already put up on the GameSalad Arcade site. (You may simply want to keep a Word document handy with text and descriptions so that you can simply copy and paste.)

4. Next, click on the "App on Facebook" from the list on the bottom of your screen.

5. Put the "Embed" code from GameSalad Arcade into the box listed as "Canvas URL." However, you will need to clip off everything before "http" and after the last number. Essentially, you will take something like this:

<iframe src="http://e.gamesalad.com/play/147861" width="480" height="353" allowtransparency="true" scrolling="no"></iframe>

and rewrite it like this:

http://e.gamesalad.com/play/147861/

This abbreviated version will allow Facebook to embed your game so that players can access it.

6. Check the "fluid" box and be sure the "Social Discovery" button is checked as well. This is an important part of how Facebook allows players to discover your game through their friends.

7. Fill out any remaining information and click on "Save Changes."

8. A new/reorganized window for your game will appear. You will need to select the "App Details" from the tabs on the left. This is where you will to provide a screenshot, icon, and other descriptive information.

9. On the "Application Profile" page, you will need to add your screenshots and other images and information about your game. An important part of getting people to discover your game will revolve around getting "likes" on this page—so be sure to choose your best screenshots and some concept art and quotes from your team.

10. From here, click "Go to App" to see how your game will look to players.

Facebook is constantly reinventing its app submission process. Its developer site will most likely continue to grow and evolve as security requirements change and developer feedback is received.

Screens & Banners

Facebook offers the opportunity to create screenshots, banners, and icons at a number of different sizes. While minutiae such as banners may be tedious, including them will help your game maintain a more professional appearance on Facebook.

Design Limitations

There are a few *limitations* that you should keep in mind when designing for HTML5. A good practice is to pick a middle-of-the-road computer specification and design so your game runs well on that. You are not going to be able to adapt your game so it looks good on *every* screen that displays out, and trying to do so will quickly drive you off the deep end. Here are a few components that you should consider—including audio, file sizes, download speeds, and acquisition.

Audio

Keep your *audio* elements simple. You don't need to have more than 3-5 sound effects going off at once—especially if you are including music as well. Compress these files as much as possible—and keep in mind that your primary player will most likely be listening to the sound on a set of crappy, built-in laptop speakers (or might even keep the sound turned off).

File Sizes

Keep your *file sizes* as small as possible and work with .png rather than .jpg files. Once your folder full of assets exceeds 10 MB, you will need to start thinking about what to cut—unless you are building a very detail-rich game.

Source Apple Inc.

Games such as *The Secret of Grisly Manor* that rely on higher levels of detail and atmosphere for storytelling will have larger image sizes.

Download Speeds

While broadband may be close to total penetration in the United States, online gamers exist in all parts of the globe—not to mention those who try to play your game in coffee shops and Internet hotspots. GameSalad recommends the 480 x 320 screen in order to ensure that games can be played on every device, from every type of Internet connection. Increasing download speeds can be tricky, you cannot force a connection to go more quickly—but you can get clever with how your players perceive the length of download time. Some games have small mini-games that help to cover a long load time, and others take advantage of this load by using the time and space to display video ads that can drive revenue for their games. Long load times can be a liability, but there are ways to turn this into an asset.

At Your Fingertips

Not everyone plays games at their home desktop computers. With the popularization of laptops, more players are traveling light—which means no mouse. Can your game be played with the trackpad if your player is trapped in an airport somewhere?

Acquisition

Another limitation to consider is *acquisition*. How will players find your game? Currently, it's possible to publish a game to the Apple App Store, Google Play, or Amazon—allowing players to have a "one-stop shop" where they can find all the games for their device of choice. The same goes for the Mac App Store and the Windows Store. If you have a Mac, you can go straight to the Mac App Store to access games and software that has been vetted by Apple and will be compatible right out of the box. The same goes for most legally purchased Windows software. For HTML5, however, centralized collections are few and far between. When you do find a web site that focuses on HTML5, you're likely looking at a collection that is not curated and that can run the gamut from brilliant and high-quality games to "what were they *thinking*?"

Deployment

No matter what type of device your HTML5 game will be deployed on (e.g., desktop computer, iOS device, Android tablet), keep in mind that you are building a game experience to be delivered on the web. While this is nothing new, there are hundreds of web sites devoted to games of every stripe. Working with HTML5 means that your game is will be somewhat bulletproof for the next few years. A common issue with higher-end web games was always the installation of particular end-user software such as "Unity3d Web Player" and the "Shockwave plugin." Flash games took off because the Flash Player was a broadly used plugin that could handle all kinds of video and visual elements for web design. Almost everyone already had installed it, so the barrier to entry was almost non-existent. In the case of HTML5, you will bypass all that plugin/player drama. HTML5 games will work on any major browser and require no special additives. There is nothing to keep you from your players.

Evolution Over Time

HTML5 is more than just a shiny news item; it is the official next evolution of the "language" of the web—and as such, it's here to say. The question becomes: Where does HTML5 go from here? It is a much more robust and well-documented product than earlier versions, and it seems as of now that it will continue to evolve over time rather than be replaced. Note that HTML5 was designed specifically with backwards-compatibility in mind, which means that there are places on the web than cannot or will not upgrade until they absolutely, positively *must* do so. This means that your new HTML5 game may not be able to be deployed absolutely everywhere. The good news is that almost every major browser (including Firefox, Internet Explorer, Chrome, and Safari) has already updated to support HTML5—so your players find the game, they'll be able to play it. The next big step for HTML5 games will be when a major publisher starts to back HTML5 as a delivery platform. Once HTML5-specific sites that provide the same kind of consistent quality as the Mac App Store or Windows Store start to pop up online, we will see a shift in the way web games are regarded. There is value in the "walled garden" approach; it provides players with a curated list of games that they can access easily without having to do extensive searches online. As the next generation of web delivery, HTML5 is a solid, quality piece of work. The problems it faces are not related to whether or not the new update crashed your game; instead, they will lie in the unstructured nature of the web—with companies scattering games around content aggregate sites like a bridesmaid throws confetti. Finding your players—engaging them and establishing a relationship with them over the course of several projects—will prove to be a key element in how to handle user acquisition for online games of the future.

Additional material based on these exercises and chapter topics is available as part of the Instructor Resources package.

157

:::CHAPTER REVIEW EXERCISES:::

1. What design components would need to be altered in order to deliver a game as an HTML5 vs. mobile game?

2. Take a look at your folder of game-ready art assets. Did you manage to keep the whole set under 10 MB? If so, what techniques did you use to optimize the art?

3. Does your current UI design lend itself to touchscreens or monitors? What changes might you make to increase your game's cross-compatibility?

4. What visual feedback elements are you planning on including in your game? Will they translate from one platform to another?

5. When designing gameplay for HTML5, GameSalad recommends that you use 480 x 320 pixels. Why is this the case?

6. Tags are an important part of the discoverability process. List five tags that you feel are a good fit for your game.

7. How might publishing to a social media site help your game more than a content aggregation site?

Part III:
Focus

CHAPTER

8

Social Games
"you've got to have friends"

Key Chapter Questions

■ What elements make a game a *social* game?

■ Can a *single-player* game be social?

■ How do social media games *connect* to each another?

■ How does *GameSalad Creator* add social components to a game?

■ What game *genres* make viable social games?

Social games come in all shapes and sizes. Technically, any kind of game that pits player against player or requires two or more people to cooperate toward an end goal is actually a "social" game. More recently, the term has been given a particular focus: games that utilize social media to connect players. At times, the games are played head-to-head—and the only interaction between players involves a quick troll through each player's contacts (e.g., email, Facebook, Twitter, Google+) to let everyone know what game they're playing (or to invite a specific player to join). These games fill a niche that had gone untapped by designers and players, and they continue to evolve—testing and reinventing gameplay styles and goals. The way these games connect players can run the gamut from invasive to nearly unnoticeable. They can take people who have never played games and turn them into "whales" overnight. Some social games can move beyond gameplay mechanics and into the meta—where the social component (telling your friends and roping them in to join you) can become an even bigger game itself.

Meet Me at the Gaming Tables

For basic GameSalad Creator tutorials, see Appendix.

Historically, a game is a social construct. Card games, board games—games of skill, luck, or chance—almost all games required the interaction of two or more people. Single-player games such as solitaire were the exception to the rule. The term "social game" is a recent invention and specifically refers to games that make use of social media constructs to pit players against one another (or make them interdependent) and encourage new players to join the game. These types of games have actually been around for decades—but over time, designers added certain elements that evolved them into their current forms.

When games moved from the real, physical world into the digital realm, it became more common to play against the game itself—rather than against another person. While this didn't entirely remove the "social" aspect from traditional games (many were still played in a group setting such as a video game arcade or living room), it did catalyze the use of games as a solitary activity—fostering the now long-standing assumption that most players spend hours or days alone in their parents' basement staring at the cold, soulless glow of a CRT screen.

As Internet accessibility became more widespread, games naturally began to take advantage of this new level of connectivity. Early game hubs such as Games.com (AOL Games) and Yahoo! Games that offered web-delivered casual games such as *Bejewelled* and *Breakout* began to provide players with the ability to brag about their high scores to their friends as a way to pull in and introduce new players to the service. *Leaderboards* and scoreboards within games have been around since the days of *Pac-Man*, but now they were made public on the various gaming portals—allowing players to showcase their victories in a more public forum.

Image courtesy of Kimberly Unger.

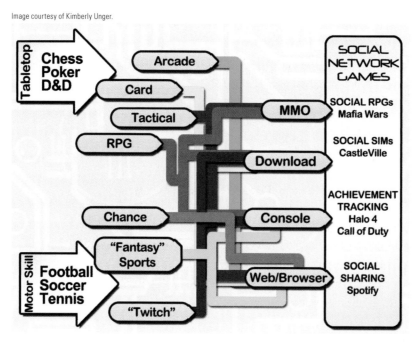

Games are inherently social constructs, with most forms of traditional games requiring two or more people to play. When games moved into the virtual, players increasingly pitted their wits against the computer as opposed to human opponents—but the desire to play against other human minds eventually made its way back in.

Home consoles such as the Xbox and PlayStation 3 took the idea of socializing (or "re-socializing") their games by enhancing and evolving multiplayer capability to allow real-time voice chat in their online games and adding *achievements* (challenges set by the developer that, when met, appear as part of the player's profile—allowing players to asynchronously compare their game stats). By 2002, the "social" was brought back to games—but these titles were still loved and played by "gamers" rather than the broader population.

In 2005, social media really began to take off—beginning with social networking sites such as Friendster, Myspace, Twitter, and eventually Facebook. The goal of having and maintaining an online presence was previously emphasized by the technically minded, or those who had a need to be online for business purposes—but social media drew in hundreds of thousands of people who had previously only dabbled in email and web searches. In a 2009 interview for *mediabistro.com*, Zynga founder Mark Pincus said that social media is like a series of cocktail parties and "the ultimate thing you can do—once you bring all of your friends and their friends together—is play games."

Source Google.

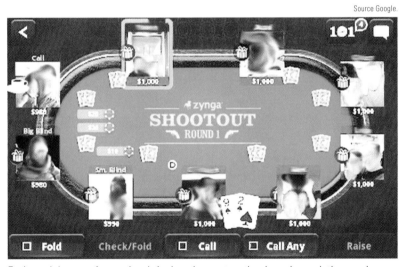

Early social games focused on bringing players together based on existing gaming models. *Zynga Poker* took advantage of poker's resurgence in popularity and combined it with the online social apect—allowing groups of friends to play together even if they were in different parts of the world.

Games dedicated to engaging and monetizing the new flood of "social media" users comprised a natural next step. Companies such as Zynga and Habbo began building *free-to-play* products that were quick to learn and, most importantly, encouraged players to get their friends to play the game as well by rewarding them with different forms of in-game incentives. As social media sites gained membership in the millions and billions, game developers that best took advantage of this "cocktail party" social setting went along for the ride—resulting in companies and products that have been valued in the billions of US dollars.

Social Design

There are a number of distinct features that tend to come together to make a game "social" rather than just "casual." Most of these features encompass game design decisions—with a smattering of connectivity and platform issues. Most social games have at least three of these elements and will often adopt more as the game is updated and evolves over time. These elements include: asynchronous gameplay, community, endless play, virtual currency, reciprocity, drop in/drop out, buyouts, and advertising. Let's take a closer look at these social design elements.

Asynchronous Gameplay

The definitions of the terms "synchronous" and "asynchronous" with regard to gameplay are currently under debate. For the purposes of this book, we'll define *synchronous* games as those that are predominantly played in real time—with all parties interacting together. This might include console games such as *Call of Duty* or *Halo* (where players connect online to participate in multiplayer "deathmatch" or "capture the flag" scenarios)—or a game of poker you host at your home on Thursday nights.

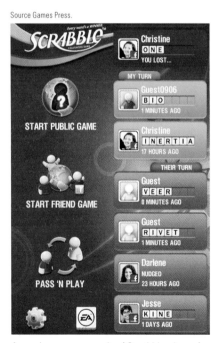

Source Games Press.

Asynchronous gameplay (*Scrabble*, shown) allows several games to be played at once with multiple opponents. The risk with asynchronous games is that one player will simply lose interest and fail to take a turn—orphaning the game before it is complete.

Asynchronous games are those that do not require both players playing at the same time. A play-by-mail game of chess or billiards played in a local pool hall would be asynchronous.

In an asynchronous social game such as *Words with Friends* or *Draw Something*, the players both interact—and the game moves forward only with the input of either player. It gives players the experience of playing together, and outcome of the game is dependent on their direct interaction—or on taking turns. This frees the players up to play at their own pace, based on their own availability—rather than requiring them to both be online at the same time.

Many multiplayer "social" games are designed for asynchronous play, and several innovations in social games have been derived from the need to prevent games from being "orphaned." Games are designed to encourage the player to get more friends involved, to allow the game to post to their social media feeds, and to remind and encourage (perhaps even "harass") players to keep their games alive. At this time, Creator does not incorporate asynchronous multiplayer gameplay—but GameSalad is working on building in these capabilities.

Community

Social media is, of course, "social"—implying *community* right from the start. Historically, a game had to build its own community through word of mouth and through forums and web sites dedicated to the product. In the case of social games, the community is pre-existing. The games are tied into a social platform such as Facebook or Google+—and the player provides the community by bringing in friends, recommending the game, and including high scores and achievements in their social stream. Included with this is the subset of players who are not interested in bombarding their friends and family with game requests, but instead choose to play anonymous "pickup" games with people outside their social circles.

Image courtesy of PlayScreen, LLC.   Image courtesy of PlayScreen, LLC.

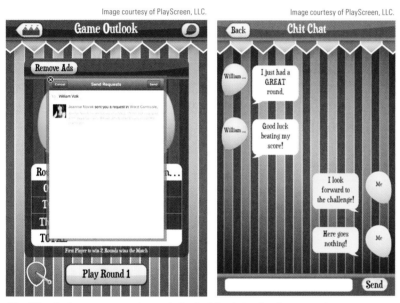

Word Carnivale encourages players to invite friends to play the game at every opportunity—and even provides in-game "chit chat."

This seamless connection between people and the games they play is one of the key elements in social games. In a more traditional online community, forums and games are accessed by players who are interested in participating in them and are willing to go through a sign-up process. In a social media community, there is a much greater chance of discovery by players who have not yet seen or experienced a product. Creator provides you, as a designer, the ability to connect with a player's social media community—thereby allowing the pool of players who know about a game to jump by leaps and bounds, rather than by a single trickle via word of mouth. Although Creator doesn't currently incorporate the "invitation" device (e.g., inviting friends to play), tweets can be sent from Mac Creator. With the iOS 6 Social Framework, there may be additional features used in the future.

::::: Tutorial: Check This Out! (Facebook Link-Up)

Kimberly Unger (Chief Executive Officer, Bushi-go, Inc.)

Social games (as their name suggests) rely on social activity to draw in more and more players. At the most basic level, this means posting your in-game activity to your social stream. Upon completion of a task or a quest, players will usually receive a prompt suggesting that they link to their Twitter or Facebook accounts along with a pre-scripted message and a link to the game. Players have the option to personalize, delete, or simply skip sending these messages each time they pop up—but there is usually no option to avoid them entirely. You can direct your players to post their successes on Facebook using the Pro version of GameSalad Creator by using the following steps:

Image courtesy of GameSalad®.

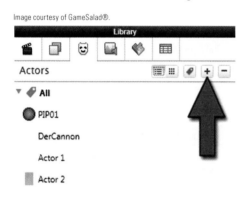

1. Import the artwork you would like to use to create a "Facebook" button. Players will be able to click/touch this button, and it will take them to Facebook to post their boast.

2. Create a "button" actor under the "Actors" tab by clicking on the + symbol on the top right of the window.

3. Add your image to the Actor and drag it to the Stage where you are setting up your game. This will create an "instance" or a copy of the Actor.

4. In the "Backstage" window below the Stage, click on the lock to change your instance (leaving the original Actor untouched) and drag the "Rules" Behavior from the Library into the instance window. Set the dropdown to "When *All* of the following are happening."

Image courtesy of GameSalad®.

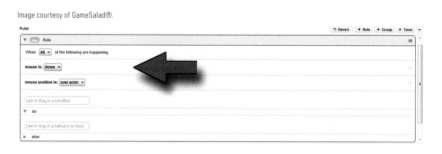

5. Drag the "Mouse Position" and "Mouse Button" conditions into your new Rule and set them to: "mouse is *down*" and "mouse position is *over actor.*"

6. Under "do" in your Rule, drag over the "Open URL" behavior. Pause working with Creator here and switch over to the web browser of your choice.

7. Be sure to set up your app as a developer with Facebook by accessing https://developers.facebook.com/setup/. This will give you the keys you need to link to so that your game can talk to the Facebook *application programming interface* (*API*). The API is the point of access between your game and the social networking site. Almost all companies that have a site or service that can be used by an external third party (e.g., Tapjoy, Facebook, Twitter) will be able to provide you with an API.

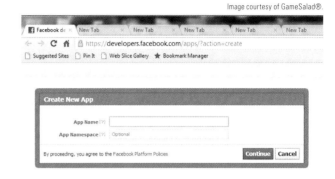

Image courtesy of GameSalad®.

8. Once you have your Facebook developer account set up, you will need to collect the *App ID* (the unique code that identifies your app) from Facebook. This method doesn't access the Facebook API directly, so the API key and the "app secret" are not needed for this method.

Different social media sites have distinct ways to link into their application programming interface. This takes a little extra effort at the moment and requires that you have GameSalad Creator Pro.

9. Open the text editor of your choice and create a URL based on the following. You'll need to include your own App ID and whatever you want the post to say in the appropriate places. This entire URL will probably be too long to include in GameSalad Creator's "Open URL" rule, so you may need to use bit.ly, goo.gl or another URL shortener of your choice.

```
http://www.facebook.com/dialog/feed?
app_id=PUT YOUR APP ID IN HERE&
link=INSERT A URL LINK TO YOUR APP HERE (iTUNES
OR OTHER)&
picture=INSERT A URL TO A JPG ICON FOR YOUR APP
HERE&
name=INSERT%20TITLE%20HERE&
caption=INSERT%20CAPTION%20HERE&
description=THIS%20IS%20WHERE%2
DESCRIPTIVE%20COMMENT%20GOES&
message=THIS%20IS%20TO%20PUT%20THE%20USERS%20
COMMENT&
redirect_uri=http:// INSERT A URL LINK
TO REDIRECT THE USER TO AFTER POSTING
```

10. Test your button. Something to note: This gives you the option to redirect players to a different URL after they post. This will open a new tab in your default browser (e.g., Safari, Chrome, Internet Explorer).

chapter 8

Endless Play

Often turning into the "Big Bad" of discussions revolving around social games, the concept of *endless play* means that you never really have an overall "win" or "lose" in a social game—but rather the game is structured as a series of never-ending smaller quests or missions that players can continue to work through, as long as their attention is held. This serves as a double-edged design issue. It's necessary to have a critical mass of content up front to keep the player engaged, but you should also keep pushing changes and new content to keep players coming back for more. Therefore, while a traditional casual game might be built, released, and be "done with," a social game is constantly revisited and becomes an ongoing experience for the designer and developer as well as the player.

Source Apple Inc.

Games such as *DragonVale* are almost infinitely expandable—and designers need to continue to release new content, quests and rewards in order to keep players engaged.

In essence, you are employing a "feed the beast" style of design where the player is being satisfied by a steady stream of new content and small victories rather than by the difficulty associated with completing any given task or level. When publishing with Creator to the GameSalad Arcade or using the HTML publishing option, you can update your game immediately when a change is made. On mobile, you will need to push a revision through the various app stores.

Virtual Currency

Most social games involve some sort of *virtual currency* that can always be bought with real-world money and can sometimes be earned through dedication and cleverness (or by clicking on lots of ads). Many players are not at all averse to dropping a dollar on a virtual good that will give them temporary godlike powers within a game—or that will allow them to miraculously bring all their fish back from the dead. Mac Creator helps to support virtual currencies in game by connecting to Apple's in-game purchases. Virtual currency is one of the strongest ways for a developer to monetize a game and forms the basis for the free-to-play model that underlies most, if not all, social games.

Virtual currency is exactly that: *virtual*. It isn't "real" and is composed of bits and bytes. There are several ways to handle virtual currency: You can design your own that works only in your game(s), or you can partner with services such as Playhaven to work with its virtual currency. The advantage of the first option is that you retain complete control with regard to how much the currency costs in real-world dollars and how much it is worth in game. The advantage of the second option is that you can use the cross-compatibility of currency from a third party to bring in players from other games who spend currency they earn through clicking on banner ads or other rewards in your game.

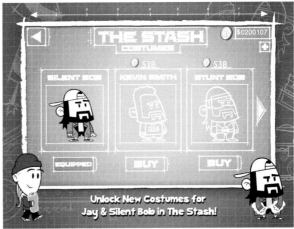
Image courtesy of GameSalad®.

Virtual currencies can often be purchased in games such as *Too Fat to Fly* for cash or platform (e.g., Facebook) credits—or they can sometimes be earned through pop-up advertising or in-game rewards.

Reciprocity

"If you scratch my back, I'll scratch yours." As the saying goes, players are encouraged to help one another out through *reciprocity*—either by "gifting" in game goods to one another or throwing the weight of their in-game stats behind a conflict. Many games,

such as Zynga's *Ville* games (e.g., *FarmVille*, *CityVille*), allow players to earn additional resources—such as an extra brown cow—that they can gift to another player via Facebook. Gifting the resource to a friend who is not yet playing the game can prove to be a powerful tool to bring the friend in as a player. These types of "gifts" (e.g., in-game resources, coins, credits) are of little or no cost to the developer—yet they provide an immense benefit in increasing the virality of their game and drawing in new, casual players.

Source Zynga. Image courtesy of Kimberly Unger.

In social games such as *FarmVille 2*, players may be offered extra resources that they themselves cannot use but that can be gifted to a friend. The game then reminds players that after sending the gift to a friend, the recipient can reciprocate by gifting an item to the player.

Along with the reciprocity element, social games often invoke "guilt" by either encouraging players to either return to the game after a long absence or invite their friends to the game. This "guilting" can get fairly serious—with more aggressive games requiring you to either get the help of a friend or pay in virtual currency for the right to continue a game. One of the more popular fish-raising mobile games requires the player to invite a friend to help remove dead fish from a tank. (Otherwise, the player's dead fish will float in there indefinitely!)

::::: Tutorial: Impulse Buy!

Kimberly Unger (Chief Executive Officer, Bushi-go, Inc.)

Social games operate on the same principle as the checkout line at your local supermarket. Items are brought to your attention, priced low enough to be paid for by the change under your couch cushions. It might be a pack of gum or a pair of new shoelaces, or . . . a cow! GameSalad Creator allows you to connect your social game to Apple's *In-App Purchase* (*IAP*) solutions so that your game can be monetized through these types of virtual goods. To build out your IAP, use Creator's Tables to build your lists of items and set up the game so it can record which items have been purchased and their associated categories. This is a bit more complex than many Creator functions—but once in place, it provides flexibility with regard to monetizing the game. (Remember: IAP only works in iOS games.)

It's important to note that many of the online distribution options require that developers set up games to work with their own purchasing system. For example, Apple requires that developers offer an IAP option to players if there are virtual goods in the game. This makes the transaction quick and painless for players (since the purchase is billed directly to their iTunes accounts) and allows Apple to keep some modicum of control over the purchasing process and content.

Image courtesy of GameSalad®.

1. Click on the "Tables" tab to create a new table. (Tip: When working on your game, create a mockup of your Table to make it easier to transfer information rather than having to keep track of all your Goods and saleable items on the fly.)

2. In both versions of Creator, the new table will appear in the same space you use to edit your Actors (the Backstage in Windows Creator and the Editor in Mac Creator)—allowing for easy reference to the Actors in your Library.

3. Populate your new Table with a series of rows that can be completed with individual information relating to the Goods in your game. You can build your own Table to suit your needs, but the image on the left (and the list below) provides a simple breakdown for the purposes of this tutorial.

   - *ID:* This is the ID number of your Virtual Good. This ID# *must* match the one you have set up in iTunes.

   - *Description:* This is a brief text description of the Good.

   - *Consumable:* This is a "yes/no" box. If your Good is consumable (i.e., it can be used once and then goes away), check this box.

   - *Quantity of Consumable:* This shows the maximum number of this Good that can be purchased/held by the player in the game. As the player consumes these, they can then purchase more until they reach the max again.

- *Price:* How much does it cost to purchase one unit of this Good?

- *Purchase Status:* This is another "yes/no" box. It should be left unchecked and will be changed/checked by the game if and when the player purchases the Good.

- *Total Quantity Purchased:* How many of the Good did your player purchase?

- *Attempting Purchase:* This is checked by the game when the player has initiated a purchase, and it is unchecked by the game when the purchase has been completed. It serves a few useful functions—including being able to verify if a player attempted to purchase an object and never received it.

4. Create a new Actor in the Library to hold your IAP. (No image needs to be associated with it.) You will need to drag the IAP Behavior over to the Editor to begin setting up your Rules.

Image courtesy of GameSalad®.

5. Tie your IAP Actor to the table you created in the first part of this tutorial. Next to the "Product ID" box on the right, you'll see an "e"; click it to open the "expression" editor. Next to "insert function," click the dropdown menu and roll down to "table CellValue(table,row,col)"; this will tell the game which Cell in the table it looks at to match the Product ID of the purchase.

6. Notice the word "table" in that expression; replace this with the name of the table you created at the start of the tutorial. Next, replace the values "row" and "col" with the row and column of the Product ID for this Good.

7. Check to be sure you have the "Consumable" box checked if your Good is a consumable. If you don't check the "Consumable" box, the purchase of the Good will be a one-time event—and the change will stay as long as the player owns the game.

Image courtesy of GameSalad®.

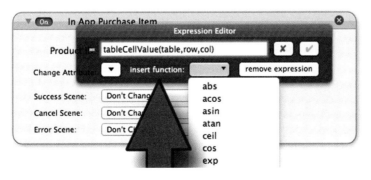

Image courtesy of GameSalad®.

8. Tell the game which attribute to change in response to this purchase. Is it for a Good such as an extra life or an in-game currency purchase? Under the "Change Attribute" expression, set these parameters again using the Expression Editor.

9. Set up what happens after the purchase has occurred. There are three options: "Success Scene," "Cancel Scene," and "Error Scene." Set up a separate scene in your game for each of these options.

Mano a Mano

You can manually enter the Product information for each of your IAP Actors. However, if you create and use the Tables in Creator, you can modify those tables and have all of the product information in the game update from a single source—rather than needing to manually change each expression by hand.

Drop In/Drop Out

Social games are known for being "bite sized"; players need to be able to *drop in/drop out*: pausing them on a moment's notice and pick them up again pretty close to where they left off. The amount of time a player spends on the game may not be short; some players of online social games may spend hours of time in the game of their choice. However, the length of time it takes to complete any given task or quest should be fairly short. If you have longer levels or goals, you'll want to consider how to break them up into smaller pieces. Since GameSalad Creator games are in essence single-player only, the drop in/drop out feature isn't really an issue; as long as a player pauses the game (and doesn't quit it), the player may do something else and then return to the game later after unpausing it.

Source Zynga. Image courtesy of Kimberly Unger.

Games such as *Bubble Safari* are broken up into small, easy-to-play levels that are usually tracked on a map of some sort. Each point on the map represents a level of short, puzzle based gameplay—and the game can be turned off and on at the player's convenience.

Buyouts

The *buyout* option allows a player with more money than time to pay a fee to be a superhero for a bit. A player can simply *buy* the "big sword," an extra life, or a potion that will make all the bad guys shrivel up and blow away. In the same vein, your game can also contain *paywalls* (points at which the player simply *cannot* progress any further without the purchase of a specific Good).

Image courtesy of GameSalad®.

Battle Legend Infinity allows players to level up by playing, buying a level up, or purchasing a max out to reach max level.

Not all paywalls are absolute; in fact, if they're "soft" (i.e., players can get around them through an extra day of patience), you can appeal to *both* kinds of players— those who derive satisfaction from thinking they "beat" you by avoiding the paywall, and those who really just want to *get on* with playing the game. Paywalls can also be tied to advertising opportunities: The player can click on an ad or install another game (e.g., provided via Tapjoy or Playdom) to unlock the paywall. The developer gets a kickback for the install, and the player doesn't have to pay anything out of pocket. In *Candy Crush Saga*, a paywall might be disguised as an in-game powerup. For example, it might appear on the menu bar next to the "candy hammer" powerup—but when it is clicked on, it sends the player to a purchase screen to buy the extra moves (instead of providing the player with the needed boost). This presents the player with a dilemma: Does the player end the game or simply buy the moves needed to finish?

Advertising

You cannot escape *advertising*. The majority of online games, web sites, and mobile games are supported at least partly (and often wholly) through advertising. It's possible to provide players with the option of earning more cash to spend in your game through the installation of other games—not only games by other developers, but your own games as well. Types of in-game advertising include:

- *Banner ads:* These are ubiquitous, especially in mobile and web-based games—popping up at the top or bottom of a game or app.

- *Offerwalls:* These are pop-ups that show up at key points—offering to award players coins or points in exchange for trying out other goods or services. Offers can be as varied as coins in exchange for signing up for a web site such as Travelocity—or as points for downloading and installing a different game.

- *Interstitial ads:* These often take the form of video ads (though they can be still images as well) that are shown to players while the game is loading a new level.

Image courtesy of GameSalad®.　　　　　　　　　　　Image courtesy of GameSalad®.

Social games incorporate various forms of advertising, including interstitial ads (*Shred Neffland*, left) and offer walls—such as *Ice Cap Games: Black Jack* (right), which advertises other games on its distribution network.

Social games are all about engagement. They are, by their very definition, social constructs—talking to you and your friends via "pushes" and "posts" to your stream or wall or timeline. They can, in fact, sometimes get *too* pushy—but since they're often free-to-play, many players have a much higher tolerance for being harassed by this entertainment. However, social games measure success by downloads and the number of eyeballs that scan their pages—rather than by direct purchases or even IAPs within the game. GameSalad Creator allows Pro developers to incorporate both banner and interstitial ads in order to monetize their games.

Hive Mind

Social games continue to progress—drawing in many people who never considered themselves "gamers" by offering a point of commonality: playing games together. As games move to the mainstream, social games become part of "water cooler" conversations—creating a shift in how people look at friends, co-workers, and complete strangers both online and in the real world. Social games make it easy to create a "soft" connection or re-connection between individuals. Unlike a phone call or an email out of the blue, they allow a more casual contact that can be acted upon or ignored with (ideally) less risk of offense to either party. The social media climate is slowly but surely taking us to a place where making and keeping friends is a delightful game rather than a social chore. Social games make it that much easier to plant the seeds for lasting friendships (and immediate rivalries)—transforming human relationships forever.

Additional material based on these exercises and chapter topics is available as part of the Instructor Resources package.

:::CHAPTER REVIEW EXERCISES:::

1. Does your game lend itself to be categorized as a "social" game? If not, what are some social elements that could be incorporated to help raise visibility for your game?

2. Are you planning on working with GameSalad Creator's mobile (iOS/Android) or HTML5 publishing for your social game? (See Chapters 6 and 7, respectively, for more information on online/HTML5 and mobile development.) Discuss the rationale for your choice.

3. Are there places in your game where players should connect with friends via Facebook or Twitter? Compile a list to see where ideal contact points might be and compose a few promotional tweets.

4. Does your game design lend itself to new and expanded content updates? Are these sorts of updates best suited to virtual goods or levels? Why or why not?

5. Does your game have an "end"? What happens when a player gets to the end of your game and why might they want to announce this to their friends?

6. Does your game lend itself to in-game advertising? What types of ads might work best in your game?

7. Do you plan on utilizing virtual currency in your game? Why or why not?

CHAPTER

9

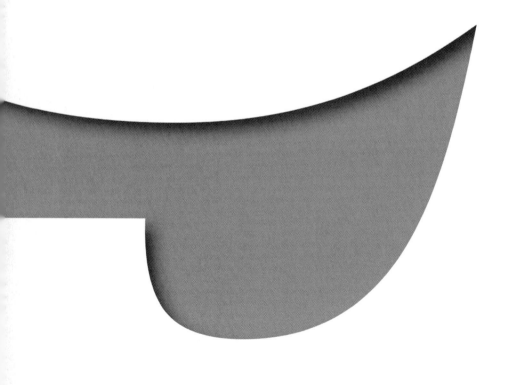

Serious Games
why so serious?

Key Chapter Questions

- What distinguishes a *serious* game from other games?

- What distinct *design features* are associated with serious games?

- How is *learning* and *progression* handled in serious games?

- What *industry sectors* are associated with serious games?

- What types of serious games are best suited to *GameSalad Creator*?

- What are some unique features of the *publishing and delivery* process associated with serious games?

The *serious games* sector is really a class unto itself. Unlike games created solely for entertainment purposes, serious games are deliberately constructed to serve a wide variety of non-entertainment purposes. While commercial games such as *Assassin's Creed* and *Sid Meier's Civilization* contain accurate historical settings, figures, and technology—sparking the player to conduct additional historical research—their primary function is not to teach, but to entertain. In games created solely for entertainment, any science serves the story and as such can be tweaked, modified, or wholeheartedly altered for the sake of engaging the player. In contrast, serious games focus on specific non-entertainment objectives—such as instructing, informing, persuading, or healing. Games have been used throughout history to train others to perform tasks accurately, operate within a team, and apply specific lines of logic to certain situations. The more recent trend of "gamification" is a second cousin to serious games with a much tighter focus: to make simple, repetitive tasks more palatable. Gamification encourages a pattern of behavior through a system of encouragements and rewards. Serious games, by contrast, focus on a much more comprehensive form of training—one that can teach players *how* to think in a given situation, rather than just handing them food pellets for pecking at the red button instead of the green.

Games Get Serious

For basic GameSalad Creator tutorials, see Appendix.

In the 1950s, computer scientists researching the nascent field of *artificial intelligence* (*AI*) created early versions of chess and checkers with an emphasis on developing a computer mind that could "think" well enough to beat a human player (or at least prove to be a challenge). These were some of the first examples of computer "games" being built with a larger purpose: *not* for entertainment, but to test the development of early logic systems. Another example was *OXO* (a.k.a. *Noughts and Crosses*)—a tic-tac-toe game programmed by A.S. Douglas in 1952 to illustrate and support a research thesis on human-computer interfacing.

Source Martin Campbell-Kelly. Image courtesy of Jeannie Novak.

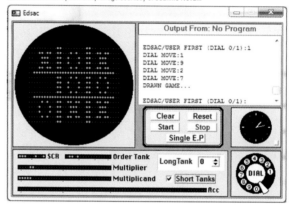

OXO (a.k.a. *Noughts & Crosses*)—considered to be the world's first "video" game—was not designed as a commercial product but to illustrate new forms of human-computer interface design. This image depicts the game running on a simulator of the EDSAC—possibly the very first computer ever built (in 1949 at the University of Cambridge).

During the Cold War, computer games began to serve a role in the military. These games were usually *simulators* (games focusing on real-world rules and situations) such as *HUTSPIEL*, which simulated the impact of nuclear weapons on a global battlefield and resulting supply-chain issues. Like many of their predecessors, these games were never meant to reach consumers—but they are early (and accurate) prototypes for many strategy games (such as *Civilization*) that appeared on home computers in the 1980s.

Serious Consumers?

Serious games are always designed with a specific purpose: a task to teach, a tale to tell, a concept to illustrate. Traditionally, they are not intended for consumer release—though several have gone on to be runaway commercial successes (e.g., *America's Army, Secure the Deck, Skillrex Quest*). It's becoming more common for serious game projects to have two (or more) "versions" focusing on their respective markets (e.g., educational and consumer editions).

The term "serious games," as coined by Ben Sawyer and David Rejeski in 2002, was defined as "games that do not have entertainment, enjoyment or fun for their primary purpose." At first glance, the term might seem to be an oxymoron—but consider that many formalized games, even if they are often played purely for enjoyment, were initially created for a "serious" purpose. Games such as polo and chess were derived as forms of physical and intellectual exercise—one being used to teach four-dimensional thinking, and the other to increase mounted combat skills. Even branches of the modern military continue to engage in "war games" with the intent of training their personnel—even during peace time.

Although formal military exercises and corporate team-building efforts are rarely thought of as "games," they usually involve codified rules, direct competition between players or teams—and even scorekeeping methods. This incorporation of gameplay features can partly be attributed to the rise during the late '80s and early '90s of *edutainment* products (games that were designed to teach in a scholastic setting). Real-life classroom simulations of historical events and economic processes, developed by companies such as Interact, *did* exist in an analog form before—but as society has continued to embrace new technologies, there has been a natural inclination to use digital simulations as a way to improve the mind. These new technologies came with a much broader reach. No longer were edutainment products advertised solely in the back of Scholastic Book Club pamphlets or kids' magazines. The net was cast as wide as possible; advertising on television and the Internet ensured that almost *everyone* (parents, kids, gamers, non-gamers) with access to a screen was exposed to the existence of edutainment products. Well-known edutainment brands included LeapFrog (games and hardware) and Knowledge Adventure (*JumpStart* franchise). The instructional aspect in edutainment titles tended to be heavy-handed, possibly because the connection between "education" and "edutainment" needed to be clearly shown.

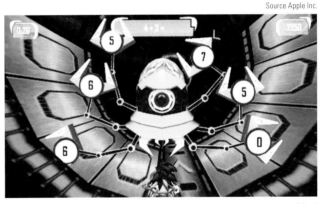

Source Apple Inc.

Games that were born of the "edutainment" era, such as the *Math Blaster* franchise (*Math Blaster: Hyperblast 2*, shown), attempted to make learning fun by incorporating gameplay into core basics (multiplication tables, logic puzzles, spelling).

In 2002, the US Army released *America's Army* as a recruitment tool—a 3D first-person shooter (FPS) built using the then cutting-edge Unreal Engine. *America's Army* was game-changing—with its real-world military scenarios and one-shot-one-kill scoring. It opened up a dialogue between the reality of combat and the hyper-reality that was rapidly taking over the AAA console scene at the time.

What, Me *Serious?*

"Serious" does not mean *photoreal*. Serious does not mean ragdoll physics and AI that can make Deep Blue curl up and shed silicon tears in the corner. Serious games are often clean and simple; they fulfill their purpose through design and execution; as such, a tool like GameSalad Creator is an ideal fit—especially in situations where an in-house solution needs to be cost-effective and quickly executed. In serious games, concept and design are both driven by the product's goal; this is often a quantifiable, real-world objective—as opposed to simply the completion of the game.

Styles

Serious games come in several distinct gameplay styles. However, rather than focusing on attracting players, the priority of a particular style choice is to match the game's subject matter. Styles help designers define and focus a game so that it can achieve its primary goal. Let's look at just a few of the *many* styles of serious games; you'll notice that each corresponds to a particular market segment.

Educational

Educational games (or *game-based learning* products) are sometimes seen as an outgrowth of the edutainment market—but the lessons learned over 15 years ago have resulted in more emphasis on gameplay and the "fun factor" rather than merely converting educational topics into animated environments and characters. Games such as *Zoo Vet: Endangered Animals* target instruction and education with an emphasis on real-world situations and concerns.

Source Legacy Interactive. Image courtesy of Jeannie Novak.

Educational games teach players real-world skills—such as treating sick animals at the zoo with veterinary tools and techniques (*Zoo Vet: Endangered Animals*, shown).

::::: Case Study: *Body Adventure with Captain Brainy-Pants!*

Image courtesy of Power Up Education Inc.

In Fall 2010, I created a game for the iPad entitled *A sciTunes Human Body Adventure* (the precursor to *Body Adventure with Captain Brainy-Pants!*) and entered it in the 2011 National STEM Video Game Challenge. I was selected as one of three finalists in the Developer category and went on to win an award for the best teacher-developed game. Under this label, I have published a dozen or so non-educational games—a few of which were chosen by Apple to be in their main SERIOUS: New and Noteworthy games section.

— *Dan Caldwell (Owner & Founder, Power Up Education Inc.)*

Simulation

When it comes to getting serious, a *simulation* is one of the broadest types of games. Simulations are used in training in any number of skills (e.g., critical thinking, resource management, economic theory, aerodynamics, exploring extreme conditions—such as space). Although simulations are often utilized in research, government, and military institutions, these types of games are also administered in both public and privately held corporations to train employees.

Image courtesy of GameSalad®.

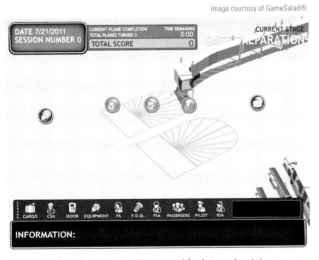

Many simulations (particularly those used for internal training purposes such as *Alaska Airlines: Turn Pro*) are never intended to see the light of consumerism—so the focus tends to be on the accuracy of the simulation, rather than the depth and quality of the visuals.

Marketing and Advertising

Games focusing on *marketing and advertising* (including *advergames*) are often used to either provide brand awareness or *persuade* players to purchase associated products or services. Most often, advergames are classic puzzle games done over with custom or branded art and sound. Advergames often appear with more traditional banner advertisements either within the game or as *bookending* (advertising before and/or after the game, like bookends corralling books on a shelf)—and they can easily be *re-skinned* (same game, new art) to match several different sub-brands.

Image courtesy of GameSalad®.

Most major brands or properties (including television series such as *2 Broke Girls*, shown) incorporate advergames that are predominantly used to connect with an existing audience rather than drawing in new fans.

Consciousness and Change

While advergames are used almost exclusively for brand engagement, *consciousness and change* games (also known as *games for change*) target current informational or social mores with an emphasis on engaging in some form of dialogue. These games seek to *persuade* the player to change their mind about some topic through exposure and instruction—and they can run the gamut from social commentary and change (*Amnesty: The Game*) to resource conservation (*The Voltinator*). It is interesting to note that both sides have the opportunity to influence one another—but this is not the case with persuasive games; despite some level of interactivity, the persuasion is always one-sided.

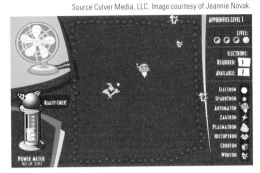

Source Hellenic Game Developers Association. Image courtesy of Kimberly Unger.

Source Culver Media, LLC. Image courtesy of Jeannie Novak.

Social networks are giving social consciousness games such as *Amnesty: The Game* (left) a broader audience (at a much lower cost). Through *The Voltinator* (right)—which gets wide online distribution through power company web site links—kids learn about energy conservation by pushing electrons to a circuit to power an electric appliance.

Change Agent

We use GameSalad Creator to create Games for Change. The students' games address topics such as energy, water conservation and the prevention of child obesity. In addition to GameSalad, I'm working with the Mozilla Open Badges project, Gamestar Mechanic, and Adobe Educational Leaders.

David Conover (Game Design Instructor, Connolly High School)

I've used GameSalad Creator to develop an application for Project Reach—a contest run by the New Jersey government to see who can come up with the best application to help in the aid of the homeless.

John Papiomitis (Developer, Papio Games)

Health and Fitness

A recent trend fueled by a subcategory of *health and fitness* games known as *exergames* encourages players to get "off the couch" and engage physically as well as mentally. Many exergames can be played with traditional controllers and screens but the more advanced forms can include specialized workout equipment. Major sporting brands such as Nike often work directly with console publishers to deliver gaming experiences that target fitness and health. Smaller companies focus on a blend of hardware and software—such as Motion Fitness, which has developed the Exerbike GS to fit the emerging exergaming market.

Source Games Press.

With the ever-increasing sophistication of motion controllers, exergames have increased in popularity as well. Local gyms in some areas now offer aerobics classes that utilize *Dance Dance Revolution* playmats or take advantage of the Kinect's ability to track multiple bodies (*Dance Central 2*, shown).

Case Study:
3Start Trainer

Image courtesy of Part12 Studios.

TIME   BEST

A collaboration between Coach Ivra Warren and Part12 Studios, *3Start Trainer* was developed as a unique and useful training tool to help increase athletes' response times to a track starter pistol. The app was designed for track athletes; each race has a unique graphic background to help the athlete get into the frame of mind of being in that position on a track. The app simulates an environment where you can hear a background audience and a voice that says, "Runners take your marks, set, BANG" spaced out in random intervals to keep the runner guessing. An athlete who is doing live training should wear an iPhone or iPod touch armband. When the BANG of the gun is heard through the earbuds of the athlete, the accelerometer measures the time it takes for a runner's arm to tilt a full 90 degrees. The app measures this reaction time—allowing athletes to gauge current reaction times and strive for shorter times. GameSalad Creator's access to the accelerometer and straight-forward development process allows both fast responsive measurements of a runner's reaction time and also a text-to-voice system for runners who keep the device strapped to their arms—saving them the trouble of having to look at their arms each time they complete a fully dedicated sprint from the starting blocks.

Caleb Garner (Game Producer, Part12 Studios)

Health games (also known as *games for health*) differ from exergames in that they are designed for a range of medically therapeutic purposes. These games may be used for psychological therapy and diagnosis, physical therapy, and other services associated with medicine and healthcare. While the medical benefits for many of these games may be incidental to their original entertainment purpose, gameplay elements are being studied and quantified in an effort to develop serious games that might help to improve brain function beyond the capabilities of more conventional methods.

Understanding where your serious game fits into these styles will help narrow the design focus and determine the criteria used to analyze a game. For example, an advergame designed to connect with an audience will be deemed successful by a different set of criteria than an educational game designed to teach multiplication to 10-year-olds.

Source Games Press.

Source HopeLab Foundation.

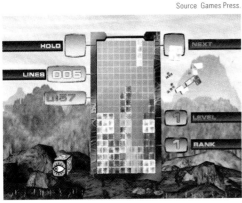

Commercial games requiring cognitive focus can have a surprisingly broad range of therapeutic applications; the *Tetris* franchise (*Tetris Worlds*, left) has been found to help alleviate symptoms of post-traumatic stress disorder in recovering military personnel. *Re-Mission* (right), a non-commercial game, provides emotional therapy for cancer patients; it allows players to pilot a nanobot traveling through bodies of fictional cancer patients—destroying cancer cells, battling bacterial infections, and managing side effects associated with cancer and cancer treatment.

Gamification

Gamification is a system of rewards and encouragement. Not as intrusive or obvious as the branding in advergaming—nor as in-depth as a simulation—gamification is often used as support for other types of products (e.g., games, web sites, social media) and as a form of viral advertising.

Source Foursquare Labs, Inc. Image courtesy of Jeannie Novak.

Source GetGlue. Image courtesy of Jeannie Novak.

Services such as Foursquare (left) and GetGlue (right) have used gamification to make repetitive tasks entertaining by including reward systems in exchange for check-ins (at locations and entertainment media, respectively).

Substance Over Style

Some serious games—particularly those developed for in-house training purposes—lack visual polish compared to commercial releases. However, the gameplay is often more refined.

Learning

It seems simple enough to develop a serious game. After all, we have all played games that taught us something—and some argue that *all* games teach, even if by accident. You might have learned how to: spell "supercalifragilisticexpialidocious"; bake chocolate cookies; or determine the average number of bees that can be found in an underground nest. The information learned may not always consist of external, real-world facts and figures—but having it at your fingertips at the right moment was a crucial part of playing the game. Therefore, how hard can it be to swap in boring history factoids or number puzzles for the player to memorize instead? Surprisingly hard—as it turns out!

Image courtesy of GameSalad®.

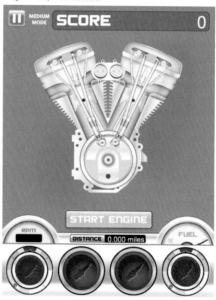

Many serious games such as *Popular Mechanics: Be the Spark* introduce a new element of information and require the player to use it immediately. By walking the player through the use of the item, memorization is improved.

The current crop of young players has, for the most part, never known a world without some sort of digital input. Whether in traditional broadcast media (e.g., cable, network television) or "interactive" content (e.g., online, mobile), an established learning pattern of serious content design needs to be taken into consideration. Several features associated with digital learning—put forth by Rockwell and Kee (*GameStudies*), Futurelab, and Adobe—include the following:

1. Digital learners tend to *process information quickly from multiple sources.* A player can understand a blend of spoken, iconic, and written instruction quickly and easily—with the different elements complementing rather than conflicting with one another.

2. *Sounds, video, and images are processed before text.* We are already seeing this being incorporated into existing social/mobile game design—where sounds and icons replace instructional and informational text.

3. Digital learners are capable of *parallel processing and "multitasking."* This is not "true" multitasking (the ability to focus on multiple elements simultaneously), but rather the ability to quickly switch focus between several tasks and needs.

4. *Information needs to be immediately relevant* for stronger retention. Instruction needs to be given and then immediately applied. This is put to good use in many casual games where players' hands are held through the tutorial. They are given a task and asked to execute it immediately—without any detriment to their scoring or status in game.

5. A varying *system of rewards* is needed. Players need to know how they are doing and whether the information they are applying is correct via immediate feedback or reward systems. These do not necessarily have to be significant resources on the part of the game—but badges, congratulatory screens, and other incentives work well to motivate players.

6. *Learners can adapt to changing scenarios.* Endless repetition is just what serious games are trying to avoid. Don't be afraid to add another task or decrease the time required for it to be successfully executed. Players expect scalable difficulty levels and will rise to the challenge.

Not all of these elements will be a good fit for the type of serious game you're interested in building. (For example, a health game utilizing repetitious puzzle elements might not be a good fit for the collection of information from multiple sources.) However, careful consideration of teachable moments in your game will allow you to build a stronger and more easily codified product.

Check the Box

A key component to serious games is the ability to record and track improvements in specific areas of learning. Being able to show how the game is affecting behavior and demonstrating the learning through *assessment* is necessary to prove the efficacy of a game.

Markets

Serious games comprise a rapidly growing market. Games with non-entertainment purposes are created and utilized by a broad range of industries—including education, healthcare, and even multinational corporations such as McDonald's. Different industries have distinct uses and designs depending on how the games are used (e.g., job training, diagnosis) and how the results need to be measured.

Sector	Advergames	Educational	Simulation	Persuasive	Exergames	Health
Government	Political	Public Awareness	Economic Simulations	Public Awareness	Health & Welfare	Emergency Response
Military	Recruitment	Education & Training	Deployment Simulations	Cultural Training	Rehab	Therapy & Wellness
Health	Awareness Campaigns	Therapy & Management	Therapy	Patient Awareness	Therapy & Rehab	General Health & Wellness
Marketing	Brand Awareness	Product Information	Immersive Games	Brand Preference	Third-Party Sales	Sales & Distribution
Education	Social Issues	Learning	Mathematic & Historical	Current Issues	Student Wellness	Student Wellness
Corporate	Customer Education	Certification	Strategic Planning	Employee Education	Employee Health	Employee Health
Industry	Sales & Recruiting	Workforce Education	Process & Optimization	Process Adoption	Health & Rehab	Health & Rehab

Different types of serious games are well-suited to certain industries and topics. This table lists some of the more common game types and associated industries.

Not all game styles will be a good fit for all serious situations. As you consider features designed to drive the development of your game concept, you will be able to find a fit between the needs of the game and the styles of gameplay suited for different types of information.

::::: Tutorial: Tracking Progress

Kimberly Unger (Chief Executive Officer, Bushi-go, Inc.)

Tracking progress is essential in many types of serious games. Whether recording the number of tutorials a player has completed, use players' progress to deliver in-game rewards, or even deliver external game rewards (e.g., coupons for products associated with advergames), it's important to include a way to keep track of what a player has accomplished.

Referring to the *Pachinko Madness* game that we have been using in other tutorials in this book, let's take a look at the steps needed to use Windows Creator's Tables to keep track of your players' progress and to pop up a reward icon at the end of the level. In this case, we will build a simple, writeable table that will record whether or not a player has completed an action. There are other ways to do this through the game attributes, but this will allow you to easily access the table information through all levels of your game.

1. Open up your game-in-progress and create a new table by clicking on the "Tables" tab. Set the size of this table to three columns wide and five rows tall. This can be modified for your own project, but let's keep it simple for the purposes of this tutorial.

Image courtesy of GameSalad® and Kimberly Unger.

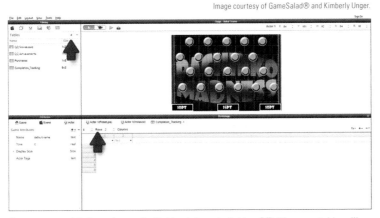

Create your table by going to the Tables tab and clicking ➕ . The new table will appear in the Backstage area (Windows Creator).

2. Set your first column type to "Text." You'll add the names of your different rewards here to easily keep track of them.

3. Set your second and third column types to "Boolean," which gives you a simple checkbox. If unchecked, the answer is "no"; if checked, the answer is "yes."

4. Fill in your reward names. These don't have to be names people will see but are there to help you keep track of what you are doing. However, if you will be working with in-game text (generated by the game rather than having a pre-made image), you can call these names when the reward is given to the player—so having "player-friendly" names is certainly an option.

Image courtesy of GameSalad® and Kimberly Unger.

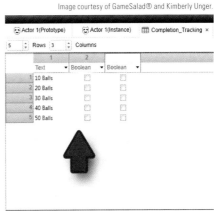

The names in the first column are up to you. We will be able to call this data—so if you want to use "in-game" names the player will see, that is an option.

5. Now that the table is set up, you'll need to make an exact copy that will be kept as a backup. Since you're working with writeable tables, there is always the possibility that something will glitch (a slim possibility in this tutorial) but a more complex table results in more chances for something to go awry. Create a second table that duplicates the first.

Image courtesy of GameSalad® and Kimberly Unger.

Create a new rule attached to the object that will trigger the change in the table. For this tutorial, the change will be triggered when the PIP_01 ball hits the bucket—but for game design purposes, tie it more directly to your game's rewards.

6. To add a change to your Table, select the object that will trigger a change in the table's value. In this tutorial, we want the table value to change when the ball that drops (PIP_01) hits the 10-point bucket at the bottom of the screen. Set the rule to "when ALL of the following are happening" and place the "Change Table Value" Attribute under the "do" section of the Rule.

7. The next step is to ask the game to check the table at the appropriate time, to see if the value we want has been filled in. First, go to "Scene: Attributes" and create a new Attribute called "Level 01."

8. Create an "empty" Actor (one without an image) and place it in the scene. Be sure to uncheck the "Movement" Attribute under Physics; just because this Actor doesn't have an image doesn't mean it is unaffected by physics.

9. Double-click the Actor to open the Backstage (in Windows Creator), and click the lock to add Behaviors and Rules to this Actor.

10. Add the "Constrain Attribute" Behavior to the Actor. Set the constrain attribute box to "scene.Level01" (the new scene attribute you just created) to tableCellValue(table,col,row)—where "table" is the name of your Table, "col" is the column number, and "row" is the row number of the cell you want to copy. This will constantly update our new "Level 01" Attribute with the value found in the table.

11. Add a Rule to your Actor. Set your first line to "When *All* of the following are happening." This will allow you to set multiple Attribute checks. (This tutorial only does one check, but you can set up as many as you need.)

You can set as many requirements as you need under the Rule. For this tutorial, we only instructed the game to check to see if scene.Level01 hits 0 or higher, but you could have it check a whole list of Attributes if necessary before it executes the Behaviors listed under "do."

12. Drag the "Attribute" Condition into your Rule. Set the "if" box to scene. Level01 and note that a new pair of boxes pops up: a dropdown box with an "=" and a new expression box. In the expression box, choose your value. (For this example, we set the value to "0" to match the "0" value in the Table—just to test the tutorial.)

13. Under "do" in your Rule, place the "Spawn" Behavior. This will spawn the object of your choice in the location of your choice. You could use this to spawn a medal to reflect an achievement ("Congratulations, you finished all 5 tasks"), to open a new scene, or access a Web URL to receive a printable certificate.

Backup Plan

It is important to note that any changes that are made to a Table are permanent—and even restarting the game will not change them back to their default values. This is the reason you should create a backup copy of your original Table. Building a "reset" button into the game's menu that will copy the backup table's values into the current table is a painless way to ensure that players can get the game back to its default state.

Design

Serious design is no less serious than formal entertainment-based game design. Rather than simply adding algebraic equations to a re-skin of *Monster Drop*, you're developing a product that is going to have a clear and well-defined goal. After playing your game, the player should come away with useable information and experience; how well your game delivers that end result will determine your product's success.

1. *What skills will be taught?* Determine the skills that your game should teach—such as cognitive (e.g., critical thinking, memory), psychomotor (e.g., timing, accuracy), or affective (e.g., identification, understanding differing points of view). Breaking down this first design component will help you to assess whether or not your game is accomplishing its primary goals.

2. *What type of content will be included?* Determine what the player needs to learn—such as facts (e.g., elements in the periodic table, names of all the countries of the world), procedures (e.g., following a recipe, understanding a chemical process), and concepts (e.g., deductive reasoning, logic, principles, rules). Concepts might better apply to advergames because their aim is to persuade—whereas procedures might be a better fit for exergames, which focus on elements such as physical technique and feedback.

3. *What is the game's outcome?* Determine the game's goal—such as memorization (e.g., vocabulary words in a new language highest grossing films), categorization (e.g, differentiate between a mouse and a rat), identification, analysis, or procedural knowledge (e.g., driving a stick-shift automobile).

4. *What gameplay elements will your game require?* This is where answering the first three questions comes into play, and where entertainment-oriented game design has some crucial effect. Examples of common elements in serious games include:

    ■ *Breakdown of information.* Are you delivering your information incrementally or presenting it to the player in one large piece?

    ■ *Linear instruction.* Can the player jump around to learn things or do the elements need to be learned in strict order?

    ■ *Length of play sessions.* Do you need to design for short attention spans? Can players pop in and out of the game at will or do they need to sit and play for an extended time?

    ■ *Support and scaffolding.* How will your game help the player as they learn what they need to know?

- *Leveling information.* Do elements the player learned in earlier levels apply and be reinforced in later levels?

- *Rewards systems.* While studies in training have shown that intermittent rewards work better than consistent rewards (the pigeon will get a pellet every 3-5 times it pushes the level, as opposed to every time), serious games illustrate that human players can respond very effectively to consistent, predictable rewards.

5. *Does the player have a chance to review?* Depending on the goal of your game, you may want to consider a way for the player to review and reaffirm the essential game elements. This can apply even to advergames, where your goal might simply be trying to achieve a higher level or brand recognition.

6. *Can players measure their progress?* Is it possible to measure progress within the game itself *and* after it game is over? Showing players what they have learned and how they have progressed can be done through different elements by building it into the reward structure.

Many commonly available serious games tend to fall into the "educational games" category. Browsing through app stores for iOS, Mac, Android, or Windows, you will find dozens of variations on learning the alphabet, multiplication tables, or other basic preschool and elementary school facts that are traditionally taught with flash cards or some other form of rote memorization. However, serious games go far beyond this concept—and their design is more involved than in most mid-level titles. One of the more difficult aspects to achieve in serious games is assessment—and a significant amount of time should be spent testing it.

Image courtesy of Bharat Battu.

In educational games such as *Bartley Does Boston*, the player controls Bartley—who encounters different iconic landmarks in the Public Garden of Boston as he progresses through the level. Reaching a landmark provides the player with a real-world snapshot of the object and some educational facts delivered via audio.

Down the Rabbit Hole . . .

Serious games can get incredibly complex—sometimes requiring approval from a number of subject matter experts and other specialists. If their input is required, these individuals should be brought into the process as early as possible to help avoid design issues further down the line.

Distribution

Distribution of serious games is handled a differently than other titles. Most projects are require an extensive amount of pre-production in the form of detailed game design documentation, content analysis—and sometimes even curriculum development. Serious games that are *proprietary* (used within a company or an organization for training purposes) are usually created on a contract basis—with payment received as milestones are passed, rather than building the game upfront and recouping costs through public sales.

External

There are some types of *external* serious games that provide a revenue stream outside of the initial development cost. Advergames are paid for on a project basis by advertisers. While the end goal is to sell to Internet users, the developer does not normally receive a cut from clicks or social media shares. The sole goal of an advergame is to promote a brand by making a product (or related intellectual property) playable. School-related distribution for serious games is on the rise. A number of game-based learning web sites are now providing materials that tie directly into elementary school level curricula. The games on sites such as *Everyday Math Online* are used to provide supplemental practice for the basic lessons taught in some schools. Children are provided with account information through their teachers and are directed to the appropriate games. Large-scale recruitment games such as the *America's Army* franchise are also made available online with an emphasis on maximizing distribution among "hardcore" gamers. (It should be noted that *America's Army* is a rare case in that its popularity has increased based on the quality and the content of the game itself—both elements of which overshadow the PR/recruitment aims of the product in the eyes of many players.)

Internal

Games designed for *internal* use only are often a bit rougher in look and feel than games released to the public. These games are only rarely available online; instead, they come pre-installed on company computers or distributed to employees via CD/DVD-ROMs or portable flash drives. In many cases, these games can only be accessed at corporate training center—where the gameplay can be monitored and the players observed to ensure they're not "gaming" the system in any form (pun intended). These games are often followed up with written or web-based tests—and the scores are used to determine how well or poorly the game works to train/educate the employee. Medical games designed for therapy or rehabilitation can often only be obtained through a prescription—or they can only be utilized in a setting where a nurse or licensed physical or psychological therapist is present.

Image courtesy of US Army.

Image courtesy of US Army.

Games used for recruitment or advertising (*America's Army*, left) are often made widely available on the web—utilizing web portals and third-party distributors such as Steam to allow players to access them from any Internet-enabled location. In *Adaptive Thinking & Leadership* (right)—an internal simulation built on the *America's Army* engine—two Special Forces soldiers negotiate with a host national.

A Not-So-Serious Future?

Serious games are already changing the way education and training are distributed at an international level. The shortage of teachers is not just a problem in schools and colleges; it crosses into all areas of instruction. Finding qualified people—whether to train employees how to work with automated equipment, instruct children in reading and spelling, or demonstrate how to cook six pieces of bacon for a breakfast meal—is a problem that strikes everywhere. Any subject that can be taught through a game will find a way into that format simply because the demand for training is so high in comparison to the number of qualified personnel available. As the natural learning aspects of gameplay prove to be successful, serious games will be able to pull back a bit on the obvious lessons, tests, codification, and matching to a curriculum—and provide more "covert" or "stealth" learning. The message associated with advergames and persuasive games can be delivered with more subtlety—and players will be drawn in increasing numbers to games that are based around a social idea or a brand. The serious game sector is the sleeping giant of game development, and the market is ubiquitous. For best results, experts in game design and in the content's subject matter should work together to ensure the most effective use of the medium. Ideally, subject matter experts who also understand game design will be key members of the development team. As proof of game-based and experiential learning's effectiveness continues to emerge, the notion of games as being *just* for fun will become a thing of the past.

Additional material based on these exercises and chapter topics is available as part of the Instructor Resources package.

:::CHAPTER REVIEW EXERCISES:::

1. Choose a serious game sector and classification. Create a short summary of an original serious game that fits your chosen category, and describe the ultimate goal of your game.

2. How do you plan on testing the results of your game? Will there be a quiz at the end or will you track progress through the entire game?

3. How will new information be presented in your game? Avoid rote memorization and other overt methods.

4. How will your rewards system encourage the player to progress? What kinds of rewards do you plan to offer?

5. How will your serious game be distributed? Will you develop games on spec and try to find them a home (perhaps for both industry and consumer markets), or will you develop them for internal use by corporations or training centers?

6. How do you plan to test the effectiveness of your game? What criteria will you use to ensure that the outcomes are being met?

7. Choose three serious game categories and discuss their similarities and differences.

Appendix
Basic Terms & Tutorials

Kimberly Unger (Chief Executive Officer, Bushi-go, Inc.)

Topics

- Projects
- Library/Inspector (Scenes, Layers, Actors, Media/Media Library, Behaviors, Tables)
- Attributes
- Stage
- Backstage/Actor Editor

::

GameSalad Creator allows developers to create games without having to know how to program. It's possible for developers to import their own original art, use it to create Actors, and then assign Behaviors and Attributes to those Actors to generate gameplay—all without having to understand the difference between an object and a function. With mobile and indie game development in full swing, there has never been a better time to take the plunge and create your first project. GameSalad Creator simplifies the process of developing games for multiple desktop (Windows and Mac) and mobile (iOS and Android) platforms and operating systems—ensuring that your game reaches a large majority of non-console players worldwide. Each piece of software requires some basic rules and information that often needs to be accessed numerous times—but all this can be difficult to categorize into one area or another. It's like learning the basic controls in the first level of a game (such as how to change weapons, create a portal, and get a longer-lasting jump): If you put the game away for a while, you can always come back for a refresher course—a quick tour through the basics to help you get back up to speed.

Projects

Projects include sets of files and folders that are created by the software to keep all related assets together in the same place. As assets are imported, copies are placed into the appropriate Project folders so that they can be easily accessed when needed. If any folder or its contents is deleted or modified, you run the risk of temporarily breaking your game. (Although this is fixable, it's troublesome!)

Image courtesy of GameSalad®.

GameSalad Creator automatically creates a set of files and folders associated with a project's assets (Windows Creator, shown). These files don't need to be accessed directly until you archive your Project after completion.

A great way to learn how a software platform or engine works is to look at pre-built games that have already been created using it. Fortunately, not only does GameSalad provide many example templates to choose from, the community at large is also fairly generous when it comes to sharing works in progress that can be used by others. However, keep in mind that these are often the basic elements of a game—so simply adding new art assets won't necessarily give you a polished product. When Mac Creator is opened, it reveals a number of icons associated with templates that can be used to begin a project. Focus on templates that are central to your type of project. (If you are working with mobile devices, for example, find templates that are built for iOS or Android.)

The first option, "My Great Project," is blank—but it is scaled to fit a mobile device, rather than a desktop screen. Others are simple pre-built templates that incorporate games in many different genres and gameplay styles (e.g., *Pong*, *Breakout*, *Space Invaders*—and even a template showing how to add a reminder to rate a game). Instead of starting from scratch, use an existing template that incorporates a genre or gameplay style associated with the game you want to create. It will be necessary to replace the graphics and otherwise modify the template to make it your own, but a template will give you a head start.

Mac Creator

Unlike a Windows program (where all of the needed content is contained in a single window), Mac Creator handles the entire screen as a window; the menu bar is at the top, and there are several smaller popup panels or windows onscreen at any given point in time.

Image courtesy of GameSalad®.

In order to create a wholly new Project in Mac Creator—where you may determine the delivery platform and screen sizes from the outset—it's necessary to either choose "Blank Project" from the initial window or use the File menu button at the top of the screen.

After opening Creator by double-clicking the icon, you will see the Dashboard—the first window that pops up in the center of your screen; it contains a number of pre-fabricated templates and starting points, along with a list of projects you are already working on (if applicable). From here, you can choose to open a project (including a free or paid template), visit the Marketplace, or access links to GameSalad's knowledge base. In order to create a wholly new project—and determine parameters such as delivery platforms and screen size/ratio—choose either "Blank Project" from the window in the center or go to the "File" menu in the upper left hand corner of your screen.

The next window that opens is the Project window; it's here that you have the chance to set the proper resolution for your new Project. Note that resolution choices are arranged by platform rather than pixels. When planning on building a project that is to be distributed on iPad or iPhone, for example, choose the appropriate resolutions here. (These can be changed later on.) To return to the Project window at any time, click the "Home" icon on the upper left hand corner of the window.

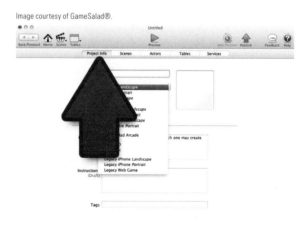

Image courtesy of GameSalad®.

The Project Window in Mac Creator is available at all times through the "Home" icon on the top left of the screen. From here, you can adjust the game's resolution and get an outline of you're your game's Scenes, Actors, and other resources.

If you go back to the Project screen to change the resolution and orientation of your game (e.g., from iPhone horizontal to Kindle horizontal), Creator will do its best to keep your in-game objects and Actors in their proper places—but in all likelihood, it will be necessary to go back and make changes to better suit the new format. Once you have made resolution and orientation selections, access the Scenes tab in the Project window—and you'll find that the first Scene is already listed. Double-click on the Scene to open it up for editing, and you are ready to begin.

Windows Creator

Windows Creator is visually designed along the same lines as most Windows software—with all relevant elements contained within a single primary window. As with Mac Creator (or any GUI driven OS), Windows Creator is opened by double-clicking the icon. This will open a brand new Project and take you straight to editing the first Scene. The initial Project automatically defaults to the legacy standard of 320 x 480, which is the same ratio and pixel depth on the original iPhone. While you can change the display size in the game Attributes, keep in mind that this will not change the camera boundaries—so your design area will be much smaller than your game's display, unless you manually adjusted the game camera to match.

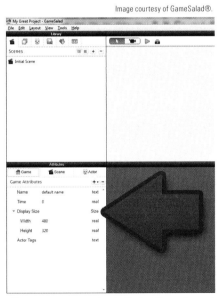

Image courtesy of GameSalad®.

Windows Creator opens up a basic Project from the outset. Sizes and ratios need to be changed manually in the game Attributes area, or a new Project should be opened up from the File menu.

Rather than adjusting the resolution and camera so they match at this stage, it is simplest to use the File menu to open a brand new Project. This will give you the opportunity to choose a resolution and make a decision about resolution independence as in Mac Creator. The display area and camera will have already been created to match—so you run less risk of having your game appear distorted or stretched.

Production Area

Creator uses a number of specific terms when it comes to defining elements that make up a game. Knowing and understanding basic terms can make navigating and learning the software a much simpler task—even if you are already well versed in other types of game production software. In both Mac and Windows Creator, you are developing your game in a central suite of windows. Each area (Library, Stage, Attributes—and Backstage [Windows Creator only]) can be resized (within limits) by dragging the edges with the mouse—much the same way most windows can be resized on both Mac and Windows operating systems. Note: When initially opening Windows Creator, the Backstage area (in the lower right portion) may not be visible; it will appear when after opening an Actor for editing, or when you click on the "Open Backstage" icon (📷)—found just above the Stage to the left.

Image courtesy of GameSalad®. Image courtesy of GameSalad®.

The main production area is broken into four sections: Library, Stage, Attributes, and Backstage (Windows Creator, left); or Inspector, Scene Editor, Library, and Actor Editor (Mac Creator, right).

Library/Inspector

The *Library* (Windows) or *Inspector* (Mac) window can be found in the top left section of the production area. This is where assets may be imported, found, or used. In the Windows version, there are six tabs (in order from left): Scenes, Layers, Actors, Media, Behaviors, and Tables. In the Mac version, there are two buttons: Scene (which provides access to scene-level Attributes and Layers) and Game (which provides access to game-level Attributes and Layers). You'll notice that the Mac version displays a few less tabs than the Windows version. In order to access the remaining tabs, click the Home button and return to the Project screen.

Scenes

Scenes (under Library in Windows Creator and as an icon on the menu bar in Mac Creator) will display a listing of all Scenes that have been created for this game. Using Scenes is an easy way to break your game into different levels. (You might have one Scene for your title screen and menu, a second Scene for your sound and social media options, a third Scene for your tutorial or instructions, etc.) It's a good idea to initially set up all the anticipated Scenes. To add blank Scenes (starting with "Initial Scene"), click on ✚ at the top of the Scenes screen (Windows) or bottom left (Mac).

Each Scene represents a level or a piece of the game. For example, you may notice that many games have a Scene that handles title image and main menu, a second Scene for the first game level, another Scene for the second game level, etc. Scenes can be duplicated, which is useful when there are several levels with identical assets but distinct layouts. Rather than starting from scratch every time, set up the first Scene, duplicate it as needed, and then rearrange the assets.

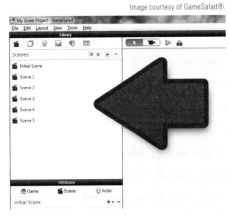

Image courtesy of GameSalad®.

Double-clicking on any Scene accessed through the Scenes tab will open it up in the "Scene" panel on the right.

Double-clicking on a Scene will cause it to open up on the Stage to the right. Once there, everything you do to the Scene will be saved within that Scene only; changes to one Scene will not propagate across all the Scenes in your game. If there are a handful of Scenes that will be similar in some way (e.g., user interface), you can save development time by working on the similar elements first in a single Scene—and then copying that Scene over and over again to serve as a starting point for more.

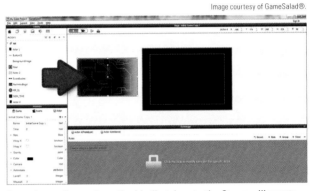

Image courtesy of GameSalad®.

Dragging an image from the Media tab onto the Stage will create an Actor under the Actor tab in the Library to the left.

In *Pachinko Madness*, the demo game discussed throughout this book, the exact same background image and a 10PT "bucket" are used in the first five levels. To save some work, it's a good idea to place the background image and bucket in the first Scene and then make several copies to work from. Using *Pachinko Madness* as a reference, here are the steps that are taken to accomplish this:

1. Double-click on "Initial Scene" under the Scenes tab so that it opens up. Then choose one of your images (in our case, a black/white circuit pattern) to use as a background and drag it over to the Stage area to the immediate right.

2. Drag the 10PT bucket Image or Actor to the Stage.

3. Arrange the Scene as it should appear in the game.

4. Return to the Library and select the Scenes tab.

5. Select "Initial Scene" and then select "Edit/Copy" from the menu bar at the top. Finally, select "Edit/Paste" to create an exact copy of your existing Scene.

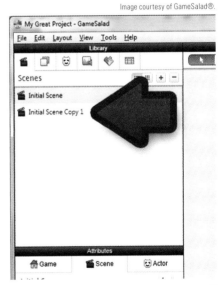

Image courtesy of GameSalad®.

Selecting Edit/Copy followed by Edit/Paste will make an exact copy of the selected Scene and will add it to the list.

Layers

Layers allows a game to be broken into background, middle ground, foreground, user interface—and any number of other Layers you might choose to work with. Layers allow different game elements to be separated so they are easier to work with. For example, it's possible to place a static, non-animated background image on the "Background" Layer and the user interface on the "Foreground" Layer.

Creating a layer is fairly simple: On the upper right corner of the Layer tab (Windows) or the bottom corner (Mac), you will see ⊞ and ⊟ buttons. The ⊞ adds a new Layer to the list, and the ⊟ removes the selected Layer. There are also a few useful elements within the Layer tab that should be addressed:

Changing the order of the Layers can be accomplished through simple "drag and drop." However, it's also possible to use the up/down arrow buttons to move the selected Layer up and down in the queue (which could come in handy if you're working on a laptop using a touchpad, for example). Next to any given Layer, there's a "Scrollable" checkbox. When designing a side-scrolling game, this box needs to be checked; it will set up a "looping" background so that you only need a single background image, which will be replicated over and over again as your character runs across the screen. This provides the seamless rolling background seen not only in side-scrolling games such as *Canabalt* but in chase scenes in cartoons such as *Scooby-Doo!*

Actors

You will probably create more *Actors* than anything else in your game design. They will make up your obstacles, your characters, your weapons, your projectiles, and even those little puffy clouds. Creating an Actor—the backbone of game development in Creator—is a fairly simple task:

1. Find the Actor tab in the Library (Windows Creator) or Inspector (Mac Creator) window on the upper left. Click ⊞ in the upper right corner of the Library tab to create a new Actor, which will be empty and invisible—just a container into which you may place all of your components. The Actor is created at a default size of 120 x 120 pixels (Windows Creator) or 100 x 100 pixels (Mac Creator) and is ready for images and Behaviors to be added to it.

2. To make adjustments to your new Actor, select it and then move down to the Attributes window. The third (Actor) tab will display all the parameters for your new Actor.

3. To add an image to your Actor, you have the option of either dragging it into place from the Media tab in the Library accessing the drop-down menu button next to "Image." All images in your Library will appear here.

4. Add a collision shape to your Actor by going down to the "Physics" Attribute under the Attributes tab. Here you can choose the shape best suited to your gameplay. Consider whether this particular object will work best with a circle or a square (or a rectangle or an oval), for example. The collision shape tells the game roughly where your object is so that other objects—and the ground or walls—can collide with it.

5. Set the movability of the Actor in the Scene. If the Actor will be static (such as a bush or rock), uncheck the "moveable" checkbox under Attributes. If the Actor will be moveable, leave the checkbox on. (Note that the default state for this box is checked.)

6. At this point, you have a basic, functional Actor that will react to collisions and physics (such as gravity) in your Scene. In order to use this Actor, simply drag it from the Actor Library onto the Stage to the right.

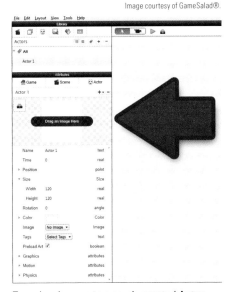

Image courtesy of GameSalad®.

To make changes to a newly created Actor, first select the Actor, then drop down to the Attributes window. Select the Actor tab, and you will be given a list of options to change. Keep in mind that an Actor is created at a default size at 120 x 120; after adding an image, be sure to adjust the size to fit.

Media/Media Library

Media (Windows Creator) or *Media Library* (Mac Creator) includes the sound and art that are imported and stored. In Windows Creator, imported sound and art assets may be found under the Media tab on the upper left. In Mac Creator, all Behaviors, Images, and Sounds are collected under separate tabs in the Media Library on the bottom left of the screen. When you begin to assemble the assets for your game, you will find that almost everything is tied to Media. These elements need to be loaded through the Images tab before they can be assigned to the Actors—and they're the bits and pieces you will use to build your Actors, such as set dressing or costumes. Most of your Media will be created in another program such as GIMP or SoundForge, and then imported into Creator. You can also purchase sets of assets from the Creator Marketplace to help enhance your game.

Sprite

Sprites (small, moveable images used within a game) may be animated (as in the case of a character or enemy) or may simply be affected by the programming (falling leaves or rocks). These sprites are invariably painted on a transparent background—allowing them to be used anywhere they are applicable within the game. Creator will automatically mask any image that has been saved out with transparency. The most efficient format is an indexed .png. Be sure to check the "transparency" box when compressing it in Photoshop.

Creator accepts a broad range of flattened images—from .jpg to .png files. In order to save space, compress the images as small as possible. Save high-color depth images for key places such as title screens and backgrounds—and compress anything else down to as few colors as possible.

Imported media files, both image and sound files, are held under the Media tab in the Library (Windows Creator, shown).

Audio

Audio files may be used for background music and sound effects. The .m4a format, which can be played on most smartphones, might seem like the obvious choice. However, these files lose quality due to the way they are compressed; they may also not be the best choice for looping audio, since the format adds empty space at the start and end that could cause it to loop incorrectly. Many indie game studios prefer the open-source .ogg format. Audio assets can be memory-intensive, but they can also have the biggest effect on players—letting them know when they have failed or succeeded—and when they need to fight or flee. Mac Creator handles many of the most popular types of sound files—from the open-source .ogg to the tried and true .wav. However, files must be converted to .ogg, .m4a, or .wav before they can be imported by Windows Creator.

Importing

The two most common forms of media for import will be images and sounds. Both will need to be created in external programs. Most popular sound or image editing tools provide the ability to export into formats that Creator can use.

1. Under the Library/Media tab, click on ⊞ —located on the top right corner (Windows Creator) or bottom left corner (Mac Creator) of the Library window. This will open up a "Select File" dialogue box where you can browse to find the files you wish to import.

2. Select your file. For image files, Creator supports .png, .jpg, .jpeg, .gif, .wdp, and .tiff file formats. If you have built transparency or masking into your image file, Creator will account for this automatically on import.

Image courtesy of GameSalad® and Kimberly Unger.

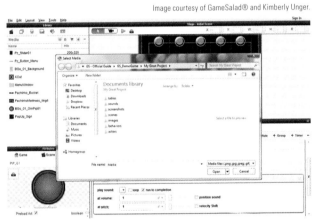

All Media files (sound, images or sequential images) are imported through the Media tab in the Creator Library window (Windows Creator, shown). Creator recognizes a variety of the most common formats for both images and sound.

3. If you are importing a sound file, note that Creator will recognize and import .ogg, .m4a, and .wmv. (Windows version).

4. If you are importing a sequence of files (e.g., a series of individual frames of a character running or jumping), name those files in sequence (e.g. Bob001.png, Bob002.png, Bob003.png, etc.). After import, having the files named sequentially will prove to be a valuable tool in setting up your animations.

Behaviors

GameSalad provides a comprehensive package of tools for developers. These tools or *Behaviors* can all be found under the Behaviors tab on the upper left (Windows Creator) or lower left (Mac Creator) of the screen. When a game object needs to interact with the player and the game world (even if it is as simple a command as telling it to bounce up and down once every five seconds), these Behaviors act as clear cut instructions for the Actor to follow.

Image courtesy of GameSalad®.

The Behavior tab holds all the individual pieces of instructions that convey what should be done with the Actors during the game (Windows Creator shown).

For the more experienced user, Creator also incorporates the ability to assemble and group commonly used Attributes into custom Behaviors—adding them under the Custom tab in the browser. This provides a small team with even greater flexibility in game design and execution, and it allows for a higher level of customization that can set a game apart from the rest of the pack.

Code pieces are dragged and dropped into the object properties from the Behaviors browser to create a set of commands for it to follow when the game is run. Creator does an excellent job of laying this out graphically and working in a very straightforward conditional ("when-then") format to allow designers of all skill levels access to complex Behavior sequences.

To add a Behavior to an Actor in Windows Creator: Double-click on an Actor, and then check the tabs at the top of the Backstage window. Be sure to add Behaviors to the Actor designated as "Prototype"—which is the original version of the Actor; any changes you make to the Prototype will show up in all copies of the Actor—even those you are already using in the game.

1. Double-click on any Actor under the Library. This should open up the Prototype in the Backstage window on the bottom right side of Creator.

2. Click on the "Rule" button at the top of the Backstage; this will set up a "when-then" condition (i.e., WHEN something is happening, THEN do this thing). This will add a Rule box to the Prototype.

3. Choose your Behavior, Condition, or Attribute from under the Behaviors tab and drag it into the newly added Rule. In this case, let's add sound to the Actor so it plays a noise when it collides with another Actor. First, choose the Condition "Collision" from under the Behaviors tab and drag it into the Rule box indicating "type or drag in a condition."

4. Near "actor overlaps or collides with actor of type," use the drop-down menu to find the Actor with which it should collide.

5. Find the "Play Sound" Attribute under the Behaviors tab and drag it onto the "do" dropdown in our Rule. This Rule reads: "WHEN the Actor Collides, THEN Play Sound."

Image courtesy of GameSalad® and Kimberly Unger.   Image courtesy of GameSalad®.

After double-clicking on an Actor in the Library, the Actor will automatically open up in the Backstage window of Creator (Windows Creator, left) or the Actor Editor (Mac Creator, right).

Tables

Tables are created and used for storing information that can be accessed by any Scene in your game. You might be keeping track of how many times a particular level has been played through—or you might use them to store clues from Level One that the player will need later to complete Level Five. You use them to allow you to cleanly save data that needs to be accessed by any Scene at any time.

Attributes

Attributes may be accessed from the bottom window on the left hand side of the screen (Windows Creator) or under the Attributes tab in the Inspector (Mac Creator). This is where the Attributes of any given Actor or game element may be modified. Under the Attributes window, there are three tabs: Game Attributes, Scene Attributes, and Actor Attributes.

Game

Game Attributes is used to change the attributes across the entire game. You can add new Attributes here (text data or number data) by clicking ⊕ in the upper right corner of the Game Attributes tab and choosing the type of Attribute to add. These Attributes can be accessed from any Scene at any time—so if there's a value that needs to be stored or changed across multiple levels, it can be stored in Game Attributes and retrieve it from any point in the game.

A common and simply way to use the Game Attributes is to set a "Tutorial Complete" Attribute. The purpose of this Attribute is to tell the game that the player has already completed the tutorial and is ready to play the game. If this Attribute is set to "no," the game will throw up a pop-up window asking whether the player wants to review the tutorial at the start of each level.

1. Access the Game Attributes tab under the Attributes window on the bottom left corner of Creator. Click ⊕ in the upper right corner.

2. Set the new Attribute as *Boolean* (a simple "yes/no" answer in the form of a checkbox—where "checked" = yes and "unchecked" = no) and name the Attribute "Tutorial Complete."

Image courtesy of GameSalad®.

3. The new Attribute will now show up in the Game Attributes list. Set it to "unchecked." This will be the starting state of the Game Attribute.

4. In order to change this Attribute, set up a Behavior that is triggered at the end of your Tutorial. This Behavior should be set to change the Game Attribute from "no" to "yes" when a certain event occurs.

New Attributes can be created to encompass the entire game, a single Scene, or a single Actor. Upon creation, you may choose the type of information needed within the Attribute—such as a text string, a number or a simple yes/no checkbox (Windows Creator, shown).

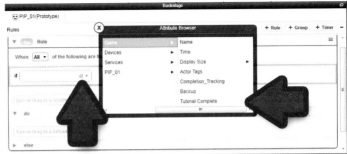

5. When building a second level, check this new Attribute to see if the box has been checked (set to "yes") by adding a Behavior that will check the Game Attribute you have created: IF the Attribute is set to yes, it will destroy the Tutorial Prompt; IF the Attribute is set to no, it will run the Tutorial prompt Actor to see if the player wants to try the tutorial first.

Attributes affecting the entire game (or that will be accessed throughout) can be created and set in Game Attributes.

Scene

Scene Attributes is used to change the Attributes of a selected Scene. For example, you might set the gravity in your first Scene to pull a balloon downward, then set the gravity in your second Scene to pull the balloon upward. Note: Changes made here will affect the selected Scene only and will not affect the rest of the game.

Actor

The majority of development time will most likely be spent within the *Actor Attributes* area. Under this tab, you can change the Attributes of the selected Actor—making it transparent, changing its color, setting it so that it's always in motion, or "locking" it so that it cannot ever be moved at all. This is where you make an Actor larger or smaller, rectangular or square—or to tell the game whether an Actor's collision shape is a circle or if it is heavier than a box of horseshoes.

Stage

The *Stage* is found in the top right section of the production area; it represents the "stage" upon which your game will be played, and where you will drag and drop your Actors—placing them in their starting positions and setting up the gameplay to follow.

Backstage/Actor Editor

The *Backstage* is found in the bottom right section of the production area in Windows Creator. This is where you will be spending time placing Behaviors for the selected Actor and laying out instructions that tell it what to do—and when to do it. In Mac Creator, this section opens up as a completely separate *Actor Editor* window. In both cases, the quickest way to get to the editing area is to double-click on any Actor.

Resources

There's a wealth of information on game development and related topics discussed in this book. Here is just a sample list of books, news sites, organizations, and events you should definitely explore!

Communities, Directories & Libraries

Android Developers developer.android.com

Android Game Programming Tutorial (DZone) eclipse.dzone.com/articles/beginning-android-game

APM Music   www.apmmusic.com

Apple Developers   developer.apple.com

ArtBarf.com   www.artbarf.com

Betawatcher.com   www.betawatcher.com

Beyond3D   www.beyond3d.com

Bitmob.com   www.bitmob.com

CG Society   www.cgtalk.com

CG Textures   www.cgtextures.com

David Janes' Code Weblog code.davidjanes.com/blog/2009/11/20/how-to-use-xcode-for-android-projects

Design Instruct   www.designinstruct.com

Destructoid   www.destructoid.com

DevMaster.net   www.devmaster.net

DevShed Forum   forums.devshed.com/game-development-141

Eclipse Game Development Community www.touchofdeathforums.com/eclipse

Facebook Developers https://developers.facebook.com

Gamasutra   www.gamasutra.com

Game Audio Forum www.gameaudioforum.com

Game Audio Pro Tech Group   groups.yahoo.com/group/gameaudiopro

GameDev.net   www.gamedev.net

Game Development Search Engine www.gdse.com

GameDevMap www.gamedevmap.com

GameFAQs   www.gamefaqs.com

Game Music.com   www.gamemusic.com

Game Music Revolution (GMR) www.gmronline.com

GamesMuseum gamesmuseum.pixesthesia.com

GameSalad Cookbook cookbook.gamesalad.com

Games Tester   www.gamestester.com

Gaming (Reddit) www.reddit.com/r/gaming

GarageGames   www.garagegames.com

Giant Bomb   www.giantbomb.com

Guide to Sound Effects www.epicsound.com/sfx/

iDevGames Forum www.idevgames.com/forum

Indiegamer Forum forums.indiegamer.com

IndustryGamers www.industrygamers.com

International Dialects of English Archive (IDEA)   web.ku.edu/idea/

iOS Human Interface Guidelines developer.apple.com/library/IOs/#documentation/UserExperience/Conceptual/MobileHIG/Introduction/Introduction.html

iPhone Game Programming Tutorial (iCode[blog])   www.icodeblog.com/2009/01/15/iphone-game-programming-tutorial-part-1/

Machinima.com   www.machinima.com

Mayang's Free Texture Library www.mayang.com/textures

Microsoft Developer Network msdn.microsoft.com

mobiForge   www.mobiforge.com

MobyGames   www.mobygames.com

NeoGAF   www.neogaf.com

Nokia User Experience Library
www.developer.nokia.com/Resources/Library/
Design_and_UX

Northern Sounds
www.northernsounds.com

Overclocked Remix   www.overclocked.org

PAL Gaming Network   palgn.com.au

Professional Sound Designers Forum   psd.
freeforums.org

PS3   www.ps3.net

Sketching, wireframing & note-taking PDF templates
www.smashingmagazine.com/2010/03/29/
free-printable-sketching-wireframing-and-note-
taking-pdf-templates/

Sound Design Forum   groups.yahoo.com/group/
sound_design

Superior Web Solutions
www.superiorwebsys.com

3D Buzz   www.3dbuzz.com

3D Total   www.3dtotal.com

Tongue Twisters   www.geocities.com/Athens/8136/
tonguetwisters.html

TrueGaming (Reddit)   www.reddit.com/r/

Unity Tutorials
www.unity3d.com/support/resources/tutorials/

UX Stack Exchange   ux.stackexchange.com

VGMix   www.vgmix.com

Video Game Music Database (VGMdb)
www.vgmdb.net

Voicebank.net   www.voicebank.net

Voiceover Demos   www.compostproductions.com/
demos.html

Wii-Play   www.wii-play.com

w3schools.com   www.w3schools.com/browsers/
browsers_display.asp

Xbox.com   www.xbox.com

Xbox 360 Homebrew   www.xbox360homebrew.com

XNA Creators Club   creators.xna.com

Organizations

Able Gamers   www.ablegamers.com

Academy of Interactive Arts & Sciences (AIAS)   www.interactive.org

Academy of Machinima Arts & Sciences   www.machinima.org

Association of Computing Machinery (ACM)   www.acm.org

Audio Engineering Society (AES)   www.aes.org

Business Software Alliance (BSA)   www.bsa.org

Digital Games Research Association (DiGRA)   www.digra.org

Entertainment Software Association (ESA)   www.theesa.com

Entertainment Software Ratings Board (ESRB)   www.esrb.org

Game Audio Network Guild (GANG)   www.audiogang.org

Game Audio Technical Committee   www.aes.org/technical/ag

Interactive Audio Special Interest Group (IASIG)   www.iasig.org

International Computer Games Association (ICGA)   www.cs.unimaas.nl/icga

International Game Developers Association (IGDA)   www.igda.org

Usability Professionals Association   www.upassoc.org

News, Reviews & Research

AppAddict.net   www.appaddict.net

The APPera   www.theappera.com

Appolicious   www.appolicious.com

Ars Technica   www.arstechnica.com

Blues News   www.bluesnews.com

Buzzle.com: intelligent life on the web   www.buzzle.com/articles/history-of-video-game-consoles.html

Classic Gaming   classicgaming.gamespy.com

CNET   www.cnet.com

Computer & Video Games   www.computerandvideogames.com

Computer Games Magazine   www.cgonline.com

Curse.com   www.curse.com

Develop Magazine   www.developmag.com

Digital Playroom   www.dplay.com

DIYgamer   www.diygamer.com

Edge Online   www.edge-online.com

Electronic Gaming Monthly (EGMi)   www.egmnow.com

The Escapist   www.escapistmagazine.com

Eurogamer   www.eurogamer.net

FingerGaming   www.fingergaming.com

Game Developer Magazine   www.gdmag.com

Gamers Hell   www.gamershell.com

Game Industry News   www.gameindustry.com

GameInformer.com   www.gameinformer.com

Game-Machines.com   www.game-machines.com

GamePolitics   www.gamepolitics.com

GamePro   www.gamepro.com

GameRankings   www.gamerankings.com

Game Revolution   www.gamerevolution.com

Games.com (blog)   blog.games.com

GamesBeat (VentureBeat)   www.venturebeat.com/category/games

GameSetWatch   www.gamesetwatch.com

GamesIndustry.biz   www.gamesindustry.biz

GameSlice Weekly   www.gameslice.com

GameSpot   www.gamespot.com

Games Radar (PC Gamer)   www.gamesradar.com/pc

GameTrailers   www.gametrailers.com

Gamezebo   www.gamezebo.com

GamingAngels   www.gamingangels.com

GayGamer   www.gaygamer.net

Girl Gamer   www.girlgamer.com

IndieGames.com   www.indiegames.com

Internet Gaming Network (IGN)
    www.ign.com

Jay is Games   www.jayisgames.com

Joystiq   www.joystiq.com

Kotaku   www.kotaku.com

The Loop   www.theloopinsight.com

Mac|Life   www.maclife.com

Macworld.com   www.macworld.com

MCV   www.mcvuk.com

Metacritic   www.metacritic.com

MMOGChart.com   www.mmogchart.com

MMORPG.com   www.mmorpg.com

MPOGD.com   www.mpogd.com

MTV Multiplayer
    multiplayerblog.mtv.com

Music4Games.net   www.music4games.net

NetMarketShare
    www.netmarketshare.com

Nine Over Ten   www.nineoverten.com

148Apps   www.148apps.com

PC Gamer   www.pcgamer.com

Penny Arcade   www.penny-arcade.com

Planet Unreal   planetunreal.gamespy.com

Pocket Gamer   www.pocketgamer.co.uk

PolyCount   www.polycount.com

Recording History: The History of
    Recording Technology
    www.recording-history.org

Ripten   www.ripten.com

Rock, Paper, Shotgun
    www.rockpapershotgun.com

Shacknews   www.shacknews.com

Showfax   www.showfax.com

Slashdot   games.slashdot.org

Slide to Play   www.slidetoplay.com

Star Tech Journal
    www.startechjournal.com

Ten Ton Hammer
    www.tentonhammer.com

TouchArcade   www.toucharcade.com

TouchGen   www.touchgen.net

UnderGroundOnline (UGO)
    www.ugo.com

Unreal Technology
    www.unrealtechnology.com

Unreal Wiki   wiki.beyondunreal.com

Xbox Developer Programs
    www.xbox.com/ en-US/dev/
    contentproviders.htm

Wired Game | Life   blog.wired.com/games

WorkingGames   www.workinggames.co.uk

Events

Month	Title	Location	Site
January	Consumer Electronics Show (CES)	Las Vegas, NV	www.cesweb.org
February	DICE Summit (AIAS)	Las Vegas, NV	www.dicesummit.org
March	Game Developers Conference (GDC)	San Francisco, CA	www.gdconf.com
	Penny Arcade Expo East (PAX East)	Boston, MA	east.paxsite.com
April	Engage! Expo	San Francisco, CA	www.engagedigital.com
	LA Games Conference	Los Angeles, CA	www.lagamesconference.com
May	LOGIN Conference	Bellevue, WA	www.loginconference.com
	Games For Health	Boston, MA	www.gamesforhealth.org/index.php/conferences/
June	Electronic Entertainment Expo (E3)	Los Angeles, CA	www.e3expo.com
	Games For Change Festival	New York, NY	www.gamesforchange.org/festival/
	Game Education Summit (GES)	varies	www.gameeducationsummit.com
	Origins Game Fair	Columbus, OH	www.originsgamefair.com
July	Comic-Con	San Diego, CA	www.comic-con.com
	Casual Connect	Seattle, WA	seattle.casualconnect.org
August	SIGGRAPH	varies	www.siggraph.org
	GDC Europe	varies	www.gdceurope.com
	BlizzCon	Anaheim, CA	www.blizzcon.com
	Gen Con	Indianapolis, IN	www.gencon.com
September	Dragon*Con	Atlanta, GA	www.dragoncon.org
	NY Games Conference	New York, NY	www.nygamesconference.com
	Tokyo Game Show (TGS)	Tokyo, Japan	tgs.cesa.or.jp/english
October	MIPCOM	Cannes, France	www.mipworld.com/mipcom
	Brasil Game Show	Rio de Janeiro, Brazil	www.brasilgameshow.com.br/
	IndieCade	Los Angeles, CA	www.indiecade.com
	SIEGE (Southern Interactive Entertainment & Game Expo)	Atlanta, GA	www.siegecon.net
	FailCon	San Francisco, CA	www.failcon.com
	IGDA Leadership Forum	Los Angeles, CA	www.igda.org/leadership
	Project Bar-B-Q	Lake Buchanan, TX	www.projectbarbq.com
November	GDC Next	Los Angeles, CA	www.gdcnext.com
	Social Gaming Summit	London, UK	www.mediabistro.com/socialgamingsummit
	GDC China	Shanghai, China	www.gdcchina.com
December	Dubai World Game Expo	Dubai, UAE	www.gameexpo.ae

Adams, E. (2003). *Break into the game industry.* McGraw-Hill Osborne Media.

Adams, E. & Rollings, A. (2006). *Fundamentals of game design.* Prentice Hall.

Ahearn, L. & Crooks II, C.E. (2002). *Awesome game creation: No programming required. (2nd ed.).* Charles River Media.

Ahlquist, J.B., Jr. & Novak, J. (2007). *Game development essentials: Game artificial intelligence.* Cengage Delmar Learning.

Aldrich, C. (2003). *Simulations and the future of learning.* Pfeiffer.

Aldrich, C. (2005). *Learning by doing.* Jossey-Bass.

Allison, S.E. et al. (2006, March). The development of the self in the era of the Internet & role-playing fantasy games. *The American Journal of Psychiatry.*

Allmer, M. (2009, February 27). The 13 basic principles of gameplay design. *Gamasutra* (www.gamasutra.com/view/feature/3949/the_13_basic_principles_of_.php).

Atherton, J. S. (2011). Learning and teaching; Piaget's developmental theory. *Learning and Teaching.* (www.learningandteaching.info/learning/piaget.htm).

Atkin, M. & Abercrombie, J. (2005). Using a goal/action architecture to integrate modularity and long-term memory into AI behaviors. *Game Developers Conference.*

Axelrod, R. (1985). *The evolution of cooperation.* Basic Books.

Bartle, R.A. (1996). Hearts, clubs, diamonds, spades: Players who suit MUDs. *MUSE: Multi-User Entertainment Ltd* (www.mud.co.uk/richard/hcds.htm).

Bates, B. (2002). *Game design: The art & business of creating games.* Premier Press.

Beck, J.C. & Wade, M. (2004). *Got game: How the gamer generation is reshaping business forever.* Harvard Business School Press.

Beshera, T. (2008). *Acing the interview: How to ask and answer the questions that will get you the job.* AMACOM.

Bethke, E. (2003). *Game development and production.* Wordware.

Birdwell, K. (1999). The cabal: Valve's design process for creating *Half-Life. Gamasutra* (www.gamasutra.com/view/feature/3408/the_cabal_valves_design_process_.php).

Birn, J. (2006). *Digital lighting and rendering (2nd ed.).* New Riders Press.

Boer, J. (2002). *Game audio programming.* Charles River Media.

Brandon, A. (2004). *Audio for games: Planning, process, and production.* New Riders.

Brin, D. (1998). *The transparent society.* Addison-Wesley.

Broderick, D. (2001). *The spike: How our lives are being transformed by rapidly advancing technologies.* Forge.

Brooks, D. (2001). *Bobos in paradise: The new upper class and how they got there.* Simon & Schuster.

Busby, A., Parrish, Z. & Van Eenwyk, J. (2004). *Mastering Unreal technology: The art of level design.* Sams.

Byrne, E. (2004). *Game level design.* Charles River Media.

Campbell, J. (1972). *The hero with a thousand faces.* Princeton University Press.

Campbell, J. & Moyers, B. (1991). *The power of myth.* Anchor.

Castells, M. (2001). *The Internet galaxy: Reflections on the Internet, business, and society.* Oxford University Press.

Castillo, T. & Novak, J. (2008). *Game development essentials: Game level design.* Cengage Delmar Learning.

Castronova, E. (2005). *Synthetic worlds: The business and culture of online games.* University of Chicago Press.

Chang, J. (2011, October 17). Two extremes of touch interaction. *Microsoft Research* (research.microsoft.com/en-us/news/features/touch-101711.aspx).

Chase, R.B., Aquilano, N.J. & Jacobs, R. (2001). *Operations management for competitive advantage (9th ed.).* McGraw-Hill/Irwin

Cheeseman, H.R. (2004). *Business law (5th ed.).* Pearson Education, Inc.

Chiarella, T. (1998). *Writing dialogue.* Story Press.

Childs, G.W. (2006). *Creating music and sound for games.* Course Technology PTR.

Christen, P. (2006, November). Serious expectations. *Game Developer Magazine.*

Clayton, A.C. (2003). *Introduction to level design for PC games.* Charles River Media.

Co, P. (2006). *Level design for games: Creating compelling game experiences.* New Riders Games.

Cooper, A., & Reimann, R. (2003). *About face 2.0: The essentials of interaction design.* Wiley.

Corashaniti, N. (2010). How do people use their smartphones? *New York Times* (bits.blogs.nytimes.com/2010/09/14/report-looks-at-trends-with-mobile-apps/?src=twt&twt=nytimesbits).

Cornman, L.B. et al. (1998, December). A fuzzy logic method for improved moment estimation from Doppler spectra. *Journal of Atmospheric & Oceanic Technology.*

Cox, E. & Goetz, M. (1991, March). Fuzzy logic clarified. *Computerworld.*

Crawford, C. (2003). *Chris Crawford on game design.* New Riders.

Crinnion, J. (1992). *Evolutionary systems development.* Springer.

Crowley, M. (2004). "A" is for average. *Reader's Digest.*

Csikszentmihalyi, M. (1991). *Flow: The psychology of optimal experience.* Perennial.

Dawson, M. (2006). *Beginning C++ through game programming.* Course Technology.

Decker, M. (2000). Bug reports that make sense. *StickyMinds.com* (www.stickyminds.com/sitewide.asp?Function=edetail&ObjectType=ART&ObjectId=2079).

DeKoven, B. (2012). Playing for laughs. *Deep Fun with Bernie DeKoven* (www.deepfun.com/playing-for-laughs).

DeMaria, R. & Wilson, J.L. (2003). *High score!: The illustrated history of electronic games.* McGraw-Hill.

Demers, O. (2001). *Digital texturing and painting.* New Riders Press.

Derryberry, A. (2007). Serious games: Online games for learning. *Adobe* (www.adobe.com/products/director/pdfs/serious_games_wp_1107.pdf).

Dickens, C. (2004, April 1). Automatic testing basics. *Software Test Engineering @ Microsoft* (blogs.msdn.com/chappell/articles/106056.aspx).

Dickheiser, M. (2006). *C++ for Game Programmers.* Charles River Media.

Digital Media Wire. (2008). *Project Millennials Sourcebook (2nd ed.).* Pass Along / Digital Media Wire.

Djaouti, D. et al. (2011). Origins of serious games. *Serious Games & Edutainment Applications.* Springer (www.ludoscience.com/files/ressources/origins_of_serious_games.pdf).

Donovan, T. (2010). *Replay: The history of video games.* Yellow Ant.

Duffy, J. (2007, August). The bean counters. *Game Developer Magazine.*

Dunniway, T. & Novak, J. (2008). *Game development essentials: Gameplay mechanics.* Cengage Delmar Learning.

Eberly, D. H. (2004). *3D game engine architecture: Engineering real-time applications with wild magic.* Morgan Kaufmann.

Edwards, B. (2009, October 9). Evolution of the cell phone. *PCWorld* (www.pcworld.com/article/173033/cell_phone_evolution.html).

Egri, L. (1946). *The art of dramatic writing: Its basis in the creative interpretation of human motives.* Simon and Schuster.

Eischen, C. W. and Eischen, L. A. (2009). *Résumés, cover letters, networking, and interviewing.* South-Western College Pub.

Eisenman, S. (2006). *Building design portfolios: Innovative concepts for presenting your work.* Rockport Publishers.

Erikson, E.H. (1994). *Identity and the life cycle.* W.W. Norton & Company.

Erikson, E.H. (1995). *Childhood and society.* Vintage.

Escober, C. & Galindo, J. (2004). Fuzzy control in agriculture: Simulation software. *Industrial Simulation Conference 2004.*

Evans, A. (2001). *This virtual life: Escapism and simulation in our media world.* Fusion Press.

Fagerholt, E. and Lorentzon, M. (2009). Beyond the HUD: User interfaces for increased player immersion in FPS games. *Chalmers University of Technology.*

Fay, T. (2003). *DirectX 9 audio exposed: Interactive audio development.* Wordware Publishing.

Feare, T. (2000, July). Simulation: Tactical tool for system builders. *Modern Materials Handling.*

Flacy, M. (2011, October 6). App turns any Windows Phone into Xbox 360 media controller. *Yahoo! News* (news.yahoo.com/app-turns-windows-phone-xbox-360-media-controller-043932112.html).

Fling, B. (2009). *Mobile design and development.* O'Reilly.

Fradera, X. (2011, December 22). Classic design lessons: What free-to-play can learn from arcades. *Gamasutra* (www.gamasutra.com/view/feature/6575/classic_design_lessons_what_.php).

Friedl, M. (2002). *Online game interactivity theory.* Charles River Media.

Fristrom, J. (2003, July 14). Production testing and bug tracking. *Gamasutra* (www.gamasutra.com/view/feature/2829/production_testing_and_bug_tracking.php).

Fruin, N. & Harringan, P. (Eds.) (2004). *First person: New media as story, performance and game.* MIT Press.

Fullerton, T., Swain, C. & Hoffman, S. (2004). *Game design workshop: Designing, prototyping & playtesting games.* CMP Books.

Galitz, W.O. (2002). *The essential guide to user interface design: An introduction to GUI design principles and techniques (2nd ed.).* Wiley.

Gamma, E., Helm, R., Johnson, R. & Vlissides, J. (1995). *Design patterns: Elements of reusable object-oriented software.* Addison-Wesley.

Gardner, J. (1991). *The art of fiction: Notes on craft for young writers.* Vintage Books.

Gazarov, N. (2010, December 21). The usability of accelerometer controls on iOS. *Gamasutra* (www.gamasutra.com/blogs/NikitaGazarov/20101221/6675/The_Usability_of_Accelerometer_Controls_on_iOS.php).

Gee, J.P. (2003). *What video games have to teach us about learning and literacy.* Palgrave Macmillan.

Gershenfeld, A., Loparco, M. & Barajas, C. (2003). *Game plan: The insiders guide to breaking in and succeeding in the computer and video game business.* Griffin Trade Paperback.

Giarratano, J.C. & Riley, G.D. (1998). *Expert systems: Principles & programming (4th ed.).* Course Technology.

Gibson, D., Aldrich, C. & Prensky, M. (Eds.) (2006). *Games and simulations in online learning.* IGI Global.

Gladwell, M. (2000). *The tipping point: How little things can make a big difference.* Little Brown & Company.

Gladwell, M. (2007). *Blink: The power of thinking without thinking.* Back Bay Books.

Gleick, J. (1987). *Chaos: Making a new science.* Viking.

Gleick, J. (1999). *Faster: The acceleration of just about everything.* Vintage Books.

Gleick, J. (2003). *What just happened: A chronicle from the information frontier.* Vintage.

Godin, S. (2003). *Purple cow: Transform your business by being remarkable.* Portfolio.

Godin, S. (2005). *The big moo: Stop trying to be perfect and start being remarkable.* Portfolio.

Goldratt, E.M. & Cox, J. (2004). *The goal: A process of ongoing improvement (3rd ed.).* North River Press.

Gorden, R. L. (1998). *Basic interviewing skills.* Waveland Press.

Gordon, T. (2000). *P.E.T.: Parent effectiveness training.* Three Rivers Press.

Graafland, M. et al. (2012). Systematic review of serious games for medical education and surgical skills training. *Wiley Online Library* (onlinelibrary.wiley.com/doi/10.1002/bjs.8819/pdf).

Guilfoyle, E. (2007). *Half Life 2 mods for dummies.* For Dummies.

Guilfoyle, E. (2006). *Quake 4 mods for dummies.* For Dummies.

Habgood, J. & Overmars, M. (2006). *The game maker's apprentice: Game development for beginners.* Apress.

Hall, R. & Novak, J. (2008). *Game development essentials: Online game development.* Cengage Delmar Learning.

Hamilton, E. (1940). *Mythology: Timeless tales of gods and heroes.* Mentor.

Hart, S.N. (1996-2000). A brief history of home video games. *geekcomix* (www.geekcomix.com/vgh/main.shtml).

Heim, M. (1993). *The metaphysics of virtual reality.* Oxford University Press.

Hight, J. & Novak, J. (2007). *Game development essentials: Game project management.* Cengage Delmar Learning.

Hirschman, D. (2009, September 16). So what do you do, Mark Pincus, CEO of Zynga? *mediabistro.com* (www.mediabistro.com/So-What-Do-You-Do-Mark-Pincus-CEO-of-Zynga-a10636.html).

Hofferber, K. & Isaacs, K. (2006). *The career change résumé.* McGraw-Hill.

Hornyak, T.N. (2006). *Loving the machine: The art and science of Japanese robots.* Kodansha International.

Hsu, F. (2004). *Behind Deep Blue: Building the computer that defeated the world chess champion.* Princeton University Press.

Hunt, C.W. (1998, October). Uncertainty factor drives new approach to building simulations. *Signal.*

Ipsos MediaCT. (2012). Essential facts about the computer and video game industry. *Entertainment Software Association* (www.theesa.com/facts/pdfs/esa_ef_2012.pdf).

Isla, D. (2005). Handling complexity in the *Halo 2* AI. *Game Developers Conference.*

Jensen, E. (2006). *Enriching the brain: How to maximize every learner's potential.* John Wiley & Sons.

Jobs, S. (2010). Thoughts on Flash. *Apple* (www.apple.com/hotnews/thoughts-on-flash).

Johnson, S. (1997). *Interface culture: How new technology transforms the way we create & communicate.* Basic Books.

Johnson, J. (2010). *Designing with the mind in mind.* Morten Kaufmann Publishers.

Johnson, S. (2006). *Everything bad is good for you.* Riverhead.

Jung, C.G. (1969). *Man and his symbols.* Dell Publishing.

Kennedy, J. L. (2007), *Résumés for dummies.* For Dummies.

Kent, S.L. (2001). *The ultimate history of video games.* Prima.

King, S. (2000). *On writing.* Scribner.

Knoke, W. (1997). *Bold new world: The essential road map to the twenty-first century.* Kodansha International.

Koster, R. (2005). *Theory of fun for game design.* Paraglyph Press.

Krawczyk, M. & Novak, J. (2006). *Game development essentials: Game story & character development.* Cengage Delmar Learning.

Kurzweil, R. (2000). *The age of spiritual machines: When computers exceed human intelligence.* Penguin.

Laramee, F.D. (Ed.) (2002). *Game design perspectives.* Charles River Media.

Laramee, F.D. (Ed.) (2005). *Secrets of the game business. (3rd ed.).* Charles River Media.

Levy, L. (2012). Trailers: Win the YouTube wars, get ink, make it a hit. *Novy PR* (novypr.com/post/21939549035/trailers-win-the-youtube-wars-get-ink-make-it-a-hit).

Levy, L. & Novak, J. (2009). *Game development essentials: Game QA & testing.* Cengage Delmar Learning.

Levy, P. (2001). *Cyberculture.* University of Minnesota Press.

Lewis, M. (2001). *Next: The future just happened.* W.W. Norton & Company.

Mackay, C. (1841). *Extraordinary popular delusions & the madness of crowds.* Three Rivers Press.

Marks, A. (2008). *The complete guide to game audio.* Elsevier/Focal Press.

Marks, A. & Novak, J. (2008). *Game development essentials: Game audio development.* Cengage Delmar Learning.

Mathis, L. (2011). *Designed for use: Create usable interfaces for applications and the Web.* Pragmatic Programmers, LLC.

Maurina III, E. F. (2006). *The game programmer's guide to Torque: Under the hood of the Torque game engine.* AK Peters Ltd.

McAllister, G. (2011, March 30). A guide to iOS twin stick shooter usability. *Gamasutra* (www.gamasutra.com/view/feature/6323/a_guide_to_ios_twin_stick_shooter_.php).

McConnell, S. (1996). *Rapid development.* Microsoft Press.

McCorduck, P. (2004). *Machines who think: A personal inquiry into the history and prospects of artificial intelligence (2nd ed.).* AK Peters.

McKenna, T. (2003, December). This means war. *Journal of Electronic Defense.*

Meigs, T. (2003). *Ultimate game design: Building game worlds.* McGraw-Hill Osborne Media.

Mencher, M. (2002). *Get in the game: Careers in the game industry.* New Riders.

Meyers, S. (2005). *Effective C++: 55 specific ways to improve your programs and designs (3rd ed.).* Addison-Wesley.

Michael, D. (2003). *The indie game development survival guide.* Charles River Media.

Montfort, N. (2003). *Twisty little passages: An approach to interactive fiction.* MIT Press.

Montfort, N. & Bogost, I. (2009). *Racing the beam: The Atari video game computer system.* The MIT Press.

Moore, M. & Novak, J. (2009). *Game development essentials: Game industry career guide.* Cengage Delmar Learning.

Moore, M. E. & Sward, J. (2006). *Introduction to the game industry.* Prentice Hall.

Moravec, H. (2000). *Robot.* Oxford University Press.

Morris, D. (2004, September/October). Virtual weather. *Weatherwise.*

Morris, D. & Hartas, L. (2003). *Game art: The graphic art of computer games.* Watson-Guptill Publications.

Muehl, W. & Novak, J. (2007). *Game development essentials: Game simulation development.* Cengage Delmar Learning.

Mulligan, J. & Patrovsky, B. (2003). *Developing online games: An insider's guide.* New Riders.

Mummolo, J. (2006, July). Helping children play. *Newsweek.*

Murphy, D. (2011, September 11). Tablet sales to take off, PC sales suffer. *pcmag* (www.pcmag.com/article2/0,2817,2392768,00.asp).

Murray, J. (2001). *Hamlet on the holodeck: The future of narrative in cyberspace.* MIT Press.

Negroponte, N. (1996). *Being digital.* Vintage Books.

Nielsen Company, The. (2011, May 5). Connected devices: How we use tablets in the US. *nielsenwire* (blog.nielsen.com/nielsenwire/online_mobile/connected-devices-how-we-use-tablets-in-the-u-s/).

Newheiser, M. (2010, June 28). Adventure game puzzles: Unlocking the secrets of puzzle design. *Adventure Classic Gaming* (www.adventureclassicgaming.com/index.php/site/features/423/).

Newstead, S. (2012, July 6). A/B testing your icon (good, better, best). *Iterating Fun* (iteratingfun.com/post/26646957216/ab-testing-your-app-icon).

Nielsen, J. (1999). *Designing web usability: The practice of simplicity.* New Riders.

Nomadyun. (2006, February 23). Game testing methodology. *CN IT Blog* (www.cnitblog.com/nomadyun/archive/2006/02/23/6869.html).

Novak, J. (2011). *Game development essentials: An introduction (3rd ed.).* Cengage Delmar Learning.

Novak, J. & Levy, L. (2007). *Play the game: The parent's guide to video games.* Cengage Course Technology PTR.

Novak, J. (2003). MMOGs as online distance learning applications. *University of Southern California.*

Nutt, C. (2011, February 14). Bill Roper: Making MMOs work again. *Gamasutra* (www.gamasutra.com/view/feature/6285/bill_roper_making_mmos_work_again.php).

Omernick, M. (2004). *Creating the art of the game.* New Riders Games.

Oram, A. (Ed.) (2001). *Peer-to-peer.* O'Reilly & Associates.

Patow, C.A. (2005, December). Medical simulation makes medical education better & safer. *Health Management Technology.*

Peck, M. (2005, January). Air Force's latest video game targets potential recruits. *National Defense.*

Pham, A. (2008, October 20). Mom, I want to major in video games. *Los Angeles Times* (articles.latimes.com/2008/oct/20/business/fi-gamesschools20).

PHP Quality Assurance Team. Handling bug reports? *PHP-QAT* (qa.php.net/handling-bugs.php).

Piaget, J. (2000). *The psychology of the child.* Basic Books.

Piaget, J. (2007). *The child's conception of the world.* Jason Aronson.

Pohflepp, S. (2007, January). Before and after Darwin. *We Make Money Not Art* (www.we-make-money-not-art.com/archives/2007/01/before-and-afte.php).

Poole, S. (2004). *Trigger happy: Videogames and the entertainment revolution.* Arcade Publishing.

Prensky, M. (2006). *Don't bother me, Mom: I'm learning!* Paragon House.

Rabin, S. (2009). *Introduction to game development.* Concept Media.

Ramirez, J. (2006, July). The new ad game. *Newsweek.*

Rheingold, H. (1991). *Virtual reality.* Touchstone.

Rheingold, H. (2000). *Tools for thought: The history and future of mind-expanding technology.* MIT Press.

Robbins, S.P. (2001). *Organizational behavior (9th ed.).* Prentice-Hall, Inc.

Rockwell, G.M. & Kee, K. (2011). The leisure of serious games: A dialogue. *Game Studies, 11* (2). (gamestudies.org/1102/articles/geoffrey_rockwell_kevin_kee).

Rogers, E.M. (1995). *Diffusion of innovations.* Free Press.

Rollings, A. & Morris, D. (2003). *Game architecture & design: A new edition.* New Riders.

Rollings, A. & Adams, E. (2003). *Andrew Rollings & Ernest Adams on game design.* New Riders.

Rouse, R. (2001) *Game design: Theory & practice (2nd ed.).* Wordware Publishing.

Sagae, A. et al. (2010). Validation of a dialog system for language learners. *SIGDIAL 2010* (www.aclweb.org/anthology/W10-4344).

Salen, K. & Zimmerman, E. (2003). *Rules of play.* MIT Press.

Sanchanta, M. (2006, January). Japanese game aids U.S. war on obesity: Gym class in West Virginia to use an interactive dance console. *Financial Times.*

Sanger, G.A. (2003). *The Fat Man on game audio.* New Riders.

Saltzman, M. (1999, July 23). Secrets of the Sages: Level Design. *Gamasutra* (www.gamasutra.com/view/feature/3360/secrets_of_the_sages_level_design.php).

Saunders, K. D. & Novak, J. (2012). *Game development essentials: Game interface design (2nd ed.).* Cengage Delmar Learning.

Schell, J. (2008). *The art of game design: A book of lenses.* Morgan Kaufmann.

Schildt, H. (2006). *Java: A beginner's guide (4th ed.).* McGraw-Hill Osborne Media.

Schomaker, W. (2001, September). Cosmic models match reality. *Astronomy.*

Sellers, J. (2001). *Arcade fever.* Running Press.

Shaffer, D.W. (2006). *How computer games help children learn.* Palgrave Macmillan.

Smith, D. (2001, September 25). *ICO:* Dream a little dream...the most original adventure in years, a game you almost certainly must play. *IGN* (ps2.ign.com/articles/164/164833p1.html).

Spohn, S. (2011, December 7). Honduras man designs affordable eye tracker technology: The Eyeboard. *Able Gamers* (www.ablegamers.com/Hardware-News/honduras-man-designs-affordable-eye-tracker-technology-the-eyeboard.html).

Standage, T. (1999). *The Victorian Internet.* New York: Berkley Publishing Group.

Stellmach, T. and Caminos, R. (2004, March 26). Cross-platform user interface development. *Gamasutra* (www.gamasutra.com/view/feature/2085/crossplatform_user_interface_.php).

Strauss, W. & Howe, N. (1992). *Generations.* Perennial.

Strauss, W. & Howe, N. (1993). *13th gen: Abort, retry, ignore, fail?* Vintage Books.

Strauss, W. & Howe, N. (1998). *The fourth turning.* Broadway Books.

Strauss, W. & Howe, N. (2000). *Millennials rising: The next great generation.* Vintage Books.

Strauss, W., Howe, N. & Markiewicz, P. (2006). *Millennials & the pop culture.* LifeCourse Associates.

Stroustrup, B. (2000). *The C++ programming language (3rd ed.).* Addison-Wesley.

Szinger, J. (1993-2006). On composing interactive music. *Zing Man Productions* (www.zingman.com/spew/CompIntMusic.html).

Takahashi, D. (2011, April 15). Apple and Google steal market share from video game systems. *VentureBeat* (venturebeat.com/2011/04/15/apple-and-google-steal-market-share-from-video-game-systems/).

Takahashi, D. (2011, December 12). How Zynga grew from gaming outcast to $9 billion social game powerhouse. *VentureBeat* (venturebeat.com/2011/12/12/zynga-history).

Taylor, H. (August/September, 2007). The success story of a misnomer. *Offscreen, 11*(8/9).

Tidwell, J. (2011). *Designing Interfaces (2ⁿᵈ ed.)*. O'Reilly.

Trotter, A. (2005, November). Despite allure, using digital games for learning seen as no easy task. *Education Week*.

Tufte, E.R. (1983). *The visual display of quantitative information*. Graphics Press.

Tufte, E.R. (1990). *Envisioning information*. Graphics Press.

Tufte, E.R. (1997). *Visual explanations*. Graphics Press.

Tufte, E.R. (2006). *Beautiful evidence*. Graphics Press.

Turkle, S. (1997). *Life on the screen: Identity in the age of the Internet*. Touchstone.

Ulicsak, M. (2010). Games in education: Serious games. *Futurelab* (media.futurelab.org.uk/resources/documents/lit_reviews/Serious-Games_Review.pdf).

Unger, K. & Novak, J. (2011). *Game development essentials: Mobile game development*. Cengage Delmar Learning.

Van Duyne, D.K. et al. (2003). *The design of sites*. Addison-Wesley.

Ventrice, T. (2010, September 21). Evolving the social game: Finding casual by definition. *Gamasutra* (www.gamasutra.com/view/feature/6143/evolving_the_social_game_finding_.php).

Ventrice, T. (2009, May 26). The four perspectives of game design: Insight from the mobile fringe. *Gamasutra* (www.gamasutra.com/view/feature/4036/the_four_perspectives_of_game_.php?page=1).

Vitale, S. et al. (2009). Increased prevalence of myopia in the United States. *Archives of Ophthamology, 127*(12), 1632-1639 (archopht.ama-assn.org/cgi/content/full/127/12/1632).

Vogler, C. (1998). *The writer's journey: Mythic structure for writers. (2ⁿᵈ ed.)*. Michael Wiese Productions.

Weems, MD. (2008, October 5). 10 steps to becoming a video game tester. *Altered Gamer* (www.alteredgamer.com/game-development/9819-10-steps-to-becoming-a-video-game-tester-part-1/).

Welch, J. & Welch, S. (2005). *Winning*. HarperCollins Publishers.

Weizenbaum, J. (1984). *Computer power and human reason*. Penguin Books.

Wilcox, J. (2007). *Voiceovers: Techniques & Tactics for Success*. Allworth Press.

Williams, J.D. (1954). *The compleat strategyst: Being a primer on the theory of the games of strategy*. McGraw-Hill.

Wilson, G. (2006, February 3). Off with their HUDs!: Rethinking the heads-up display in console game design. *Gamasutra* (www.gamasutra.com/view/feature/2538/off_with_their_huds_rethinking_.php).

Wolf, J.P. & Perron, B. (Eds.). (2003). *Video game theory reader*. Routledge.

Wong, G. (2006, November). Educators explore *Second Life* online. *CNN.com* (www.cnn.com/2006/TECH/11/13/second.life.university/index.html).

Wysocki, R.K. (2006). *Effective project management (4ᵗʰ ed.)*. John Wiley & Sons.

Yuzwa, E. (2006). *Game programming in C++: Start to Finish*. Charles River Media.

Index

Game and publication titles are in *italic*.
GameSalad Creator terms are in **bold**.